What is Civilisation?

ANANDA K. COOMARASWAMY

What is Civilisation?

AND OTHER ESSAYS

FOREWORD BY
SEYYED HOSSEIN NASR

LINDISFARNE
PRESS

Published by
Lindisfarne Press
P.O. Box 778, 195 Main Street
Great Barrington, MA 01230

ISBN 0 94 0262 07 X

Printed in United Kingdom

Contents

Foreword

OVER forty years has passed since the death of Ananda Coomaraswamy; yet his writings remain as pertinent today as when he wrote them and his voice echoes in the ears of present day seekers of truth and lovers of traditional art as it did a generation ago. In contrast to most scholarly works which become outdated and current philosophical opuses which become stale, Coomaraswamy's works possess a timeliness which issues from their timeless character and a freshness which flows from their being rooted in the eternal present. It is therefore with joy that one can welcome a new collection of the essays of this formidable metaphysician and scholar.

During the past few decades several collections of Coomaraswamy's essays have appeared in book form, a few in his own life time and some after his death, the most noteworthy recent additions to this category being the volumes edited by R. Lipsey. Yet the writings of Coomaraswamy are so rich and diversified and printed in so many different, often inaccessible journals, that many of his major studies continue to be unavailable to the general, interested public. Brian Keeble has, therefore, rendered much service to the cause of traditional studies in making some of these essays available once again in this collection.

What is Civilisation? contains some of Coomaraswamy's most famous and seminal essays such as the title essay and 'On Being in One's Right Mind', as well as a number of essays which have never appeared in print before such as an English version of 'Beauty, Light and Sound' 'Windows of the Soul', and *'Quod factum est in ipso vita erat*'. The essays cut across the spectrum of ideas with which Coomaraswamy was especially concerned during the last and most mature period of his life. They include metaphysical and philosophical studies, including his well known essay 'On the Pertinence of Philosophy' in which he distinguishes sharply philosophy as traditionally understood from the profane meaning of philosophy, and his equally well-known scientific essay in which he contrasts and compares the traditional doctrine of gradation with the modern biological theory of evolution.

The collection also includes a number of Coomaraswamy's important studies on the soul and the human microcosm and the entelechy of the soul according to traditional doctrines. Also included are a number of important essays on symbols and myths with which Coomaraswamy was occupied throughout his life including the well known study 'On Hares and Dreams'. The essays on symbols, moreover, include not only those dealing with the meaning and interpretation of symbols, but also works on the study of specific symbols. In this category are included three of Coomaraswamy's most brilliant studies dealing respectively with the symbolism of archery in which he draws from many sources including the Japanese and Islamic, the symbolism of the fountain of life in Persian and Mughal miniatures which constitutes one of Coomaraswamy's major contributions to the study of Islamic art, and the symbolism of the Eckstein as both cornerstone and diamond in the context of traditional Christian thought. These essays reveal the author at the height of his power as a peerless interpreter of the traditional art forms of both East and West.

The final two essays of the book concern certain basic principles of traditional art dealing with the form of an art object in the 'mind' of the artist and ultimately its *paradigma* in relation to the external manifestation of this form, and the link between wisdom and technique, or the intellectual and practical elements whose harmonious wedding is necessary for the creation of any serious work of art. These last essays in a sense recapitulate through concrete examples the principles elucidated in such a magisterial manner by Coomaraswamy in his earlier writings on the traditional philosophy of art; such works as *The Transformation of Nature in Art* and *Why Exhibit Works of Art?*

All those concerned not only with the study of traditional art but also with the saving truths which are embedded in the millennial traditions of mankind will be grateful for this valuable collection of essays of one of the truly towering intellectual figures of this century. The living and timely nature of the thought presented in the pages which follow is itself proof of the continuing pertinence of traditional teachings of which Coomaraswamy was one of the major expositors in these times of spiritual eclipse. Truth is like the sun whose light and heat sustain and invigorate life never to become outmoded or stale. And so it is with works which bear the stamp of that truth or wisdom which Coomaraswamy himself called both *perennis* and *universalis.* The works of Coomaraswamy themselves bear the mark of that truth and so remain a beacon of guidance and light decades after they were written. Let us hope that these essays will be read with a view to drawing from them those universal and perennial teachings which can be applied to all times and climes and with the help of which alone man can charter in this life a path which is truly worthy of the vocation of being human.

Seyyed Hossein Nasr

BIBLIOGRAPHICAL NOTE

Of the essays that comprise the present volume 'Beauty, Light and Sound', 'Windows of the Soul', and *'Quod factum est in ipso erat'* have not previously appeared in print. These have been edited from photocopies of the typescripts deposited in the Princeton University Library and are printed here by kind permission of the Library and Rama P. Coomaraswamy. The remaining essays are here reproduced as they appeared in their original published form without changes except for obvious errors and matters of stylistic consistency. The location of the original publication of each essay can be found in *Ananda K. Coomaraswamy, Bibliography/Index,* edited by Rama P. Coomaraswamy, Prologos Books, Berwick on Tweed, 1988.

Editorial additions are enclosed in square brackets. These include occasional references to the two volumes of *Selected Papers* edited by Roger Lipsey. The abbreviated references are as follows: SP1 =

Coomaraswamy, 1: Selected papers, Traditional Art and Symbolism, edited by Roger Lipsey, Bollingen Series LXXXIX, Princeton University Press, 1977, SP2 = *Coomaraswamy, 2: Selected Papers, Metaphysics,* edited by Roger Lipsey, Bollingen Series LXXXIX, Princeton University Press, 1977. Page references follow the abbreviation. No attempt has been made to achieve total stylistic consistency in the manner in which the most frequently cited works are given. These are cited both fully, i.e. *Bhagavad Gītā* and in abbreviation i.e. BG. The works are most frequently cited are as follows.

AĀ.	*Aitareya Āraṇyaka*
AB.	*Aitareya Brāhmana*
AV.	*Atharva Veda Samhitā*
BD.	*Bṛhād Devatā*
BG.	*Bhagavad Gītā*
BS.	*Brahma Sūtra*
BU.	*Bṛhadāraṇyaka Upaniṣad*
CU.	*Chāndogya Upaniṣad*
D.	*Dīgha-Nikaya*
DhA.	*Dhammapada Attakathā*
GB.	*Gopatha Brāhmaṇa*
HJAS.	*Harvard Journal of Asiatic Studies*
IC.	*Indian Culture*
IHQ.	*Indian Historical Quarterly*
Iśā.	*Iśāvasya Upaniṣad*
J.	*Jātaka*
JAOS.	*Journal of the American Oriental Society*
JB.	*Jaiminīya-Brāhmana*
JIH.	*Journal of Indian History*
JUB.	*Jaiminīya Upaniṣad Brāhmana*
KU.	*Kaṭha Upaniṣad*
Kauṣ.	*Kauṣītaki Upaniṣad*
KB.	*Kauṣītaki Brāhmana*
Kena.	*Kena Upaniṣad*
Lib.	*Libellus (Hermes Trismegistus)*
M.	*Majjhima-Niyāka*
Maṇḍ.	*Maṇḍūkya Upaniṣad*
Mbh.	*Mahābhārata*
Mhv.	*Mahāvaṃsa*

Mil.	*Milinda Pañho*
MU.	*Maitri Upaniṣad*
Muṇḍ.	*Muṇḍaka Upaniṣad*
PB.	*Pañcavimśa Brahmana*
PTS.	*Pali Text Society*
RV.	*Ṛg Veda*
SAr.	*Sāṇkhāyana Āraṇyaka*
SB.	*Śatapatha Brāhmaṇa*
SBB.	*Sacred Book of the Buddhists*
Sum. Theol.	*Summa Theologica* (St Thomas Aquinas)
Śvet.	*Śvetāsvatara Upaniṣad*
TU.	*Taīttirīya Upaniṣad*
TS.	*Taīttirīya Saṃhitā*
VS.	*Vājasaneyi Saṃhitā*

Full details of these and other abbreviations and editions used by Coomaraswamy are listed in both volumes of *Selected Papers*.

What is Civilisation?

ONE

What is Civilisation?

FROM Albert Schweitzer's own writings it is clear that, aside from his more active life of good works, his theoretical interest centres in the questions: What is civilisation? And how can it be restored? For, of course, he sees very clearly that the modern 'civilised world, so self-styled, is not really a civilised world at all, but as he calls it, a world of 'Epigoni', inheritors, rather than creators of any positive goods.

To the question: What is civilisation? I propose to contribute a consideration of the intrinsic meanings of the words 'civilisation', 'politics' and 'puruṣa'. The root in 'civilisation' is Kei, as in Greek, *keisthai,* Sanskrit śī, to 'lie', 'lie outstretched', 'be located in'. A city is thus a 'lair', in which the citizen 'makes his bed' on which he must lie. We shall presently ask 'Who?' thus inhabits and 'economises'. The root in 'politics' is Pla as in Gr. *pimplēmi,* Skr. *pṛ(piparmi)* to 'fill', Gr. *polis,* Skr. *pur,* 'city', 'citadel', 'fortress', Lat. *plenum,* Skr. *pūrṇam,* and English 'fill'. The roots in *puruṣa* are these two and the intrinsic meaning therefore that of 'citizen', either as 'man' (this man, So-and-so) or as the Man (in this man, and absolutely); in either way, the *puruṣa* is the 'person' to be distinguished by his powers of foresight and understanding from the animal man (*paśu*) governed by his 'hunger and thirst'.[1]

In Plato's thought there is a cosmic city of the world, the city state, and an individual body politic, all of which are communities (Gr. *koinōnia,* Skr. *gaṇa*). 'The same castes (Gr. *genos,* Skr. *jāti*), equal in number are to be found in the city and in the soul (or self) of each of us';[2] the principle of justice is the same throughout, viz. that each member of the community should perform the tasks for which he is fitted by nature; and the establishment of justice and well-being of the whole in each case depends upon the answer to the question, Which shall rule, the better or the worse, a single Reason and Common Law or the multitude of moneyed men in the outer city and of desires in the individual (*Republic*, 441, etc.)?

Who fills, or populates, these cities? Whose are these cities, 'ours' or God's? What is the meaning of 'self-government'? (a question that, as Plato shows, *Republic*, 436B, implies a distinction of governor from governed). Philo says that 'As for lordship (*kyriōs*), God is the only citizen' (*monos polites, Cher.* 121), and this is almost identical with the words of the Upaniṣad, 'This Man (*puruṣa*) is the citizen (*puruṣaya*) in every city', (*sarvasu pūrṣu, Bṛhadāraṇyaṇka Up.* II.5.18), and must not be thought of as in any way contradicted by Philo's other statement, that 'Adam' (not 'this man', but the true Man) is the 'only citizen of the world' (*monos kosmopolites*) *Opif.* 142). Again, 'This city (*pur* is these worlds, the Person (*puruṣa*) is the Spirit (*yo'yam pavate=Vāyu*), who because he inhabits (*śete*) this city is called the "Citizen" (*puru-ṣa*)', *Śatapatha Brāhmaṇa*, XIII.6.2.1—as in *Atharva Veda*, X.2.30, where 'He who knoweth Brahma's city, whence the Person (*puru-ṣa*) is so-called, him neither sight nor the breath of life desert ere old age', but now the 'city' is that of this body, and the 'citizens' its God-given powers.

These macrocosmic and microcosmic points of view are interdependent; for the 'acropolis', as Plato calls it, of the city is within you and literally at the 'heart' of the city. 'What is within this City of God (*brahmapura*, this man) is a shrine[3] and what therein is Sky and Earth, Fire and the Gale, Sun and Moon, whatever is possest or unpossest; everything here is within it.' The question arises, What then is left over (survives) when this 'city' dies of old age or is destroyed? and the answer is that what survives is That which ages not with our inveteration, and is not slain when 'we' are killed; *That* is the '*true* City of God';[4] *That* (and by no means this perishable city that we think of as 'our' self) is our Self, unaging and immortal,[5] unaffected by 'hunger and thirst', (*Chāndogya Up.* VIII.1.1–5, slightly abbreviated), 'That art thou' (*ibid.* VI.8.7); and 'Verily, he who sees That, contemplates That, discriminates That, he whose game and sport, dalliance and beatitude are in and with that Self (*ātman*), he is autonomous (*sva-rāj, kreittōn heautou*, self-governing), he moveth at will in every world;[6] but those whose knowing is of what is other-than-That are heteronomous (*anyarāj, hettōn heautou*, subject), they move not at will in any world' (*ibid.* VII.25.2).

Thus at the heart of this City of God inhabits (*śete*) the omniscient, immortal Self, 'this self's immortal Self and Duke', as the Lord of all, the Protector of all, the Ruler of all beings and the Inward-Controller of all the powers of the soul by which he is surrounded, as by subjects,[7] and 'to Him (*Brahma*), thus proceeding in Person (*puruṣa*), as he lies there extended (*uttānāya śayānaye*), and enthroned (*brahmāsandhīm ārūdhā, atrasada*), the powers of the soul (*devatā, prāṇā*), voice, mind, sight, hearing, scent, bring tribute'.[8]

The word 'extended' here states a meaning already implied in the etymology of the 'city', Kei including the sense to lie at full length or outstretched.[9] The root in 'extended' and *ut-tāna* is that in Gr. *teinō* and Skr. *tan*, to extend, prolong, in Gr. *tonos*, a string, and hence also, tone, and in *tenuis*, Skr. *tanu*, thin.

Not only are these worlds a city, or am 'I' a city, but these are populated cities, and not waste lands, because He fills them, being 'one as he is in himself there, and many in his children here' (*Śatapatha Brāhmaṇa*, X.5.2.16). 'That dividing itself, unmeasured times, fills (*pūrayati*)[10] these worlds . . . from It continually proceed all animate beings' (*Maitri Up.* V.26). Or with specific reference to the powers of the soul within the individual city, 'He, dividing himself fivefold, is concealed in the cave (of the heart . . . Thence, having broken forth the doors of the sensitive powers, He proceeds to the fruition of experience . . . And so this body is set up in the possession of consciousness, He is its driver' (*ibid.* II.6.d).[11] This 'division', however, is only as it were, for He remains 'undivided in divided beings' (*Bhagavad Gītā*, XIII.16, XVII.20), 'uninterrupted' (*anantaram*) and thus is to be understood as an undivided and total presence.

The 'division', in other words, is not a segmentation, but an extension, as of radii from a centre or rays of light from a luminous source with which they are con-tinuous.[12] Con-*tin*uity and in-*ten*sity (*samtati, syntonia*) are, indeed, a necessary quality in whatever can be tensed and extended but, like the immanent Spirit, 'cannot be severed' (*acchedya, Bhagavad Gītā*, II.23)—'no part of that which is divine cuts itself off and becomes separated, but only extends (*ekteinetai=vitanute*) itself' (Philo, *Det.* 90). It is then, the same thing to say that the Person 'fills' these worlds as to say that Indra saw this Person 'as the most widely extended (*tatamam*) Brahma' (*Aitareya Āraṇyaka*, II.4.3). In this way all the powers of the soul, projected by the mind towards their objects, are 'extensions' (*tetomena*) of an invisible principle (*Republic*, 462E), and it is this 'tonic power' by which it is enabled to perceive them (Philo, *Leg. Alleg.* I.30, 37). Our 'constitution' is a habitation that the Spirit makes for itself 'just as a goldsmith draws-out-for-himself (*tanute*) from the gold another shape' (*Bṛhadāraṇyaka Up.* IV.4.4).[13]

This is an essential aspect of the 'thread-spirit' (*sūtrātman*) doctrine, and as such the intelligible basis of that of the divine omniscience and providence, to which our partial knowledge and foresight are analogous. The spiritual Sun (not that 'sun whom all men see' but that 'whom few know with the mind', *Atharva Veda*, X. 8.14)[14] is the Self of the whole universe, (*Ṛg Veda*, I.11.5.1) and is connected to all things in it by the 'thread' of his luminous pneumatic rays, on which the 'tissue' of the universe is woven—'all this universe is strung on Me, like rows of gems on a thread' (*Bhagavad Gītā*, VII.7); of which thread, running through our intellect, the ultimate strands are its sensitive powers, as we have already seen.[15] So, just as the noonday sun 'sees' all things under the sun at once, the 'Person in the Sun', the Light of lights, from the exalted point and centre 'wherein every where and every when is focussed' (*Paradiso*, XXIX.23) is simultaneously present to every experience, here or there, past or future, and 'not a sparrow falls to the ground' or ever has or ever will without his present knowledge. He is, in fact, the only seer, thinker, etc., in us (*Bṛhadāraṇyaka Up.* III.8.23), and whoever sees or thinks, etc., it is by *His* 'ray' that he does so (*Jaiminīya Up. Brāhmaṇa*, I.28,29).

Thus, in the human *City of God* which we are considering as a political pattern, the sensitive and discriminating powers form, so to speak, a body of guardsmen by which the Royal Reason is conducted to the perception of sense objects, and the heart is the guardroom where they take their orders (Plato, *Timaeus*, 70B, Philo, *Opif.* 139, *Spec.* IV.22 etc.). These powers—however referred to as Gods,[16] Angels, Aeons, Maruts, Ṛṣis, Breaths, Daimons, etc.—are the people (*viśa*, yeomanry, etc.) of the heavenly kingdom, and related to their Chief (*viśpati*) as are thanes to an Earl or ministers to a King; they are a troop of the 'King's Own' (*svā*), by which he is surrounded as if by a crown of glory—'upon whose head the Aeons are a crown of glory darting forth rays' (*Coptic Gnostic Treatise*, XII), and 'by "thy glory" I understand the powers that form thy bodyguard' (Philo,

Spec. I, 45).[17] The whole relationship is one of feudal loyalty, the subjects bringing tribute and receiving largesse—'Thou art ours and we are thine' (*Ṛg Veda*, VIII.92.32), 'Thine may we be for thee to give us treasure' (*ibid.* v.85.8, etc.).[18]

What must never be forgotten is that all 'our' powers are not our 'own', but *delegated* powers and ministries through which the royal Power is 'exercised' (another sense of Gr. *teino*); the powers of the soul 'are only the names of His acts' (*Bṛhadāraṇyaka Up.* I.4.7, I.5.21. etc.).[19] It is not for them to serve their own or one another's self-interests—of which the only result will be the tyranny of the majority, and a city divided against itself, man against man and class against class—but to serve Him whose sole interest is that of the common body politic. Actually, in the numerous accounts we have of a contest for precedence amongst the powers of the soul, it is always found that none of the members or powers is indispensable to the life of the bodily city, except only their Head, the Breath and immanent Spirit.

The right and natural life of the powers of the soul is then, precisely, their function of bringing tribute to their fountain-head, the controlling Mind and very Self, as man brings sacrificial offerings to an altar, keeping for themselves only what remains. It is the task of each to perform the functions from which it is fitted by nature, the eye seeing, the ear hearing, all of which functions are necessary to the well-being of the community of the whole man but must be co-ordinated by a disinterested power that cares for all. For unless this community can act unanimously, as one man, it will be working at all sorts of cross purposes. The concept is that of a corporation in which the several members of a community work together, each in its own way; and such a vocational society is an organism, not an aggregate of competing interests and consequently unstable 'balance of power'.

Thus the human City of God contains within itself the pattern of all other societies and of a true civilisation. The man will be a 'just' (Gr. *dikaios*) man when each of his members performs its own appropriate task and is subject to the ruling Reason that exercises forethought on behalf of the whole man; and in the same way the public city will be just when there is agreement as to which shall rule, and there is no confusion of functions but every occupation is a vocational responsibility. Not, then, where there are no 'classes' or 'castes' but where everyone is a responsible agent in some special field.[20] A city can no more be called a 'good' city if it lacks this 'justice' (*dikaiosynē*) than it could be were it wanting wisdom, sobriety or courage; and these four are the great civic virtues. Where occupations are thus vocations 'more will be done, and better done, and with more ease than in any other way' (*Republic*, 370C). But 'if one who is by nature a craftsman or some sort of businessman be tempted and inflated by wealth or by his command of votes or by his own might or any such thing, and tries to handle military matters, or if a soldier tries to be a counsellor or guardian, for which he is unfitted, and if these men interchange their tools and honours, or if one and the same man tries to handle all these functions at once, then, I take it, you too hold that this sort of perversion and being jack-of-all-trades will be the ruin of the city'; and this is 'injustice' (*Republic*, 434B).

Thus the ideal society is thought of as a kind of co-operative work-shop in which production is to be for use and not for profit, and all human needs, both of the body and the soul, are to be provided for. Moreover, if the command is to be fulfilled, 'Be ye perfect even as your Father in heaven is perfect', the work must be *perfectly* done.[21] The arts are not directed to the advantage of anything but their object (*Republic*, 432B), and that is that the thing made should be as perfect as possible for the purpose for which it is made. This purpose is to satisfy a human need (*Republic*, 369B, C); and so the perfectionism required, although not 'altruistically' motivated, actually 'serves humanity' in a way that is impossible where goods are made for sale rather than for use, and in quantity rather than quality. In the light of Plato's definition of 'justice' as vocational occupation we can the better understand the words, 'Seek first the kingdom of God and his *justice*, and these things shall be added unto you' (Matthew, 6:33).

The Indian philosophy of work is identical. 'Know that action arises from Brahma. He who on earth doth not follow in his turn the wheel thus revolving liveth in vain; therefore, without attachment to its rewards, ever be doing what should be done, for, verily, thus man wins the Ultimate. There is nothing I needs must do, or anything attainable that is not already mine; and yet I mingle in action. Act thou, accordingly, with a view to the welfare of the world; for whatever the superior does, others will also do; the standard he sets up, the world will follow. Better is one's own norm,[22] however deficient, than that of another well done; better to die at one's own post, that of another is full of fear . . . Vocations are determined by one's own nature. Man attains perfection through devotion to his own work. How? By praising Him in his own work, from whom is the unfolding of all beings and by whom this whole universe is extended (*tatam, <tan*). Better is a man's own work, even with its faults, than that of another well done; he who performs the task that his own nature lays upon him incurs no sin; one should never abandon his inherited[23] vocation.'[24]

On the one hand the inspired tradition rejects ambition, competition and quantitive standards; on the other, our modern 'civilisation' is based on the notions of social advancement, free enterprise (devil take the hindmost) and production in quantity. The one considers man's needs, which are 'but little here below'; the other considers his wants, to which no limit can be set, and of which the number is artificially multiplied by advertisement. The manufacturer for profits must, indeed, create an ever-expanding world market for his surplus produced by those whom Dr. Schweitzer calls 'over-occupied men'. It is fundamentally, the incubus of world trade that makes of industrial 'civilisations' a 'curse to humanity', and from the industrial concept of progress 'in line with the manufacturing enterprise of civilisation' that modern wars have arisen and will arise; it is on the same impoverished soil that empires have grown, and by the same greed that innumerable civilisations have been destroyed—by Spaniards in South America, Japanese in Korea and by 'white shadows in the South Seas'.[25]

Dr. Schweitzer himself records that 'it is very hard to carry to completion a colonisation which means at the same time a true civilisation . . . The machine age brought upon mankind conditions of existence which made the possession of civilisation difficult[26] . . . Agriculture and handicraft are the foundation of civilisation . . . Whenever the timber trade is good, permanent famine reigns in the Ogowe region[27] . . . They live on imported rice and imported preserved foods which they purchase with the proceeds of their labour . . . thereby making home industry impossible . . . As things are, the world trade which has reached them is a fact against which we and they are powerless'.[28]

I do not consent to this picture of a *deus*, or much rather *diabolus*, *ex machina*, coupled as it is with a confession of impotence.[29] If, indeed, our industrialism and trade practice are the mark of our uncivilisation, how dare we propose to help others 'to attain a condition of well-being'? The 'burden' is of our own making and bows our own shoulders first. Are we to say that because of 'economic determination' we are 'impotent' to shake it off and stand up straight? That would be to accept the status of 'Epigoni' once and for all, and to admit that our influence can only lower others to our own level.[30]

As we have seen, in a true civilisation, *laborare est orare*. But industrialism—'the mammon of in-justice' (Gr. *adikia*)—and civilisation are incompatible. It has often been said that one can be a good Christian even in a factory; it is no less true that one could be an even better Christian in the arena. But neither of these facts means that either factories or arenas are Christian or desirable institutions. Whether or not a battle of religion against industrialism and world trade can ever be won is no question for us to consider; our concern is with the task and not with its reward; our business is to be sure that in any conflict we are on the side of Justice.[31] Even as things are, Dr. Schweitzer finds his best excuse for colonial government in the fact that to some extent (however slightly) such governments protect subject peoples 'from the merchant'. Why not protect ourselves (the 'guinea-pigs' of a well known book) from the merchant? Would it not be better if, instead of tinkering with the inevitable consequences of 'world trade', we considered its cause, and set about to re-form (*Wideraufbauen* is Schweitzer's world) our own 'civilisation'? Or shall the uncivilised for ever pretend to 'civilising missions'?

To reform what has been deformed means that we must take account of an original 'form', and that is what we have tried to do in historical analysis of the concept of civilisation, based on Eastern and Western sources. Forms are by definition invisible to sense. The form of our *City of God* is one 'that exists only in words, and nowhere on earth, but is, it seems, laid up in heaven for whomsoever will to contemplate, and as he does so, to inhabit; it can be seen only by the true philosophers who bend their energies towards those studies that nourish rather soul than body and never allow themselves to be carried away by the congratulations of the mob or without measure to increase their wealth, the source of measureless evils,[32] but rather fix their eyes upon their own interior politics, never *aiming* to be politicians in the city of their birth' (*Republic*, 591 E, F).

Is not Plato altogether right when he proposes to entrust the government of cities to 'the uncorrupted remnant of true philosophers who now bear the stigma of uselessness',[33] or even to those who are now in power 'if by some divine inspiration[34] a genuine love of true philosophy should take possession of them': and altogether right when he maintains that 'no city ever can be happy unless its outlines have been drawn by draughtsmen making use of the divine pattern' (*Republic*, 499, 500)—that of the City of God that is in heaven and 'within you'?[35]

NOTES

1. As in *Aitareya Āraṇyaka*, II.3.2 and Boethius, *Contra Evtychen*.

2. Plato's Immortal Soul (Self), and two parts of the mortal soul (self), together with the body itself, make up the normal number of 'four castes' that must co-operate for the benefit of the whole community.

3. 'The kingdom of God is within you' (Luke 17: 21); *en hautō politeia* (*Republic*, 591 E). The King survives his kingdoms and 'lives forever'. Just as, in the traditional theory of government, the Kingship immanent in kings antecedes them and survives them, 'le roi est mort, vive le roi'.

4. Plato's *polis en logois* (Skr. *śrute*), *kaimenē epei ges ge oudamou* (*Republic* 592 A.)

5. That eternally youthful Spiritual-Self of which whoever is a Comprehensor has no fear of death (*Atharva Veda*, X.8.44).

6. This liberty, so often spoken of in the Vedic tradition from *Ṛg Veda*, IX.123.9 onwards, corresponds to the Platonic term *autokinēsis* (*Phaedrus*, 245D, *Laws*, 895B, C) and to John, 10: 9 'shall go in and out, and find pasture'.

7. BU. III.8.23, IV.4.22, *Kaṭha Up*. II.18, *Muṇḍ Up*. II.2. 6. 7, *Maitri Up*. VI. 7, etc.

8. *Jaiminīya Up. Brāhmaṇa*, IV, 23.7–23.10, somewhat condensed.

9. The divine extension in the three dimensional space of the world that is thus filled is a cosmic crucifixion to which the local crucifixion in two dimensions corresponds. To the extent that we think of Him as really divided up by this extension, i.e. to the extent that we conceive of our being as 'our own', we crucify him daily.

10. Causative of *pṛ*, the root in *pūr* and so 'populates' or even 'civilises'.

11. *Psyche men estin hē periagousa hēmōn pantōn*, *Laws*, 898C; Questi nei cor mortali é permotore, *Paradiso*, I.116; 'the heart has pulled the reins of the five senses' (Rūmī, *Mathnawī*, I.3275). Throughout the Vedic tradition (most explicitly in *Katha Up*. III.3 f. and *Jātaka*, VI. 242) as in Plato, (*Phaedrus*, 246f). Philo, (*Leg. Alleg*.1.72, 73, III. 224, *Spec*. IV. 79, etc.) and Boethius, etc., man's constitution in which the spiritual Self-of-all-beings rides as passenger for so long as the vehicle holds together, mind (*manas*, *nous*) holds the reins; but being twofold, clean or unclean, disinterested or interested, may either control or be run away with by the team of the senses. The 'chariot', 'city', 'ship'

and 'puppet' symbols are equivalent, so that, for example, 'when Mind as charioteer rules the whole living being, as a governor does a city, then life holds a straight course'. (Philo, *Leg. Alleg.* III.224, cf. *Ṛg Veda*, VI.75.6). The whole conception of *yoga* (*yuj*, to 'yoke', 'harness', 'join') is connected with the symbolism of the chariot and team; we still speak of 'bridling' our passions.

12. Hence *viraj*, literally 'distributive shining' = 'ruling power'.

13. Gold in such contexts is not a figure of speech, but of thought, Gold 'is' (we should now say 'means') light, life, immortality (*Śatapatha Brāhmana*, passim, and traditionally); and to 'refine' this 'gold' is to burn away from our spiritual Self the dross of all that is not-Self. Hence it is a 'golden' cord by which the human puppet is rightly guided (Plato, *Laws* 644) and Blake gives us a 'golden' string that 'will lead you in at heaven's gate'.

14. 'Sun of the sun', *Mahābhārata*, V. 46.3 and Philo, *Spec.* I.279; 'invisible light perceptible only by mind', Philo, *Opif.* 31; 'whose body the sun is, who controls the sun from within', *Bṛhadāraṇyaka Up.* III. 7.9; 'whose body is seen by all, his soul by none' Plato, *Laws*, 898 D; 'Light of lights', *Bhagavad Gītā*, X. II. 17, *Ṛg Veda*, I. 113.1; 'that was the true Light . . . of the world', John, 1:9, 9:5; 'the Sun of men', *Ṛg Veda*, I. 146,4 and 'Light of men', John, 1:4, 'seated in every heart', *Bhagavad Gītā*, XIII.17, *Maitrī Up*, VI. 1.

15. We cannot expound the 'thread-spirit' doctrine at length here. In the European tradition it can be traced from Homer to Blake. For some of the references see my 'Primitive Mentality', *Quarterly Journal of the Mythic Society*, XXXI, 1940 and '*Literary Symbolism*' in the *Dictionary of World Literature*, 1943. See Philo, *Immut.* 35 and passim; also my 'Spiritual Paternity and the Puppet Complex' in *Psychiatry*, VIII, 1945, reprinted A. K. Coomaraswamy, *The Bugbear of Literacy*, 1947.

16. Or Sons of God. Cf. Boehme, *Signatura Rerum*, XIV. 5 'Each angelical prince is a property out of the voice of God, and bears the great name of God.' It is with reference to these powers that it is said that 'All these Gods are in me' (*Jaiminīya Upaniṣad Brāhmana*, I. 14.2), that 'All things are full of Gods' (Thales, cited Plato, *Laws* 899 B) and that 'Making the Man (*puruṣa*) their mortal house, the Gods indwelt him' (*Atharva Veda*, XI. 8.18); accordingly, 'He is indeed initiated, whose "Gods within him" are initiated, mind by Mind, voice by Voice' etc. (*Kauṣītaki Brāhmana*, VII. 4). We need hardly say that such a multiplicity of Gods—'tens and thousands'—is not a polytheism, for all are the angelic subjects of the Supreme Deity from whom they originate and in whom, as we are so often reminded, they again 'become one'. Their operation is an epiphany (*Kauṣítaki Up.* II. 12. 13.—'This Brahma, verily, shines when one sees with the eye, and likewise dies when one does not see'). These 'Gods' are Angels, or as Philo calls them, the Ideas—i.e. Eternal Reasons.

17. The double meaning of Gr, *stephanos* must be remembered: (1) as 'crown' and (2) as city 'wall'; thus both a glory and a defence. 'Children are a man's crown, towers of the "city"' (*Homeric Epigrams*, XIII). In the same way Pali *cūlikā*, usually 'turban', is also a 'city wall', as in *Samyutta Mikāya*, II. 182 *nagaram . . . cūlikā-baddham.*

Philo's interpretation of the 'glory' has an exact equivalent in India, where the powers of the soul are 'glories' (*śriyah*) and collectively 'the kingdom, the power and the glory' (*śrī*) of their royal possessors; and, accordingly, the whole science of government is one of the control of these powers (*Arthaśāstra*, I. 6; see my *Spiritual Authority and Temporal Power in the Indian Theory of Government*, 1942, p.86). Non potest aliquis habere ordinatam familiam, nisi ipse sit ordinatus [one cannot have discipline in his family, unless he (first) have it in himself], St. Bonaventura, *De don.* S. S. IV. 10. V, p.475, being applicable to everyone who proposes to govern himself, a city or a kingdom.

18. On *bhakti* ('devotion', or perhaps better 'fealty', and literally 'participation') as a reciprocal relationship, see my *Spiritual Authority and Temporal Power in the Indian Theory of Government*, 1942, note 5, and my *Hinduism and Buddhism*, 1943, p.20.

19. '"I" do nothing, so should deem the harnessed man, the knower of Ultimate Reality' (*Bhagavad Gītā*, v. 8). 'I do nothing of myself' (John 8: 28, cf. 5:19). To think that '"I" do' (*kartò' ham iti*) or '"I" think' is an infatuation, Philo's *oiēsis* (*Leg. Alleg.* 1.47, 2.68, 3.33) and Indian *abhimāna*. The proposition *Cogito ergo sum* is a *non sequitur* and non-sense; the true conclusion being *Cogito ergo EST* with reference to Him 'who Is' (Damascene, *De fid. orthod.* I; *Katha Up.* VI.12; *Milinda Pañha* p.73) and can alone say 'I' (Meister Eckhart, Pfeiffer, p.261). Cf. also the references in my *'Ākimcaññā: Self-Naughting', New Ind. Antiquary* 1940, [Rpr. SP2, pp.107–147.]

Nichts anders stürzet dich in Höllenschlund hinein
Als das verhasste Wort (merk's wohl!): das Mein und Dein

Nothing else will so readily cast one into the jaws of Hell as the detestable words (mark them well!) mine and thine (Angelus Silesius, *Der Cherubinische Wandersmann*, v. 238).

20. In which case, *every* occupation is a profession; not merely a way of earning one's living, but a 'way of life', to abandon which is to die a death. 'The man who has shifted, easily and unworried so long as the pay was good, from one job to another, has no deep respect for himself' (Margaret Mead, *And Keep Your Powder Dry*, p.222).

21. It is a commonplace of mediaeval theory that the craftsman's primary concern is with the good of the work to be done, and this means that it must be at the same time *pulcher et aptus* [beautiful and appropriate.] A Buddhist text defining the entelechies of the different vocational groups calls that of the householder whose support is an art 'perfected work' *Anguttara Nikāya*, III.363.

22. *Sva-dharma=sva-karma*, Plato's *ta heautou prattein, kata physin. Dharma* is a pregnant term, difficult to translate in the present context; cf. *eidos* in *Republic* 434A. In general, *dharma* (literally 'support', *dhr* as in *dhruva*, 'fixed', 'Pole Star', and Gr. *thronos*) is synonymous with 'Truth'. Than this ruling principle there is 'nothing higher' (*Bṛhadāraṇyaka Up.* I.4.14); *dharma* is the 'king's King' (*Anguttara Nikāya*, I.109), i.e. 'King of kings'; and there can be no higher title than that of *dharma-rājā*, 'King of Justice'. Hence the well-known designation of the veritable Royalty as Dharmarājā, to be distinguished from the personality of the king in whom it temporarily inheres. One's 'own dharma' is precisely Plato's 'justice', viz. to perform the task for which one is naturally equipped. Justice, Gr. *dikē* (Skr. √ *diś*, to 'indicate') represents in the same way the ultimate Index and standard by which all action must be judged. Dharma is *lex aeterna*, sva-dharma *lex naturalis*.

23. For our tradition, procreation is a 'debt', and its purpose is to maintain the continuity of ministerial functions in a stable society (see my *Hinduism and Buddhism*, 1943, note 146).For only so can the bases of civilisation be preserved.

24. *Bhagavad Gītā*, III.15–35 and XVIII.18–48, slightly abbreviated.

25. Cf. my 'Am I my Brother's Keeper?', *Asia and the Americas*, March 1943, reprinted in *The Bugbear of Literacy*, 1947.

26. 'The machine . . . is the achievement of which man is capable if he relies entirely on himself—God is no longer needed . . . Eventually . . . (it) transforms him into a machine himself' (Ernst Niekisch, quoted by Erich Meissner in *Germany in Peril*, 1942).

27. 'When nations grow old, the arts grow cold, and commerce settles on every tree' (William Blake).

28. Albert Schweitzer, *Zwischen Wasser und Urwald*, cited in his *My Life and Thought*.

29. 'I have no more faith than a grain of mustard seed in the future history of "civilisation", which I *know* now is doomed to destruction: what a joy it is to think of!'

(William Morris). 'For by civilised men we now mean industrialised men, mechanised societies . . . We call all men civilised, if they employ the same mechanical techniques to master the physical world. And we call them so because we are certain that as the physical world is the only reality and as it only yields to mechanical manipulation, that is the only way to behave. Any other conduct can only spring from illusion; it is the behaviour of an ignorant, simple savage. To have arrived at this picture of reality is to be truly advanced, progressive, civilised' (Gerald Heard, *Man the Master*, 1937, p.25). It is also to have arrived at what has properly been called a 'world of impoverished reality' (Iredell Jenkins), and one that can only impoverish those to whom we communicate it.

30. Cf. A. J. Krzesinski, *Is Modern Culture Doomed*? 1942, especially Msgr. G. B. O'Toole's Introduction, and Znaniecki as cited on p.54 note; and Eric Gill, *It All Goes Together*, 1944.

31. Whoever owns a single share in any manufacturing enterprise for profit is to that extent taking sides and to that extent responsible for world trade and all its consequences.

32. The body, for the sake of which we desire wealth, is the ultimate cause of all wars (*Phaedo*, 66 c); and 'victory breeds hatred, because the conquered are unhappy' (*Dhammapada*, 201). World trade and world war are congeneric evils. Whatever we have said about the government of men and cities will apply, of course, to a government of the world by cooperative and disinterested nations. Every attempt to establish 'balances of power' must end in war.

33. *Noblesse oblige*. In a city that has fostered 'true philosophers' the latter owe it to their fosterers to participate in civic affairs and so in the traditional theory of government it is incumbent upon the representatives of the spiritual authority to oversee and guide those who exercise the temporal power; to see to it, in other words, that might supports right, and does not assert itself. On the function of such philosophers in the regeneration of modern society, cf. Gerald Heard, *Man the Master*, and Aldous Huxley, *Ends and Means*, 1937.

34. I suppose that in the history of criticism nothing more inane has ever been propounded than Paul Shorey's comment, 'But we must not attribute personal *superstition* to Plato' (Loeb ed. p.64). Solecisms such as this must be expected whenever nominalists set out to expound the doctrine of realistic philosphers but *why* do men set out to expound philosophies in which they do not believe?

35. The work to be done is primarily one of purgation, to drive out the money changers, all who *desire* power and office, and all representatives of special interests; and secondly, when the city has been thus 'cleaned up', one of considered imitation of the natural forms of justice, beauty, wisdom and other civic virtues; amongst which we have here considered justice, or as the word *dikaiosynē* is commonly translated in Christian contexts, righteousness.

It may be, as Plato says, very difficult 'to bring about such a change of mind as is required if we are to "progress"' *in this way*, but as he also says, it is "not impossible"; and so we may 'not cease from Mental Fight . . . till we have built Jerusalem'.

TWO

On the Pertinence of Philosophy

'Wisdom uncreate, the same now as it ever was, and the same to be for evermore.' St. Augustine, *Confessions*, IX. 10.
'Primordial and present Witness.' Prakāśânanda, *Siddhântamuktâvali*, 44.

I DEFINITION AND STATUS OF PHILOSOPHY, OR WISDOM

TO discuss the 'problems of philosophy' presupposes a definition of 'philosophy'. It will not be contested that 'philosophy' implies rather the love of wisdom than the love of knowledge, nor secondarily that from the 'love of wisdom', philosophy has come by a natural transition to mean the doctrine of those who love wisdom and are called philosophers.[1]

Now knowledge as such is not the mere report of the senses (the reflection of anything in the retinal mirror may be perfect, in an animal or idiot, and yet is not knowledge), nor the mere act of recognition (names being merely a means of alluding to the aforesaid reports), but is an abstraction from these reports, in which abstraction the names of the things are used as convenient substitutes for the things themselves. Knowledge is not then of individual presentations, but of types of presentation; in other words, of things in their intelligible aspect, i.e. of the being that things have in the mind of the knower, as principles, genera and species. In so far as knowledge is directed to the attainment of ends it is called practical; in so far as it remains in the knower, theoretical or speculative. Finally, we cannot say that a man knows wisely, but that he knows well; wisdom takes knowledge for granted and governs the movement of the will with respect to things known; or we may say that wisdom is the criterion of value, according to which a decision is made to act or not to act in any given case or universally. Which will apply not merely to external acts, but also to contemplative or theoretical acts.

Philosophy, accordingly, is a wisdom about knowledge, a *correction du savoir-penser*. In general, philosophy (2)[2] has been held to embrace what we have referred to above as theoretical or speculative knowledge, for example, logic, ethics, psychology, aesthetic, theology, ontology; and in this sense the problems of philosophy are evidently those of rationalisation, the purpose of philosophy being so to correlate the date of empirical experience as to 'make sense' of them, which is accomplished for the most part by a reduction of particulars to universals (deduction). And thus defined, the function of philosophy contrasts with that of practical science, of which the proper function is that of predicting the particular from the universal (induction). Beyond this, however, philosophy (1) has been held to mean a wisdom not so much about particular kinds of thought, as a wisdom about thinking, and an analysis of what it means to think, and an enquiry as to what may be the nature of the ultimate reference of thought. In this sense the problems of philosophy are with respect to the ultimate nature of reality, actuality or experience; meaning by reality whatever is in act and not merely potential. We may ask, for example, what *are* truth, goodness and beauty (considered as concepts abstracted from experience), or we may ask whether these or any other concepts abstracted from experience have actually any being of their own; which is the matter in debate as between nominalists on the one hand and realists, or idealists, on the other.[3] It may be noted that, since in all these applications philosophy means 'wisdom', if or when we speak of philosophies in the plural, we shall mean not different kinds of wisdom, but wisdom with respect to different kinds of things. The wisdom may be more or less, but still one and the same order of wisdom.

As to this order, if knowledge is by abstraction, and wisdom about knowledge, it follows that this wisdom, pertaining to things known or knowable, and attained by a process of reasoning or dialectic from experimental data, and neither being nor claiming to be a revealed or gnostic doctrine, in no way transcends thought, but is rather the best kind of thought, or, let us say, the truest science. It is, indeed, an excellent wisdom, and assuming a good will, one of great value to man.[4] But let us not forget that because of its experimental, that is to say statistical basis, and even supposing an infallible operation of the reason such as may be granted to mathematics, this wisdom can never establish absolute certainties, and can predict only with very great probability of success; the 'laws' of science, however useful, do nothing more than resume past experience. Furthermore, philosophy in the second of the above senses, or human wisdom about things known or knowable, must be systematic, since it is required by hypothesis that its perfection will consist in an accounting for everything, in a perfect fitting together of all the parts of the puzzle to make one logical whole; and the system must be a *closed* system, one namely limited to the field of time and space, cause and effect, for it is by hypothesis about knowable and determinate things, all of which are presented to the cognitive faculty in the guise of effects, for which causes are sought.[5] For example, space being of indefinite and not infinite extent,[6] the wisdom about determinate things cannot have any application to whatever 'reality' may or may not belong to non-spatial, or immaterial, modes, or similarly, to a non-temporal mode, for if there be a 'now' we have no sensible experience of any such thing, nor can we conceive it in terms of logic. If it were attempted by means of the human wisdom to overstep the natural limits of its operation, the most that could be said would be that the reference 'indefinite magnitude' (mathematical infinity) presents a certain analogy to the reference 'essential infinity' as postulated in religion and metaphysics, but nothing could be affirmed or denied with respect to the 'isness' (esse) of this infinite in essence.

If the human wisdom, depending upon itself alone ('rationalism'), proposes a religion, this will be what is called a 'natural religion', having for its deity that referent of which the operation is seen everywhere, and yet is most refractory to analysis, viz. 'life' or 'energy'. And this natural religion will be a pantheism or monism, postulating a soul (*anima*, 'animation') of the universe, everywhere known by its effects perceptible in the movements of things; amongst which things any distinction of animate and inanimate will be out of place, inasmuch as animation can be defined rationally only as 'that which is expressed in, or is the cause of, motion'. Or if not a pantheism, then a polytheism or pluralism in which a variety of animations ('forces') is postulated as underlying and 'explaining' a corresponding variety of motions.[7] But nothing can be affirmed or denied as regards the proposition that such animation or animations may be merely determinate and contingent aspects of a 'reality' indeterminate in itself. Expressed more technically, pantheism and polytheism are essentially profane conceptions, and if recognisable in a given religious or metaphysical doctrine, are there interpolations of the reason, not essential to the religious or metaphysical doctrine in itself.[8]

On the other hand, the human wisdom, not relying on itself alone, may be applied to a partial, viz., analogical, exposition of the religious or metaphysical wisdoms, these being taken as prior to itself. For although the two wisdoms (philosophy (2) and philosophy (1)) are different in kind, there can be a formal coincidence, and in this sense what is called a 'reconciliation of science and religion'. Each is then dependent on the other, although in different ways; the sciences depending on revealed truth for their formal correction, and revealed truth relying upon the sciences for its demonstration by analogy, 'not as though it stood in need of them, but only to make its teaching clearer'.

In either case, the final end of human wisdom is a good or happiness that shall accrue either to the philosopher himself, or to his neighbours, or to humanity at large, but necessarily in terms of material well-being. The kind of good envisaged may or may not be a moral good.[9] For example, if we assume a good will, i.e. a natural sense of justice, the natural religion will be expressed in ethics in a sanction of such laws of conduct as most conduce to the common good, and he may be admired who sacrifices even life for the sake of this. In aesthetic (art being *circa factibilia*) the natural religion, given a good will, will justify the manufacture of such goods as are apt for human well-being, whether as physical necessities or as sources of sensible pleasure. All this belongs to humanism' and is very far from despicable. But in case there is not a good will, the natural religion may equally be employed to justify the proposition 'might is right' or 'devil take the hindmost', and in manufacture the production of goods either by methods which are injurious to the common good, or which in themselves are immediately adapted to ends injurious to the common good; as in the case of child-labour and the manufacture of poison gas. Revealed truth, on the contrary, demands a good will *a priori*, adding that the aid of the rational philosophy, as science or art, is required in order that the good will may be made effective.[10]

There is then another kind of philosophy (1), viz., that to which we have alluded as 'revealed truth', which though it covers the whole ground of philosophy (2), does so in another way, while beyond this it treats confidently of 'realities' which may indeed be immanent in time and space tissue, and are not wholly incapable of rational demonstration, but are nevertheless said to be transcendent with respect to this tissue, i.e. by no means wholly contained within it nor given by it, nor wholly amenable to demonstration. The First Philosophy, for example, affirms the actuality of a 'now' independent of the flux of time; while experience is only of a past and future. Again, the procedure of the First Philosophy is no longer in the first place deductive and secondarily inductive, but inductive from first to last, its logic proceeding invariably from the transcendental to the universal, and thence as before to the particular. This First Philosophy, indeed, taking for granted the principle 'as above, so below' and vice-versa,[11] is able to find in every microcosmic fact the trace or symbol of a macrocosmic actuality, and accordingly resorts to 'proof' by analogy; but this apparently deductive procedure is here employed by way of demonstration, and not by way of proof, where logical proof is out of the question, and its place is taken either by faith (Augustine's *credo ut intelligam*) or by the evidence of immediate experience (*alaukikapratyakṣa*).[12]

Our first problem in connection with the highest wisdom, considered as a doctrine known by revelation (whether through ear or symbolic transmission), consistent but unsystematic, and intelligible in itself although it treats in part of unintelligible things, is to distinguish without dividing religion from metaphysics, philosophy (2) from philosophy (1). This is a distinction without a difference, like that of attribute from essence, and yet a distinction of fundamental importance if we are to grasp the true meaning of any given spiritual act.

We proceed therefore first to emphasise the distinctions that can be drawn as between religion and metaphysics with respect to a wisdom that is one in itself and in any case primarily directed to immaterial, or rationally speaking, 'unreal' things.[13] Broadly speaking, the distinction is that of Christianity from Gnosticism, Sunnī from Shi'a doctrine, Rāmânuja from Śaṇkarācarya, of the will from the intellect, participation (*bhakti*) from gnosis (*jñāna*), or knowledge-of (*avidyā*) from knowledge-as (*vidyā*). As regards the Way, the distinction is one of consecration from initiation, and of passive from active integration; and as regards the End, of assimilation (*tadākāratā*) from identification (*tadbhāva*). Religion requires of its adherents to be perfected; metaphysics that they realise their own perfection that has never been infringed (even Satan is still virtually Lucifer, being fallen in grace and not in nature). Sin, from the standpoint of religion, is moral; from that of metaphysics, intellectual (mortal sin in metaphysics being a conviction or assertion of independent self-subsistence, as in Satan's case, or envy of the spiritual attainments of others, as in Indra's).

Religion, in general, proceeds from the being in act (*kāryâvasthā*) of the First Principle, without regard to its being in potentiality (*kāraṇâvasthā*);[14] while metaphysics treats of the Supreme Identity as an indisseverable unity of potentiality and act, darkness and light, holding that these can also and must also be considered apart when we attempt to understand their operation in identity in It or Him. And so religion assumes an aspect of duality,[15] viz., when it postulates a 'primary matter', 'potentiality' or 'non-being' far removed from the actuality of God, and does not take account of the principal presence of this 'primary matter' in, or rather 'of' the First, as its 'nature'.[16]

Religions may and must be many, each being an 'arrangement of God', and stylistically differentiated, inasmuch as the thing known can only be in the knower according to the mode of the knower, and hence as we say in India, 'He takes the forms that are imagined by His worshippers', or as Eckhart expresses it, 'I am the cause that God is God'.[17] And this is why religious beliefs, as much as they have united men, have also divided men against each other, as Christian or heathen, orthodox or heretical.[18] So that if we are to consider what may be the most urgent *practical* problem to be resolved by the philosopher, we can only answer that this is to be recognised in a control and revision of the principles of comparative religion, the true end of which science, judged by the best wisdom (and judgment is the proper function of applied wisdom), should be to demonstrate the common metaphysical basis of all religions and that diverse cultures are fundamentally related to one another as being the dialects of a common spiritual and intellectual language; for whoever recognises this, will no longer wish to assert that 'My religion is best', but only that it is the 'best for me'.[19] In other words, the purpose of religious controversy should be, not to 'convert' the opponent, but to persuade him that his religion is essentially the same as our own. To cite a case in point, it is not long since we received a communication from a Catholic friend in which he said 'I've been ashamed for years at the superficiality and cheapness of my attempt to state a difference between Christians and Hindus'. It is noteworthy that a pronouncement such as this will assuredly strike a majority of European readers with a sense of horror. We recognise in fact that religious controversy has still generally in view to convince the opponent of error rather than of correctness in our eyes; and one even detects in modern propagandist writing an undertone of fear, as though it would be a disaster that might upset our own faith, were we to discover essential truth in the opponent; a fear which is occasioned by the very fact that with increasing knowledge and understanding, it is becoming more and more difficult to establish fundamental differences as between one religion and another. It is one of the functions of the First Philosophy to dissipate such fears. Nor is there any other ground whatever upon which all men can be in absolute agreement, excepting that of metaphysics, which we assert is the basis and norm of all religious formulations. Once such a common ground is recognised, it becomes a simple matter to agree to disagree in matters of detail, for it will be seen that the various dogmatic formulations are no more than paraphrases of one and the same principle.[20]

Few will deny that at the present day Western civilisation is faced with the imminent possibility of total functional failure nor that at the same time this civilisation has long acted and still continues to act as a powerful agent of disorder and oppression throughout the rest of the world. We dare say that both of these conditions are referable in the last analysis to that impotence and arrogance which have found a perfect expression in the dictum 'East is East and West is West, and never the twain shall meet', a proposition to which only the most abysmal ignorance and deepest discouragement could have given rise. On the other hand, we recognise that the only possible ground upon which an effective *entente* of East and West can be accomplished is that of the purely intellectual wisdom that is one and the same at all times and for all men, and is independent of all environmental idosyncrasy.[21]

We had intended to discuss at greater length the differentia of religion and metaphysics, but shall rather conclude the present section by an assertion of their ultimate identity. Both, considered as Ways, or praxis, are means of accomplishing the rectification, regeneration and reintegration of the aberrant and fragmented individual consciousness, both conceive of man's last end (*puruṣārtha*) as consisting in a realisation by the individual of all the possibilities inherent in his own being, or may go farther, and see in a realisation of all the possibilities of being in any mode and also in possibilities of non-being, a final goal. For the Neo-Platonists and Augustine, and again for Erigena, Eckhart and Dante, and for such as Rūmī, Ibn 'Arabī, Śaṇkarācarya, and many others in Asia, religious and intellectual experience are too closely interwoven ever to be wholly divided;[22] who for example would have suspected that the words 'How can That, which the Comprehending call the Eye of all things, the Intellect of intellects, the Light of lights, and numinous Omnipresence, be other than man's last end', and 'Thou hast been touched and taken! long has Thou dwelt apart from me, but now that I have found Thee, I shall never let Thee go', are taken, not from a 'theistic' source, but from purely Vedāntic hymns addressed to the Essence (*ātman*) and to the 'impersonal' Brahman!

II. HOW DIVERS WISDOMS HAVE CONSIDERED IMMORTALITY

Let us consider the application of different kinds of wisdom to a particular problem of general significance. The pertinence of philosophy to the problem of immortality is evident, inasmuch as wisdom is primarily concerned with immaterial things, and it is evident that material things are not immortal as such (in *esse per se*) nor even from one one moment to another, but are continually in flux, and this is undeniable, regardless of whether there may or may not be in such perpetually becoming things some immortal principle. Or to regard the matter from another angle, we may say that whatever, if anything, there may be immortal in phenomenal things must have been so since time began, for to speak of an immortal principle as having become mortal is the same thing as to say it was always mortal.

It needs no argument to demonstrate that human wisdom, rationalism, our philosophy (2), will understand by 'immortality', not an everlasting life on earth, but an after-death persistence of individual consciousness and memory and character, such as in our experience survives from day to day across the nightly intervals of death-like sleep. Rational wisdom then will take up either one of two positions. It may in the first place argue that we have no experience of nor can conceive of the functioning of consciousness apart from the actual physical bases on which the functioning seems to rest, if indeed consciousness be in itself anything whatever more than a function of matter in motion, that is to say of physical existence; and will not therefore conceive the possibility of any other than an immortality in history, viz., in the memories of other mortal beings. In this sense there can also be postulated the possibility of a kind of resurrection, as when memory is refreshed by the discovery of documentary proofs of the existence of some individual or people whose very names had been forgotten it may be for millennia. Or human wisdom may maintain, rightly or wrongly, that evidences have been found of the 'survival of personality', viz., in communciations from the 'other world', of such sort as to prove either by reference to facts unknown to the observer, but which are afterwards verified, or by 'manifestations' of one sort or another, a continuity of memory and persistence of individual character in the deceased who is assumed to be in communication with the observer. If it is then attempted to rationalise the evidence thus accepted, it is argued that there may be kinds of matter other and subtler than those perceptible to our present physical senses, and that these other modalities of matter may very well serve as the suppositum of consciousness functioning on other planes of being.

It will be readily seen that no spiritual or intellectual distinction can be drawn between the two rationalistic interpretations, the only difference between them being as regards the amount or kind of time in which the continuity of individual character and consciousness can be maintained in a dimensioned space and on a material basis, theories of 'fourth dimensions' or of 'subtle matter' changing nothing in principle. Both of the rationalistic interpretations are rejected *in toto*, equally by religion and metaphysics.

Not that the possibility of an indefinite perdurance of individual consciousness upon indefinitely numerous or various platforms of being and various temporal modes is by any means denied in religion or in metaphysics (it being rather assumed that individual consciousness even now functions on other levels than those of our present terrestrial experience)[23], but that a persistence in such modes of being is not, strictly speaking, an immortality, this being taken to mean an immutability of being without development or change and wholly uneventful; while that which is thus presumed to subsist apart from contingency, viz. the soul, form or noumenal principle (*nāma*) of the individual, by which it is *what* it is, must be distinguished alike from the subtle and the gross bodies (*sūkṣma* and *sthūla śarīra*) which are equally phenomenal (*rūpa*), as being wholly intellectual and immaterial.[24]

For example, 'things belonging to the state of glory are not under the sun' (St. Thomas, *Sum. Theol.* III, Supp. q. I, a. I), i.e. not in any mode of time or space; rather, 'it is through the midst of the Sun that one escapes altogether' (*atimucyate, Jaiminīya Up. Brāhmaṇa* I. 3), where the sun is the 'gateway of the worlds' (*loka-dvāra*), (*Chānd. Up.* VIII. 6.6), Eckhart's 'gate through which all things return perfectly free to their supreme felicity (*pūrṇânanda*) . . . free as the Godhead in its non-existence' (*asat*), the 'Door' of John X, 'Heaven's gate that Agni opens' (*svargasya lokasya dvāram avṛṇot*), (*Aitareya Brāhmaṇa*, III. 42).[25] It is true that here again we shall inevitably meet with a certain and by no means negligible distinction of the religious from the metaphyscial formulation. The religious concept of supreme felicity culminates as we have already seen in the assimilation of the soul to Deity in act; the soul's own act being one of adoration rather than of union. Likewise, and without inconsistency, since it is assumed that the individual soul remains numerically distinct alike from God and from other substances, religion offers to mortal consciousness the consolatory promise of finding there in Heaven, not only God, but those whom it loved on earth, and may remember and recognise.

Nor will metaphysics deny that even in a 'Heaven', on the farther side of time, there may be, at least until the 'Last Judgment', a knowledge-of (*avidyā*) rather than a knowledge-as (*vidyā*), though it will not think of him whose modality is still in knowledge-of as wholly Comprehending (*vidvān*) nor as absolutely Enlarged (*atimukta*). Metaphysics will allow, and here in formal agreement with religion, that there may or even must be states of being by no means wholly in time, nor yet in eternity (the timeless now), but aeviternal, 'aeviternity' (Vedic *amṛtatva*) being defined as a mean between eternity and time;[26] the Angels for example, as conscious intellectual substances, partaking of eternity as to their immutable nature and understanding, but of time as regards their accidental awareness of before and after, the changeability of their affections (liability to fall from grace, etc.), and inasmuch as the angelic independence of local motion (because of which Angels are represented as winged, and spoken of as 'birds'),[27] whereby they can be anywhere, is other than the immanence of the First, which implies an equal presence everywhere. Nor is it denied by religion that 'Certain men even in this state of life are greater than certain angels, not actually, but virtually' (St. Thomas, *Sum. Theol.*, I, q. 117, a. 2, *ad.* 3), whence it naturally follows that 'Some men are taken up into the highest angelic orders' (Gregory, *Hom. in Ev.* XXXIV), thus partaking of an aeviternal being; all of which corresponds to what is implied by the familiar Hindu expression *devo bhūtvā*, equivalent to 'dead and gone to Heaven'. Precisely this point of view is more technically expressed in the critical text, *Bṛhadāraṇyaka Up.* III. 2.12, 'When a man dies, what does not forsake (*na jahāti*) him is his "soul" (*nāma*),[28] the soul is without end (*ananta*, "aeviternal"), without end is what the Several Angels are, so then he wins the world everlasting' (*anantam lokam*). Cf. Rūmī (XII in Nicholson's *Shams-i-Tabrīz*), 'Every shape you see has its archetype in the placeless world, and if the shape perished, no matter, since its original is everlasting' (*lāmkān-ast*); and St. Thomas, *Sum. Theol.* II-I, q. 67, a. 2c, 'as regards the intelligible species, which are in the *possible* intellect, the intellectual virtues remain', viz. when the body is corrupted. This was also expounded by Philo, for whom 'Le lieu de cette vie immortelle est le monde intelligible',[29] that is to say the same as the 'Intellectual Realm' of Plotinus, *passim*. If we now consider the implications of these dicta in connection with Boehme's answer to the scholar who enquires, 'Whither goeth the soul when the body dieth?' viz. that 'There is no necessity for it to *go* anywither . . . For . . . whichsoever of the two (that is either heaven or hell) is manifested in it (now), in that the soul standeth (then) . . . the judgment is, indeed, immediately at the departure of the body',[30] and in the light of *Bṛhadāranyaka. Up.*, IV. 4. 5–6, 'As is his will . . . so is his lot' (*yat kāmam . . . tat sampadyate*) and 'He whose mind is attached (to mundane things) . . . returns again to this world . . . but he whose desire is the Essence (*ātman*), his life (*prâṇāḥ*) does not leave him, but he goes as Brahman unto Brahman', it will be apparent that although the soul or intellect (Vedic *manas*) is immortal by nature (i.e. an individual potentiality that cannot be *annihilated,* whatever its 'fate'), nevertheless the actual 'fate' of an individual consciousness, whether it be destined to be 'saved' or 'liberated' (*devayāna*), or to enter into time again (*pitṛyāna*), or to be 'lost' (*nirṛtha*), depends upon itself. And therefore we are told to 'Lay up treasure in Heaven, where neither moth nor rust corrupt'; for evidently, if the conscious life of the individual be even now established intellectually (or in religious phraseology, 'spiritually'), and the intellectual or spiritual world be aeviternal (as follows from the consideration that ideas have neither place nor date), this conscious life cannot be infringed by the death of the body, which changes nothing in this respect. Or if the consciousness be still attached to and involved in ends (whether good or evil) such as can only be accomplished in time and space, but have not yet been accomplished when the body dies, then evidently such a consciousness will find its way back into those conditions, viz., of space and time, in which the desired ends can be accomplished.[31] Or finally, if conscious life has been led altogether in the flesh, it must be thought of as cut off when its sole support is destroyed; that is, it must be thought of as 'backsliding' into a mere potentiality or hell.

Space will not permit us to discuss the theory of 'reincarnation' at any length. The fundamentals are given in the *Ṛg Veda,* where it is primarily a matter of recurring manifestation, in this sense for example, Mitra *jāyate punaḥ* (X. 85. 19) and Uṣas is *punaḥpunar jāyamāna* (I. 19. 10). An individual application in the spirit of 'Thy will be done' is found in V. 46. 1, 'As a comprehending (*vidvān*) horse I yoke myself unto the pole (of the chariot of the year) . . . seeking neither a release nor to come back again (*na asyāḥ vimucaṁ na āvṛttam punaḥ*), may He (Agni) as Comprehender (*vidvān*) and our Waywise Guide lead us aright'. The individual, indeed, 'is born according to the measure of his understanding' (*Aitareya Āraṇyaka,* II. 3. 2), and just as 'the world itself is pregnant with the causes of unborn things' (Augustine, *De Trin.* III. 9); so is the individual pregnant with the accidents that must befall him; as St. Thomas expresses it, 'fate is in the created causes themselves' (*Sum. Theol.* I. q. 116, 2), or Plotinus, 'the law is given in the entities upon whom it falls, . . . it prevails because it is within them . . . and sets up in them a painful longing to enter the realm to which they are bidden from within' (*Enneads*, IV. 3. 15); and similarly Ibn 'Arabī, who says that while being is from God, modality is not directly from Him, 'for He only wills what they have it in them to become' (Nicholson, *Studies in Islamic Mysticism*, 1921, p.151). On the other hand, it may be taken as certain that the Buddhist and still more the modern Theosophical interpretations of causality (*karma*) or fate (*adṛṣṭa*), which assert the necessity of a return (except for one who is *mukta* or has 'reached' *nirvāṇa*) to the very same conditions that have been left behind at death, involve a metaphysical antinomy; 'You would not step twice into the same waters, for other waters are ever flowing in upon you' (Heracleitus). What is really contemplated in Vedic and other traditional doctrines is the necessity of a recurrent manifestation in aeon after aeon, though not again within one and the same temporal cycle,[32] of all those individual potentialities or forces in which the desire to 'prolong their line' is still effective; every Patriarch (*pitṛ*) being, like Prajāpati himself, *prajā-kāmya*, and therefore willingly committed to the 'Patriarchal Way' (*pitṛyāna*).

What is then from the standpoint of metaphysics the whole course of an individual potentiality, from the 'time' that it first awakens in the primordial ocean of universal possibility until the 'time' it reaches the last harbour? It is a return into the source and well-spring of life, from which life originates, and thus a passage from one 'drowning' to another; but with a distinction, valid from the standpoint of the individual in himself so long as he is a Wayfarer and not a Comprehender, for, seen as a process, it is a passage from a merely possible perfection through actual imperfection to an actual perfection, from potentiality to act, from slumber (*abodhya*) to a full awakening (*sambodhi*) Ignoring now the Patriarchal Way as being a 'round about' course, and considering only the straight Angelic Way (*devayāna*), with which the *Ṛg Veda* is primarily and the individual *mumukṣu* specifically concerned, we may say that this Way is one at first of a diminishing and afterwards of an increasing realisation of all the possibilities intrinsic to the fact of being in a given mode (the human, for example), and ultimately leads to the realistion of all the possibilities of being in any or every mode, and over and beyond this of those of being not in any mode whatever. We cannot do more than allude here to the part that is taken by what is called 'initiation' in this connection; only saying that the intention of initiation is to communicate from one to another a spiritual or rather intellectual impulse that has been continuously transmitted in *guru-paramparā-krama* from the beginning and is ultimately of non-human origin, and whereby the contracted and disintegrated individual is awakened to the possibility of a re-integration (*saṁskarana*);[33] and that metaphysical rites, or 'mysteries' (which are in imitation of the means employed by the Father to accomplish His own re-integration, the necessity for which is occasioned by the incontinence of the creative act), are, like the analogous traditional scriptures, intended to provide the individual with the necessary preparatory education in and means of intellectual operation; but the 'Great Work', that of accomplishing the reunion of essence with Essence, must be done by himself within himself.

We have so far followed the Wayfarer's course by the Angelic Way to the spiritual or intellectual realm; and here, from the religious point of view, lies his immortality, for indeed 'the duration of aeviternity is infinite' (St. Thomas, *Sum. Theol.* I, q. 10, a. 5, *ad.* 4). But it will be maintained in metaphysics, or even in a religion or by an individual mystic such as Eckhart (in so far as the religious experience is both devotional and intellectual in the deepest sense of both words) that an aeviternal station (*pada*), such as is implied in the concept of being in a heaven, is not the end, nor by any means a full return (*nivṛtti*), but only a resting place (*viśrāma*).[34] And likewise, it will be maintained that to conceive of the intellectual realm itself as a place of memories would be a derogation, for as Plotinus says of its natives, 'if they neither seek nor doubt, and never learn, nothing being at any time absent from their knowledge . . . what reasonings, what processes of rational investigation, can take place in them? In other words, they have seen God and they do not recollect? Ah, no . . . such reminiscence is only for souls that have forgotten' (*Enneads*, IV. 4. 6);[35] and still more must we say respecting mundane memories (*vāsanā*) that 'when the soul's act is directed to another order, it must utterly reject the memory of such things, over and done with now' (*ibid*, IV. 4. 4. 8).

The metaphysical concept of Perfection, indeed, envisages a state of being that is, not *in*human since it is maintained that such a state is always and everywhere accessible to whoever will press inwards to the central point of consciousness and being on any ground or plane of being, nor 'heartless' unless we mean by 'heart' the seat of soulfulness and sentimentality; but assuredly *non*-human. For example, in *Chāndogya Up.* v. 10. 2 it is precisely as *amānava puruṣa*, 'non-human person', that the Son and aeviternal *avatāra*, Agni,[36] is said to lead onward the Comprehending one who has found his way through the Supernal Sun to the farther side of the worlds, and this is the 'pathway of the Angels' (*devayāna*) as contrasted with that of the Patriarchs (*pitṛyāna*) which does not lead beyond the Sun but to re-embodiment in a human mode of being. And it is foreseen that this *devayāna* must lead, whether sooner or later, to what is expressed in doctrinal mysticism as a 'final death of the soul', or 'drowning', the Sūfi *al-fanā 'an al-fanā*; by which is implied a passage beyond even consciousness in deity as act, to a Supreme (Skt. *para, parātpara*) beyond all trace or even an exemplary multiplicity, nor in any way 'intelligible'. And there, so far that is from any possible 'reminiscence' of any that have been known or loved in otherness, in the words of Eckhart, 'No one will ask me whence I came or whither I went', or in Rūmī's, 'None has knowledge of each who enters that he is so-and-so or so-and-so.'[37]

If this appears to be a denial of ultimate significance to human love, the position has been altogether misunderstood. For all metaphysical formulations, assuming that an infallible analogy relates every plane of being to every other, have seen in human love an image of divine felicity (*pūrṇânanda*), imagined not as a contradiction of but as transformation (*parāvṛtti*) of sensual experience. This is the theory of 'Platonic love', according to which, as Ibn Farīd expresses it, 'the charm of every fair youth or lovely girl is lent to them from Her beauty'; a point of view implicit too in Erigena's conception of the world as a theophany, and in the Scholastic doctrine of the *vestigium pedis*, the trace or footprint of divinity in time, which has its equivalent in Vedic and Zen symbolisms. What this means in actual tradition is that the beloved on earth is to be realised *there* not as she is in herself but as she is in God,[38] and so it is in the case of Dante and Beatrice, Ibn 'Arabī and an-Niẓām,[39] and in that of Chandīdās and Rāmī.[40] The beauty of the Beloved *there* is no longer as it is here contingent and merely a participation or reflection, but that of the Supernal Wisdom, that of the One Madonna, that of the intrinsic being of the Bride, which 'rains down flames of fire' (*Convivio*) and as *claritas* illuminates and guides the pure intellect. In that last and hidden station (*guhyam padam*), nature and essence, Apsaras and Gandharva, are one and indivisible, knowing nothing of a within or a without (*na bāhyaṁ kiṁcana veda nântaram, Bṛhadāraṇyaka Up.* IV. 321), and that is their supreme felicity, and that of every liberated consciousness.

All this can only be described in terms of negation, in terms of what it is *not*, and therefore we say again that metaphysics can in no way be thought of as a doctrine offering consolations to a suffering humanity. What metaphysics understands by immortality and by eternity implies and demands of every man a total and uncompromising denial of himself and a final mortification, to be dead and buried in the Godhead. 'Whoever realises this, avoids contingent death (*punar mṛtyu*), death gets him not, for Death becomes his essence, and of all these Angels he becomes the One' (*Bṛhadāraṇyaka Up.* I. 2. 7). For the Supreme Identity is no less a Death and a Darkness than a Life and a Light, no less Asura than Deva: 'His overshadowing is both Aeviternity and Death' (*yasya chāyā amṛta, yasya mṛtyuḥ, Ṛg Veda,* X. 121. 2).[41] And this is what we understand to be the final purport of the First Philosophy.

NOTES

1. It is not pretended to lay down a final definition of philosophy.

2. Our numbering of the philosophies in inverse order as (2) and (1) is because Aristotle's First Philosophy, viz. Metaphysics, is actually prior in logical order of thought, which proceeds from within outwards.

3. This is, for example, the matter in debate as between Buddhist and Brahmanical philosophers. For the nominalist, the ultimate forms, ideas, images or reasons are merely names of the counters of thought and valid only as means of communication; for the realist (idealist) the ultimate forms are 'realities' dependent upon and inherent in being, i.e. real in their being and nominal only in the sense 'only logically distinguishable'.

4. Common sense is an admirable thing, as is also instinct, but neither of these is the same as reason, nor the same as the wisdom that is not about human affairs, but 'speculative', i.e. known in the mirror of the pure intellect.

5. When a cause is discovered, this is called an explanation. But each cause was once an effect, and so on indefinitely, so that our picture of reality takes the form of a series of causes extending backward into the past, and of effects expected in the future, but we have no empirical experience of a now, nor can we explain empirically how causes produce effects, the assumption *post hoc propter hoc* being always an act of faith.

6. As is very elegantly demonstrated by St. Thomas, *Sum. Theol.* I, q. 7, a. 3, cf. q. 14, a. 12, *ad.* 3; his 'relatively infinite' being our 'indefinite' (*ananta*), incalculable (*asaṁkhya*) but not placeless (*adeśa*) nor wholly timeless (*akāla*).

7. Science differs from animism only in this respect, that while science assumes forces in the sense of blind wills, animism (which is also a kind of philosophy) personifies these forces and endows them with a free will.

8. Pantheism is more commonly predicated of a given doctrine merely by imputation, either with unconsciously dishonest intention or by customary usage uncritically perpetuated. In every case the observer presumed to be impartial should consider the doctrine itself, and not what is said of it by hostile critics. On the general impropriety of the term 'pantheism' in connection with the Vedānta, see Lacombe, Avant-propos to René Grousset, *Les Philosophies Indiennes*, p. xiv, note 1, and Whitby, Preface to René Guénon, *Man and his Becoming according to the Vedānta*, 1945, p. ix.

9. St. Thomas, *Sum. Theol.* I, q. 1, a. 6, ad. 2.

10. Prudence is defined as *recta ratio agibilium*, art as *recta ratio factibilium*.

11. E.g. *Aitareya Brāhmaṇa*, VIII. 2.

12. 'Metaphysics can dispute with one who denies its principles, if only the opponent will make some concession; but if he concede nothing, it can have no dispute with him. . . . If our opponent believes nothing of divine revelation, there is no longer any means of proving the articles of faith by reasoning' (St. Thomas, *Sum. Theol.* I, q. 1, a. 8 c.); and *ibid.* q. 46, a. 2: 'The articles of faith cannot be proved demonstratively.'

Similarly in India it is repeatedly and explicitly asserted that the truth of Vedic doctrine cannot be demonstrated but only experienced. '*By what* should one know the Knower of knowing' (*Bṛhadāraṇyaka Up.* IV. 5. 15).

13. Throughout the present essay it is assumed that sensibility means the perception of things by the senses, not a cognition but a reaction; reason, the activity of the intelligence with respect to the causal series of accidents, sometimes called the chain of fate, or in other words an intelligence with respect to things phenomenally known in time and space and called 'material'; and intellect, the habit of first principles.

14. Thus *Chāndogya Up.* VI. 2. 1 asserts a religious point of view, as distinct from the metaphysical point of view that prevails in the Upaniṣads generally, e.g. *Taittiriya Up.* II. 7. Christian philosophy maintains that God is 'wholly in act'. Metaphysics concurs in the definition of perfection as a realisation of all the possibilities of being, but would rather say of God that 'He does not proceed from potentiality to act' than that He is without potentiality.

15. Duality, as of 'spirit and matter', 'act and potentiality', 'form and substance', 'good and evil'. This is avoided in Christianity metaphysically, when it is shown that evil is not a self-subsistent nature, but merely a privation, and can be known to the First Intellect only as a goodness or perfection *in potentia*. It is avoided in Sūfi metaphysic by considering good and evil as merely reflections in time and space of His essential attributes of Mercy and Majesty.

16. 'Matter' here must not be confused with the 'solid matter' of everyday parlance; in Christian philosophy, 'primary matter' is precisely that 'nothing' with respect to which it is said *ex nihilo fit*. Such 'matter' is said to be 'insatiable for form', and the same is implied when in the *Jaiminiya Up. Brāhmaṇa*, I. 56, it is said that 'In the beginning, the woman (= Urvaśī, Apsaras) went about in the flood seeking a master' (*icchantl salile patim*).

17. The physical analogy is represented in the assertion of the anthropologist that 'God is man-made'; a proposition perfectly valid within the conditions of its own level of reference.

18. That is mainly, of course, in Europe from the thirteenth century onwards. In Hinduism, a man is regarded as a true teacher who gives to any individual a better access to that individual's *own* scriptures; for 'the path men take from every side is

Mine' (*Bhagavad Gītā*, IV. 11). Clement of Alexandria allows that 'There was always a natural manifestation of the one Almighty God amongst all right-thinking men' (*Misc.*, v); Eckhart says almost in the words of the *Bhagavad Gītā* cited above, 'In whatever way you find God best, that way pursue', Dante will not exclude all the pagan philosophers from Heaven; in the Grail tradition, Malory says that 'Merlyn made the round table in tokenyng of the roundenes of the world for by the round table is the world sygnifyed by ryghte. For all the world crysten and hethen repayren vnto the round table' (*Mort d'Arthur*, XIV. 2); these may be contrasted with the position taken in the Song of Roland where, when Saragossa has been taken, 'A thousand Franks enter the synagogues and mosques, whose every wall with mallet and axe they shatter . . . the heathen folk are driven in crowds to the baptismal font, to take Christ's yoke upon them.'

19. The 'best for me' need not be 'truest absolutely' as judged by absolute metaphysical standards. Nevertheless, the metaphysician will not suggest that the follower of a 'second best' religion should abandon it for another (cf. *Bhagavad Gītā*, III. 26, *na buddhibhedaṁ janayed ajnānam*), but rather that he go *farther in* where he already is, and thus verify as 'true' his own images, not by those of another pattern, but rather by the prior form that is common to both.

20. 'Diverse dogmatic formulations', i.e. *dharma-paryāya* as this expression is employed in the *Saddharma Puṇḍarika*.

21. In this context the reader is recommended to René Guénon, *L'Orient et l'Occident*, 1932.

22. Cf. Erigena, *De div. naturae*, I, 66, *Ambo siquidem ex una fonte, divina scilicet sapientia, manare dubium non est*, and *Bhagavad Gītā*, V. 4–5, 'it is the children of this world, and not the men of learning who think of gnosis and works as different . . . He sees in truth who sees that gnosis and works are one' (for Sāṁkhya and Yoga as meaning gnosis and works respectively, see *ibid*, III. 3). That the Way of Gnosis and the Way of Participation have one and the same end becomes evident when we consider that love and knowledge can only be conceived of as perfected in an identity of lover and beloved, knower and known.

23. 'Even we ourselves as mentally tasting something eternal, are not in this world.' St. Augustine, *De Trin.* IV. 20.

24. Therefore incapable of 'proof', whether the phenomena adduced be 'scientific' or 'spiritualistic'.

25. While it is shown here how the formulations of different religions may express the same conceptions in almost verbal agreement, it must not be supposed that we therefore advocate any kind of eclecticism, or conceive the possibility of a new religion compounded of all existing religions. Eclecticism in religion results only in confusion and caricature, of which a good example can be cited in 'Theosophy'.

26. St. Thomas, *Sum. Theol.* I, q.10, a. 5. He says 'states of being' in the plural deliberately (cf. René Guénon, *Les États multiples de l'Être*, 1932), although for purposes of generalisation it has been necessary to speak only of three, viz. the human, angelic and divine, that is those to which the literal, metaphorical and analogical understandings pertain respectively.

With the Christian 'aeviternity', Indian *amṛtatva*, and the traditional concept of 'humanity' and 'Perfect Man' (e.g. Islamic *insanu'l kamil*), cf. Jung, *Modern Man in Search of a Soul*, p.215: 'If it were permissible to personify the unconscious, we might call it a collective human being combining the characteristics of both sexes, transcending youth and age, birth and death, and from having at its command a human experience of one or two million years, almost immortal. If such a being existed, he would be exalted above all temporal change . . . he would have lived countless times over the life of the individual, or the family, tribe and people, and he would possess the living sense of the rhythm of growth, flowering and decay. It would be positively grotesque for us to call this immense system of the experience of the unconscious psyche an illusion.' Here it may be noted that 'unconscious' presents an analogy with 'Deep-Sleep' (*susupti* = *samādhi* = *excessus* or *raptus*); on the other hand, the use of the word 'collective' betrays a purely scientific, and not a metaphysical conception.

27. 'Intellect is the swiftest of birds' (*manaḥ javiṣtam patayatsu anaḥ*, *Ṛg. Veda*, VI. 9. 5). It is as birds that the Angels 'celebrate in the Tree of Life their share of aeviternity' (*yatra suparṇā amṛtasya bhāgam . . . abhi svaṛanti, ibid.*, I. 164. 21). The traditional expression 'language of birds' (which survives in 'a little bird told me') refers to angelic communications.

28. *Nāma* is the correlative of *rūpa*, being the noumenal or intelligible part and efficient cause of the integration *nāma-rūpa*, viz. the individual as he is in himself; and therefore to be rendered not by 'name' (for this is not a nominalist but a realist doctrine), but by 'idea', 'archetype', 'form' or 'soul' (as when it is said 'the soul is the form of the body'); *ātman* on the other hand being 'essence' rather than 'soul' (*essentia*, that by which a substance has *esse* in whatever mode).

29. Bréhier, *Les Idées philosophiques et religieuses de Philon d'Alexandrie*, 1925, p.240.

30. Boehme, *On Heaven and Hell* (in Everyman's Library, volume entitled *Signatura Rerum*, etc.).

31. It is the good purpose, for example, which operates in the return of a Bodhisattva, who is otherwise fit for Nirvāṇa.

32. In *Bhagavad Gītā*, VI. 41, for example, *śāsvatī samā* is very far from implying 'forthwith'. We doubt very much whether any Aupaniṣada passage could be cited as implying a re-embodiment otherwise than at the dawn of a new cycle, and then only as the growth of a seed sown in the previous aeon, or as a tendency with which the new age can be said to be pregnant.

33. See *Aitareya Āraṇyaka*, III. 2. 6; *Aitareya Brāhmaṇa*, VI. 27; *Ṣatapatha Brāhmaṇa*, VII. 1. 2. 1 and *passim*. Cf. also Guénon, 'L'Initiation et les Métiers', *Le Voile d'Isis*, No. 172, 1934.

34. *Saddharma Pundarika*, V. 74. Similarly, the true end of the ritual acts and appointed sacrifices of the Veda is not the attainment of a temporary heaven, but the awakening of a desire to know the Essence (*ātman*) (*Siddhāntamuktāvalī*, XXXIII, with Venis' note 'Paradise is as it were but the half-way house').

35. Similarly in Dante, *Paradiso*, XXIX, 79–81, 'there sight is never intercepted by any new perception, and so there is no need of memory, for thought has not been cleft'.

36. Agni(-Prajāpati), who in the Vedas is the Herdsman of the Spheres (*gopā bhuvanasya*), Waywise Leader (*vidvān pathaḥ puraeta*), Messenger and Herald (*dūta, arati*), and stands as the Pillar of Life at the Parting of the Ways (*dyor ha skambha . . . pathāṁ visarge, Ṛg Vedā*, X. 5. 6) in cosmic crucifixion (*dharuṇeṣu sthitaḥ, ibid.*), corresponding to the 'dogmatic' Buddha, Christ as distinguished from Jesus, and to the 'Idea of Muḥammad'.

37. Nicholson, *Shams-i-Tabriz*, p. 61.

38. Cf. *Tarjumān al-Ashwāq*, XL. 2, 'She was exalted in majesty above time' and Rūmī, ' 'Tis love and the lover that live to all eternity' (XIII, in Nicholson, *Shams-i-Tabriz*). Another example could be cited in the *Shepherd of Hermas*.

39. Whom Ibn 'Arabī met at Mecca in 1201, see Nicholson, *Tarjumān al-Ashwāq*, 1911.

40. Cf. 'Sahaja' in our *Dance of Śiva*, 1917.

41. Similarly, *Śatapatha Brāhmaṇa*, X. 4. 3. 1–3 *Eṣa vai mṛtyur yat samvatsaraḥ . . . prajāpatiḥ*, 'He, the Father, who is the Year and likewise Death'.

The Darkness and Light, belonging to His *asuratva* and *devatva* respectively, remain in Him, who is both *asura* and *deva*, Titan and angel, *sarpa* and *āditya*; at the same time that from the Wayfarer's point of view their reflections in time and space are evil and good. In Hinduism, 'the Darkness in Him is called Rudra' (*Maitri Up.* VI. 2), and is represented in the names and hues of Kālī and Kṛṣṇa; in Christian *yoga*, the Dark Ray or Divine Darkness, Eckhart's 'sable stillness' and 'motionless dark that no one knows but He in whom it reigns' (cf. the 'Clouds and thick darkness' of Deut. 4: 11), is spoken of already in the Codex Brucianus and by Dionysius, and becomes the subject of the *contemplatio in caligine*. Regarding the propriety of the expression 'Christian *yoga*', we need only point out that St. Bernard's *consideratio*, *contemplatio*, and *excessus* or *raptus* correspond exactly to *dhāraṇa*, *dhyāna* and *samādhi*.

THREE

On Being in One's Right Mind

I REPENTANCE

'Swer wil werden daz er solte sīn, der muoz lāzen, daz er iezunt ist.'
Meister Eckart, Pfeiffer p. 606.

Μετάνοια,[1] usually rendered by 'repentance', is literally 'change of mind', or intellectual metamorphosis. Plato does not use the word (for the verb, see *Euthydemus*, 279C), but certainly knows the thing: for example, in *Republic*, 514F, the values of those who have seen the light are completely transformed, and, in *Laws*, 803C–804A, we are told that those who have realised their true relation to and actual de-pendence on God will be 'thinking (διανοέομαι) otherwise than they do now', and that 'it behooves our fosterlings to be of that same (new) way of thinking'; cf. St. Augustine's *reformamini in novitate mentis* (*Confessions*, XIII.13). Further, Plato distinguishes 'understanding' (συνιέναι) from 'learning' (μανθάνειν) as knowledge from relative ignorance (*Euthydemus*, 278A); and the *Shepherd of Hermas* is certainly not misinterpreting the real meaning of μετάνοια when he says that 'Repentance is a great understanding' (τό μετανοῆσαι . . . σύνεσίς ἐστιν μεγάλη), and, in fact, a transformation from the state of the fool (ἄφρων) to that of one possessed of intellect (νοῦς, *Mand.* IV.2.1, 2), In the same way Hermes (*Lib.* I. 18) opposes μετἀνοια to ἄγνοια, this 'ignorance' being, in *Lib.* XIII. 7b, the first of the 'irrational torments of matter', just as in the Buddhist *nidāna* series it is the primary source of all evils.[2]

It is, indeed, unfortunate that our word 'repentance' translates μεταμέλεια rather than μετάνοια; for the latter word imports far more than the merely moral meaning of regret for past error. The man who has really been 'converted', i.e., turned round (τρέπω, στρέφω), will have no time to spend in punishing himself, and if he does impose hardships on himself it will not be by way of penance, but (1) as a discipline like that of an athlete in training and (2) in imitation of the divine poverty. On this level of reference there can be no room for remembrance of or sorrow for past errors, to which the words, 'Let the dead bury their dead', are properly applicable, the 'dead' being the 'old man' who is now no more for those who can say with St. Paul, *vivo autem, jam non ego*. 'Such an one, verily, the thought does not torment, Why have I not done the right? Why have I done wrong?' (*Taittirīya Up.* II.9). So there comes a point in Dante's ascent at which he says 'Non mi ricorda' (*Purgatorio*, XXXIII. 91). How, indeed, should one who has ceased to be anyone either recall or regret what 'he' had done when he *was* someone? It is only when and if he returns from the unitive state to 'himself' that he can again remember or regret.

Τὸ μετανοῆσαι = τὸ συνιέναι is, then, to come to an understanding *with*. We stress the word 'with', because in order to grasp the problems involved it is essential to remember, what can easily be overlooked, that all words containing the prepositions co- or con-, *cum*, σύν, *sam-*, and all such terms as 'self-control', 'self-government', and 'self-possession' (= com-posure), imply a relation between *two* things (cf. Plato, *Republic*, 431A, B, 436B), which two are, in the last analysis, respectively human and divine. For example, 'When thou art rid of self, then art thou Self-controlled (*dīnes selbes gewaltic* = ἐγχρατής ἑαυτοῦ = *svarājan*), and Self-controlled art Self-possessed (*dīnes selbes eigen*), and Self-possessed, possessed of God (*ist got dīn eigen*) and all that he has ever made' (*Meister Eckhart*, Pfeiffer, p.598).[3] All of this will apply to σύνεσις, σύνουσια, and σύννοια, to the verbs σύνειμι and σύνιημι, to 'be together with' and 'come together with', to Sanskrit *sam-ādhi*, 'syn-thesis' or 'com-posure' and the verbs *sambhū, sampad, saṁgam, sami*, etc., all implying con-gress and unification, a 'becoming one' (*eko bhū*) in the erotic no less than in other senses, cf. τελέω, to be perfected, to marry, or to die.

In other words, the 'great understanding' is a kind of synthesis and agreement (Skr. *saṁdhi, samādhi, saṁjñāna*), by which our internal conflict is resolved, or as the Sanskrit texts also express it, in which 'all the knots of the heart are loosed'. If we ask, an agreement of what with what? the answer will be evident: unanimity (ὁμόνοια)[4] of the worse and better, human and divine parts of us, as to which should rule (Plato, *Republic*, 432C); 'assimilation of the knower with the to-be known (τῷ κατανοουμένῳ τὸ κατανοοῦν ἐξομοίωσις), in accordance with the archetypal nature, and coming to be in this likeness' (Plato, *Timaeus*, 90D, cf. *Bhagavad Gītā*, XIII.12–18, *jñeyan . . . anādimatparam brahma . . .*), 'which likeness begins now again to be formed in us' (St. Augustine, *De spir. et lit.* 37); *con-scientia* with our 'divine part', when the two parts of the mortal soul have been calmed and the third part of the soul is so moved that we are 'of one mind with our real Self' (σύννοιαν αὐτός αὐτῷ ἀφικόμενος), thus obtaining true knowledge in the stead of our opinion (*Republic*, 571, 572). In Indian terms this is also the marital agreement, or unanimity of the elemental self (*bhūtātman, śarīra ātman*) with the prescient solar Spirit (*prajñātman, aśarīra ātman*) in a union transcending the consciousness of a within or a without (*Bṛhadāraṇyaka Up*. IV. 3. 21); in other words, the fusion of the Outer King with the Inner Sage, the *Regnum* with the *Sacerdotium.*

Μετάνοια is, then, a transformation of one's whole being; from human thinking to divine understanding. A transformation of our being, for as Parmenides said, 'To be and to know are one and the same' (Diels, *Fr.* 18.5), and 'We come to be of just such stuff as that on which the mind is set' (*Maitri Up*, VI. 34. 3). To repent is to become another and a new man. That this was St. Paul's understanding is clear from Ephesians, 4:23, 'Be ye renewed in the spirit of your mind' (ἀνανεοῦσθαι δὲ τῷ πνεύματι τοῦ νοὸς ὑμῶν).

II ON THE 'TWO MINDS'

God is 'not a man, that he should repent' (1 Sam. 15:29, cf. Ps. 110:4, and Ezek. 24:4). Metanoia is a 'change of mind' differing only in its larger implication from the change of mind that has taken place when we repent of any intention. When we do this, it is because we feel ourselves to be now 'better advised' and so able to act 'advisedly', or as Plato would express it, κατὰ λόγον. Whose advice are we taking? Who gives counsel when we 'take counsel with ourselves'? On this point Socrates had no doubt, for, as he says, 'When I was about to cross the stream, the daimonian sign that usually comes to me was given—it always holds me back from what I want to do—and I thought I heard a voice from it which forbade . . .' (*Phaedrus*, 242B).[5] Or, as Plato also says, 'there is a something in the soul that bids men drink and a something that forbids, something other than that which bids', what draws us on being the passions and diseases, and that which holds us back the voice of Reason (*Republic*, 439). Everyone has had experience of this.

We hardly need to say that Plato speaks of the Leader (ἡγεμών) within us by many names, such as vocal Reason (λόγος), Mind (νοῦς), Genius (δαίμων), and most divine (θειότατος) and best or ruling (κράτιστος) and eternal (ἀειγενής) part of us, nor to be reminded that this Immortal Soul 'is our real Self' (*Laws*, 959A) and that it is for 'us' to be Its servant (ὑπηρέτης, *Laws*, 645A, *Timaeus*, 70D, etc.); how otherwise, indeed, should 'Thy will be done on earth as it is in heaven'? This immanent divinity is likewise Philo's 'Soul of the soul' (ψυχὴ ψυχῆς), Hermes' 'Good Genius' (ὁ ἀγαθὸς δαίμων), and the 'Shepherd' of Hermas. It is the Scholastic 'Synteris', Meister Eckhart's '*Funkelein*', and however attenuated, our own 'Conscience'; but not by any means *our* 'reason', or Bergson's 'intuition'. It is the Spirit that Scripture, as St. Paul points out, so sharply distinguishes from the soul, and his *jam non ego, sed Christus in me* (Heb. 4:12 and Gal. 2:20). It is 'the Self of the self, called the "Immortal Leader"' (*ātmano'tmā netāmṛtākhyaḥ, Maitri Up.* VI. 7), the 'Inner Controller' (*antaryāmin, Bṛhadāraṇyaka Up.* III. 7. 1, etc.), 'Self (or Spirit) and King of all beings', or 'of all that is in motion or at rest' (*Bṛhadāraṇyaka Up.* I. 4. 16, II. 1. 2, *Ṛg Veda* I. 115. 1, etc.), the immanent Genius (*yakṣa*) or *Atharva Veda*, X. 8. 43 and *Jaiminīya Up. Br.*IV.24, and the impassible 'immortal, incorporeal Self' of *Chāndogya Up*, VIII. 12. 1, the 'That' of the famous dictum 'That art thou'.[6] And, just as for Plato, so in the Vedic books this deathless, impassible Inner Man and very Self 'dwells together with' the human, mortal, passible self in the 'house' or 'city' of the body for so long as 'we' are alive. It is this (Holy) 'Ghost' that we 'give up' when we die: and the poignant question arises, 'In whom, when I go forth, shall I be going forth?' (*Praśna Up.* VI. 3), the answer, according to which we shall be 'saved' or 'lost' depending upon whether before the end we have known 'Who we are' (*Jaiminīya Up. Br.* IV. 19. 4, 5, *Bṛhadāraṇyaka Up.* IV. 4. 14, *Bhagavad Gītā*, IV. 40, etc.).

We still make use of such expressions as to be 'double minded', 'strong or weak minded', 'in two minds' (about a purpose), and 'not to know one's own mind'; we also 'make up our minds',[7] and only when this has been done do we really know what we are really 'minded to do'. We use these expressions (like so many other inherited phrases) without a full consciousness of their meaning, just as we speak of 'self-government' or 'self-control' without realising that 'the same thing will never do or suffer opposite things in the same context and in relation to the same thing and at the same time. So that if we ever find these contradictions in the functions of the mind we shall know that it was not the same thing functioning' (*Republic*, 436B, cf. 431A, B, and *Parmenides*, 138B).[8] Actually, all these expressions derive their meaning from the age-old doctrine of the duality of human nature,[9] stated in terms of a duality or bivalence of mind (νοῦς, Skr. *manas*). It is this doctrine which Professor Goodenough seems to find so strange in Philo:[10] and yet, without it, the notion of repentance would be unintelligible. To know one's own mind is the same as to 'know oneself' or 'love oneself' in the superior sense of Aristotle (*Nich. Eth.* IX. 8), Hermes (*Lib.* IV. 6B), St. Thomas Aquinas (*Sum. Theol.* II-II. 26. 4), and the Upaniṣads (BU. II. 4, etc.). Philo says that 'There are two minds, that of all (beings),[11] and the individual mind: he that flees from his own mind flees for refuge to the mind of all in common.' The one is ungenerated and immortal, the other generated and mortal (I. 93). The soul being 'dead' when it is entombed in the passions and vices (I. 65, and as for St Paul) he points out that 'That which dies is not the ruling part of us, but the subject laity,and for so long as the latter will not repent (μέχρις ἂν μετανοία χρησάμενον) and acknowledge its perversion (τροπή), so long will it be held by death' (I:80). The individual mind is the same thing as our 'sensibility' (αἰσθήσις),[12] and 'it is always right that the superior should rule, and the inferior be ruled; and Mind is superior to sensibility' (I. 131); 'the easy-going man sinks down into his own incoherent mind' (I. 94, cf. *Bhagavad Gītā*, II. 67 and VI. 34),[13] i.e., 'estimative knowledge' in terms of 'hunger and thirst'.

It amounts to the same thing to deny the name of 'mind' to the estimative faculties of the sensitive soul, governed by its wants. Thus in Hermes, *Lib.* I. 22, it is asked, 'Have not all men mind?' and answered, 'Mind comes only to those that are devout and good and pure' (καθαρός = *śuddha*). In Platonic terms, the soul is mindless (ἄνους) at birth and may be still unconscious (ἀνόητος) at death (*Timaeus*, 44A, C); the unchanging Mind that is contrasted with opinion subject to persuasion is to be found only in the Gods and in a small number of men (*Timaeus*, 51E). If, however, we intend by 'mind' merely the human instrument of discursive thought, then to participate in the divine manner of knowing will be, humanly speaking, to be 'out of one's mind'; so of the Prophet through whom God speaks Plato says that 'his mind is not in him' (*Ion*, 534B), a state of 'mania' that must not be confused with insanity (*Phaedrus*, 244, 265): 'the wisdom of this world is foolishness with God' (I Cor. 3:19).

We have now seen that the notion of a 'change of mind' presupposes that there are two in us: two natures, the one humanly opinionated and the other divinely scientific; to be distinguished either as individual from universal mind, or as sensibility from mind, and as non-mind from mind or as mind from 'madness'; the former terms corresponding to the empirical Ego, and the latter to our real Self, the object of the injunction 'Know thyself'. We shall conclude by briefly noticing the equivalents of these formulations in the Indian sources.

The formulation in terms of two minds is explicit in Manu, I. 14: 'From himself the Self-existent drew forth the mind, of which the nature is real and the unreal' (*sadasad-ātmakam*)[14] the mind, that is, with which one thinks 'both good and evil' (*puṇyam ca . . . pāpam ca Jaiminīya Up. Br.* I. 60. 1) and which is, therefore, a means 'either of bondage or liberation' (*Maitri Up*. VI. 34. 11). 'The mind is said to be twofold, pure and impure (*śuddhāśuddham*): impure, by connection with desire, pure by separation from desire.[15] . . . Indescribable his bliss who abides in the Self, his mind's defilement washed away by Self-composure'[16] (*samādhi-nirdhauta-malasya niveśitasya ātmani, Maitri Up*. VI. 34. 6, 9).

The distinction of Mind from sensibility (νοῦς from αἴσθησις) is analogous to that of Manas, Mind, from Vāc, the power or faculty of expression. Mind becomes a name or hypostasis of God,[17] than whom there is no other that intelligizes (*nānyad ato'timantṛ, Bṛhadāraṇyaka Up*. III. 8. 11). Manas is the sacerdotal principle that knows and wills, Vāc the power of action without whom nothing would be effected. It is her function to 'imitate' (*kanukṛ*) him[18] and to act as his follower and messenger, 'for she is by far the lesser and he by far the superior' (*Taittirīya Saṃhitā*, II. 5. 11. 5; *Śatapatha Brāhmaṇa*, I. 4. 4. 7 and 5. 11). But though the Victory depends upon her co-operation, she may be reluctant to fulfil her office (*Śatapatha Brāhmaṇa*, I. 4. 4. 12; *Taittirīya Saṃhitā* II. 5. 11. 5, etc.); she is easily seduced from her allegiance to Mind and Truth to the service of what she likes to think, and then merely babbles SB. III. 2. 4. 11, etc., cf. Philo, I. 94).

In the Indian texts we also meet with the notion of a meliorative dementation as noted above. For when 'mind' is thought of only as a part of the psychic organism, then to be 'mindless' and 'unconscious' is the superior, and conscious mental operation the inferior condition. Thus, 'When the mind has been immolated in its own source for the love of Truth, then the false controls of actions done when it was deluded by sensibilia likewise pass away' *Maitri Up*, VI. 34. 1, 2); 'None whose mind has not been immolated can attain to Him' (*Kaṭha Up*. II. 24); viz., the Person, who being devoid of all limiting attributes is necessarily 'mindless', though the source of mind (*Muṇḍaka Up*. II. 1. 2, 3). God does not think and does not know in our imperfect way of knowing in terms of subject and object; we may say that he thinks, but there is no second thing, other than himself, of which he might think (*Bṛhadāraṇyaka Up*. IV. 3. 28, etc.).[19] In this sense, then, it is said that 'when one attains to the state of dementation (*amanibhāva*), that is the last step' (*Maitri Up*. VI. 34. 7), and we recognize the like doctrine in St. Thomas Aquinas, *Cum vero intellectus jam ad forman veritatis pertingit, non cogitat, sed perfecte veritatem contemplatur* (*Sum. Theol.* I, 34. 1, ad 2). We must only be careful not to confuse this superior mindlessness of the suprarational and superconscious with the mindlessness of the Titans who are still irrational and subconscious; just as we distinguish the non-being of the divine superessentiality from the non-being of what has not yet come into being or could not be.

To resume: in the first part of this article our intention was to show that what 'repentance' really means is a 'change of mind', and the birth of a 'new man' who, so far from being overwhelmed by the weight of past errors is no longer the man who committed them; and, in the second part, to outline the doctrine of the duality of mind on which the possibility of a 'change of mind' depends, and to demonstrate its universality; to point out, in other words, that the notion and necessity of a μετάνοια are inseparably bound up with the formulations of the *Philosophia Perennis* wherever we find them.

NOTES

1. Cf. Hans Pohlmann, *Die Metanoia als Zentralbegriff der christlichen Frommigkeit, Leipzig*, 1938; *also, Fr. Tucker, Syneidesis-Conscientia*, Jena, 1928.

2. See references in PTS *Pali Dictionary*, s.v. *paticca-samuppāda*; and Gerda Hartmann in *Journal of the American Oriental Society*, Vol. 60, (1940), 356f.

3. To bring out the meaning we distinguish 'self' from 'Self', as is commonly done in translation from Sanskrit to distinguish the mortal from its immortal Self; these two 'selves' corresponding to Plato's mortal and immortal 'soul', and to St. Paul's 'soul' and 'spirit', the former being that 'soul' that we must 'hate' if we would be Christ's disciples.

4. 'Α γὰρ ὁ θεὸς διδάσκει, αὑτῶ γίγνεται ὁμονοεῖν', Xenophon, *Occ.* XVII. 3. For we then participate in his πρόνοια = Skr. *prajñāna*, Providence or Prescience.

5. It is rather strange that in one context Socrates supposes that 'the daimonian sign has come to few or none before me' (*Republic*, 496C) but this is contradicted elsewhere, notably in *Timaeus* 90D and *Phaedo* 107D and cf. *Odyssey* III. 26.

6. That 'We (I) have the mind of Christ' (I Cor. 2:16) is but another way of saying the same thing, and it will be seen that the new mind and the new man are one, or in other words that to know one's real mind is the same as to know or love one's real Self (φιλήσας δὲ σεαυτόν, νοῦν ἕξεις, Hermes, *Lib.* IV. 6b), the Self of all beings. To have that Mind is to be 'blest with a good genius' (εὐδαίμων), but sole dependence on our own unstable mind is to be 'cursed with a bad genius' (χαχοδαίμων, Philo, I. 37, 38. Our 'free will' does not consist in doing what we like (i.e. what we must, by a 'natural' compulsion) but in a choice of guides, a choice between the good and evil Genii, 'the good Daimon' and the Evil, whose name is Legion.

7. This implies a con-sent of the two wills involved.

8. Philo, I. 94 seems to contradict, but is at fault; for it is not the same man who 'rubs himself' and is also rubbed; it is, say, a finger that rubs and a leg that is rubbed, and these are not the same man but two parts of the same man. Subjectively, it may be the better part that wills to rub, and the worse that needs rubbing; or the worse part that wants to be titillated and the better part that yields.

9. Plato, *Republic*, 604B, etc; II Cor. 4:16, St Thomas, *Sum. Theol.* II.II. 26. 4; Upaniṣads, *passim*.

10. E. R. Goodenough, *By Light, Light*, 1941, pp. 382–86.

11. The plural ὅλων cannot mean 'the universe', and ought not to be rendered thus, as it is by Colson and Whitaker in the Loeb Library edition. The 'mind of all in common' (συμπάντων) is that of the 'Self of all beings' in Plato, *Phaedo* 83B: 'Philosophy exhorts the soul to trow in nothing but her Self, that she may know her Self itself, the very Self of all beings' (αὐτὸ τῶν ὄντων = Skr. *sarvabhūtānām ātmā*). Xenophon remarks that 'When the God is our teacher, we all come to think alike' (ὁμονοεῖν, *Occ.* XVII. 3). It is when we 'think for ourselves', knowing only too well what we like to think, that we disagree.

12. 'The carnal mind is enmity against God' (Rom. 8:7).

13. We ought then to 'pour out as a libation the blood of the soul and sacrifice our whole mind to God' (Philo, I. 76). Eckhart says 'the mind must be demented of itself'; that implies by no means the modern anti-intellectualism (in favour of instinctive behaviour) but Plato's 'divine madness', for 'The men whom He dements He uses as his servants . . . it is God himself who speaks through them' (*Ion* 534D).

14. *Sat* and *asat* are primarily being, reality, truth and their contraries. In the Supreme Identity (*tad ekam*), without otherness (*advaitam*), these are no longer contraries; but considered apart, where *ens et bonum convertuntur, asat* as 'non-being' is 'evil' by the same token that English 'naught-y' is 'bad'.

15. As in Hermes, x. 16, νοῦς καθαρὸς . . . των ενδυμάτων. The 'purification' enjoined (*cittam . . . śodhayet, Maitri Up*.VI.34.3) is precisely the Platonic Katharsis, 'a separation of the "soul" from the "body", as far as that is possible', the kind of 'death' that is practised by philosophers (*Phaedo* 67C,F., cf. *Sophist* 227D); for Plato, purification and liberation are coincident (*Phaedo* 82) just as in the *Maitri Up*. VI. 34. 11 the mind detached from sensible objects (*nirvisayam*) is liberation (*mokṣ*).

16. *Samādhi* (literally synthesis, composure) is the consummation of *yoga*, and what is meant by Plato when he exhorts the soul to 'collect and concentrate itself in its Self' (αὐτὴν δὲ εἰς αὐτήν, *Phaedo*, 83A).

17. *Taittirīya Saṃhitā* II. 5. 11. 5, VI. 6. 10. 1; *Satapatha Br*. X. 5. 3. 1; *Bṛhadāraṇyaka Up*. V. 5. 6, etc.

18. Cf. Hermes, *Lib*. XII. 1. 13A. ὁ οὖν λόγος ἐστὶν εἰκὼν τοῦ νοῦ, και ὁ νοῦς τοῦ θεοῦ.

19. Cf. Witelo, *Intelligentia semper intelligit . . . (sed) si se ipsam cognoscendo non cognoscit alia (De Intelligentiis*, XXIV, XXVII, the Commentary adding (*id est*) *perceptionem non intelligit, sicut anima*.

FOUR

Beauty, Light and Sound

A coincidence of sound and light (*verba, lux*) is assumed in the first chapter of John.[1] In the words of Genesis, 'Let there be Light; and there was Light', no temporal succession of events is implied. 'Whence, says Basilides, came the Light? . . . It came forth from the voice of the Speaker' (Hippolytus, *Ref. Haer.* 22). Dionysius, and with him the whole Scholastic tradition, takes for granted and argues from an identity of good or being, beauty, light, and truth in the ultimate subject and first cause, that is God. Dionysius also takes over from Plato the idea of the 'summoning' power of beauty. With these positions the Vedic doctrine is in full agreement.

In the *Ṛg Veda* we are confronted with a variety of terms which are so pregnant in their significance that it is often impossible to say that they are employed in a given context to denote only one of the meanings 'good' (desirable, appetible, or lovable), 'radiant', or 'beautiful'. A number of these roots imply at the same time 'light' and sound', cf. *Chāndogya Up.* III. 13.7, where light is seen and heard; and we can only judge that in a given context one or other of these values predominates, and translate accordingly. *Arc*, for example, means both 'to shine' and 'to intone'; *bhā*, 'to shine' or 'beam' is ultimately inseparable from *bhan* 'to speak'; *chand*, primarily 'to be bright' and hence 'to gratify', gives rise to *chandas* in the senses of 'brilliance', 'incantation', 'metre', and 'desire', and *chanda* in those of 'radiant', 'enchanting', and 'singing'; *śvar* and *svṛ* imply either 'to shine' or 'to sound'. *Sūrya* and *sūra*, 'Sun', in the Vedic tradition coincident with *ātman*, 'Spirit' and *satyam*, 'Truth', (*Ṛg Veda*, I. 115.1) is derived from the two latter roots, which can hardly be distinguished; and while the idea of brilliance seems to predominate, we meet with such texts as *Jaiminīya Up. Brāhmaṇa* III. 33, 'The Sun is sound; therefore they say of the Sun that "He proceeds resounding"' (*ādityas svara eva . . . svara etī*),[2] and *Bṛhadāraṇyaka Up.* I. 2.1, where 'Death' (the Father) proceeding from despiration to spiration[3] becomes the 'Year', the 'Sun' (the Son), and is described as going on his way 'celebrating' (*arcan*), which certainly does not exclude the idea of 'shining', but means in this context according to Śaṇkarācārya, 'singing a song of praise' (*arcate, pūjāṁ kurvate*); and what 'delight' was experienced in this officiation is called the 'sheen' (*arkatva*) of 'shining' (*arkya*), with particular reference to that of the sacrificial Fire, of which the worlds are the hypostases. One must say, to paraphrase, that the shining of the Supernal Sun *in principio* and the creative utterance of the primordial 'Word', by which all things are at the same time revealed and evoked, are one and the same coincident 'event'.

The ambivalences of *arc* and *chand* are further illustrated in the following passages: RV. I. 92.3 and 6, 'The Dawns are singing (*arcanti*) like busy women at their tasks',[4] and 'Dawn in her beauty shines with an enchanting smile' (*śriye chando na smayate vibhātī*)[5] v. 52.12 'lauding with hymns' (*chando-stubhaḥ*); and VII. 7.3.6. 'bright in glory as the Sun' (*chando na sūro arciṣā*). In *Atharva Veda* VIII. 9.12 the Dawns are described as *chando-pakṣe*, which can be rendered either by 'having metrical wings' or 'moving on wings of desire'. The values of *chandas* are of particular interest in connection with the idea of 'self-integration in the mode of the metres, or incantations' (*chando-mayam . . . ātmānaṁ saṁskurate, Aitareya Brāhmaṇa* VI. 27), which is as much as to say the building up of a spiritual 'body' of rhythmic sound, or light, or of beautitude, since for *chando-maya* might be substituted here either *mantra-maya, jyotir-maya*, or *ānanda-maya*, 'incantational', 'luminous', or 'beautific'.

It is not, however, our intention here to discuss at length the Vedic and traditional Indian terminology of the beautiful. This has indeed already been done, so far as the *Ṛg Veda* is concerned, by Oldenberg in an admirable monograph[7] which should be consulted by every student of Indian aesthetics, and especially those who are interested in the comparison of Indian and Scholastic formulae. Our present purpose is rather to call attention to a more specific parallel in the more familiar Platonic and Christian-Platonic tradition, having in mind especially such passages as in Plato's *Symposium*,

'He who has been instructed thus far . . . when he comes to the end will suddenly perceive a nature of wondrous beauty . . . absolute, separate, simple, and everlasting, which without diminution and without increase, or any change, is imparted to the ever-growing and perishable beauties of all other things. He who from these ascending . . . using these as steps only . . . arrives at the notion of absolute beauty, and at last knows what the essence of beauty is', and Dionysius, *De Divinis Nominibus*, 'But the super-beautiful is rightly called beauty absolutely, both because the beautiful that is in existing things according to their several natures is derived from it, and because it is the cause of all things being in harmony, and of illumination; because, moreover, in the likeness of light it sends forth to everything the beautifying distribution of its own fontal raying; and for that it summons all things to itself . . . self-accordant with itself and uniform with itself, and always beautiful, and as the fount of all beauty, in itself preeminently possest of all beauty. For in the simple and supernatural nature of all things beautiful, all beauty and all that is beautiful have preexisted uniformly in their cause'. A parallel to these propositions occurs in *Chāndogya Up*. IV.15, of which we offer a literal translation, assuming the value of 'beautiful' for *vāma*, and adding to this a discussion of *vāma* and other of the characteristic terms:

> They call this Spirit (*ātman*), the immortal Brahman, the 'Convent of the Beautiful' (*saṁyad-vāmaḥ*), because all things beautiful (*sarvāni . . . vāmāni*) 'convene' (*samyanti*) in it. In one who understands this, likewise, all things beautiful convene. And it is also 'Beauty-bringer' (*vāma-nīḥ*), because it brings (*nayati*)[8] all beautiful things. And it is also 'Light-bringer' (*bhāma-nīḥ*) because it illuminates (*bhāti*) all the worlds. [Cf. *rāyo budhnaḥ samgamano vasūnām . . . savitā . . . samare dhanānām, Ṛg Veda*, X. 139.3] He who understands it likewise illuminates all the worlds.

With this may be compared JUB. IV. 18.6 = *Kena Up*. 31, 'It, the Brahman, is called 'That Lovesome' (*tad-vana*). As 'That Lovesome' it is to be adored. Towards one who understandeth this, all beings' love converges (*saṁvāñchanti*).

This last text immediately follows lines in which the direct experience of the Brahman has been compared to the blinding vision of lightning, and contrasted with the formation of mental concepts and with reminiscence, and this corresponds to Plato's 'will *suddenly* perceive'. That all beauties 'coincide' (*saṁyanti*) in one immutable principle of Beauty, which principle likewise 'brings them forth' (*nayati*), at the same time that it 'enlightens' (*bhātī*) the worlds, is to say with Dionysius that the First Cause 'in the likeness of light sends forth to everything the beautifying distributions of its own fontal raying'; by which we certainly do not mean to imply that Dionysius owed any part of his doctrine to Indian sources, but only to point out the unanimity of the *Philosophia Perennis,* Sanskrit *sanātana dharma.*

Vāma and *vana* in these passages derive from *van* to 'love' or 'like', of which a verbal form occurs in *-vāñchanti;* there is also no doubt a close connection with *vena,* 'loving', commonly an epithet of the Vedic Gandharva and Sun, who is also *darśataḥ* 'sightly'.[9] *Vāma* is usually translated by some such word as 'beautiful' or 'lovely', cf. such later expressions as *vāma-bhru,* 'having beautiful eyebrows' and *vāma-netra,* 'having beautiful eyes'. The rendering by 'lovely'[10] may be preferred, as implying at the same time 'beautiful', and having the attractive qualities of what is lovely, i.e. lovable; and this again reminds us of Dionysius, who also says 'The good is praised by sainted theologians as the beautiful and as beauty; and as delight and the delectable; and by whatever other befitting names are held to imply the beautifying power or the attractive qualities of beauty'.

The word *vāma* is discussed by Oldenberg, who says, *Rūpam, loc. cit.* p.114, 'It seems to me that *vāma* is used primarily to describe those things in the attainment of which one rejoices or would wish to rejoice'. Śaṅkaracarya, commenting on *vāmāni* in our *Chāndogya* text, explains it as *vananīyāni, sambhajanīyāni, śobhanāni,* i.e. 'desirable things, things in which one would wish to participate, beautiful things'. *Sambhajanīyāni,* from root *bhaj,* to 'parcel out', 'share', and in this sense to 'give', which 'giving' is the essential significance of the Vedic Bhaga and later Bhagavan as names of God, as well as that of *bhakti* generally with reference to the 'giving back' to God of what has been received,—is noteworthy here in connection with Dionysius, who describes all partial beauties as 'participations' and all relatively beautiful things as 'participants', saying that 'The beautiful and beauty are indivisible in their cause, which embraces All in One. In existing things, these are divided into "participations" and "participants"; for we call "beautiful" whatever participates in beauty; and "beauty" that participation in the beautifying power which is the cause of all that is beautiful in things'. It is in fact in just this sense that we find in the *Ṛg Veda* such texts as IV. 30.24 addressed to the Sun, 'Bestow what is most lovely' (*vāmamvāmam . . . dadhātu*, the duplication here implying the superlative); III. 55.22, 'May we, as thy companions, Indra, participate in what is fair' (*vāmabhājaḥ syām*); and VI. 19.10, 'May we, O Indra, enjoy the lovely' *vaṅsīmahi vāmam*, explained by Sāyaṇa *vananīyaṁ dhanam . . . sambhajemahi*, 'may we participate in treasure most to be desired'.)

Vāma in the *Ṛg Veda* is employed also in particular connection with the idea of Light. In I. 48.1 for example, Dawn is said to 'shine with beauty' (*saha vāmena . . . vy uccha*); in I. 164.1 the Sun is referred to as *vāma*, which Sāyaṇa again explains by *vananīya*, to be 'desired' or 'adored'. What the Gods essentially possess and are, they can be asked to give, and hence the prayer, 'May we obtain all lovely things' (*viśvā vāmāni dhīmahi*, V. 82. 6 and VIII. 22.18).[11] In *Taittiriya Saṃhitā* V. 5.3.3 *vāmam = jyotis*, light. That *vamani* is here primarily 'whatever is beautiful and bright' is suggested by the well known incantation, III. 62.10, 'May we behold, or obtain (*dhīmahi*) that desirable lustre (*bhargas*) of the Sun', etc; and this introduces us to another connection of beauty with light and with sound, in connection with the word *bhargas*; for whereas in RV. VIII. 22.18 the Aśvins are approached for the sake of 'all beautiful things (*viśva vāmāni*), in *Atharva Veda* VI. 69.2 and IX. 1.19 we find them addressed as 'Lords of Beauty' (*śubhaspatī*) and what is asked of them is 'that I may speak splendid words amongst the people', the words for 'splendid' in these verses being respectively *bhargasvat* and *varcasvat*. We may say then, that whereas *bhargas*, in connection with the Sun or Fire, is 'lustre', in connection with speech it is precisely that of our own 'brilliant' or 'scintillating', or that of 'sparkling' when we speak of a 'sparkling wit'. With *bhargas* may be compared Latin *claris*, 'illuminated', and *claritas*, in Scholastic aesthetic, as an indispensible condition of beauty, and the modern use of 'clear' in the expressions to hear or understand 'clearly'.[12]

As for *bhāti* in our Chāndogya text, it is of course a commonplace in the *Ṛg Veda* that Fire, Sun, or any other aspect of Deity 'illuminates' these worlds, as for example is explicit in II. 8.4; VI. 68.9; VII. 9.4; X. 6.2; and X. 121.6, in natural agreement with the analogy of the light of the physical sun.[13] All that need be emphasised here is that the light of the Supernal Sun, the 'Only Light' (*jyotis ekam*, I. 93.4), the 'Light of lights' (*jyotiṣāṁ jyotis*, RV I. 113.1 and *Bṛhadāraṇyaka Up*. IV. 4.16), is an omniform and image-bearing light (*jyotir asi viśvarūpam, Vājasaneyi Saṁhitājyotiṣā* V. 35; *sarūpeṇā*, RV. X., 55.3) which when it shines 'releases all fair-forms (*viśva rūpāṇi prati muñcate*, RV. V. 81.2). The detailed significance of these expressions, in which there is involved the exemplary concept of the relation between the One and the Many, is dealt with at greater length in my 'Vedic Exemplarism', in the *Harvard Journal of Asiatic Studies*, Vol. I, No. 1, 1936. [Rpr. SP2, pp. 177–197.]

We have said enough, perhaps, to show that our Chāndogya passage, interpreted with the help of related texts, parallels the doctrine of Dionysius in particular, and generally the whole Platonic and Scholastic concept of an absolute, immutable, single and compelling Beauty of Loveliness in which all several beauties and goods inhere, and from which these derive whatever in them is beautiful or good, by way of participation (*bhāgem-bhāgam*), by an exemplary likeness to One who 'fills these worlds by a distribution of Himself' (*ātmānam vibhajya pūrayati imānlokān, Maitri Up*. VI. 26). We have briefly traced throughout the Vedic tradition the concept of an identity *in re* of the good, the beautiful, being, and light; whether conceived as visually apprehended, or as expressed in sound and apprehended by audition, the mode of apprehension being in either case speculative. It need only be added that throughout this tradition likewise, the Supernal Sun is identified with Truth (*satyam, veritas*), and is in this sense also, 'enlightening'.

NOTES

1. Cf. René Guénon, 'Verbum, Lux et Vita', *Le Voile d'Isis*, Vol. 39, 1934, p. 173.

2. Cf. Dante, *Paradiso*, X. 76, 'So singing, these burning suns' (*sì cantando, quegli ardenti soli*). Note *tam indram abhigāyata* RV. VIII. 32. 13; *abhipragā, besingen*, RV. VI. 46.10; *ya eṣa tapati prâṇo* (breath) . . . (*imam lokam*) *abhyārcat* AĀ. II. 2.1, and *sa idam sarvam abhiprâ* (*jat*) 'all sounds are one word, *prâṇa* (breath)' AĀ. II. 2.2. [*Ahiprâ* (*jāt*), 3rd person singular of *gā* to sing, sang (Ānandatīrtha) went forth to (Sāyaṇa) visited (with song), hence 'Abhipragāthas'.] Also cf. *arka* as *song* in AV. IX. 2.2 and *arko vā eṣa yad agniḥ* (with Keith's note) 'the fire is a hymn', TS. V. 3.4.6.

3. Cf. in-halation, ex-halation, breath and halation, halo, light.

4. Oldenberg, *loc. cit., infra*, 'The double meaning of *arc* "to shine" and "to sing", leads to a comparison of the gleaming light of dawn to women singing at their tasks'.

5. *Chando na* is 'like a siren', 'exerting fascination'. Our word 'enchanting', or as we might have said, 'charming', properly combines the notions of a beauty that is at once visible and musical and exercises a compelling and activating power; the light of Dawn is at once a beauty and a call to action, setting all things at work (*vayunā kṛṇoti*, RV. I. 92.6, cf. III. 59.1 and VII. 36.2 for Mitra). The original senses of 'enchant' and 'charm' imply a musical 'spell'-binding.

6. Otherwise expressed, the 'metres' are the vehicle of liberation, and hence the later Tantric expression *mantra yāna*, 'incantational path'. An ascent by means of the metres is described in JUB. I. 18: 'assemble the metres (*chandāṁsi*), enter into them as a resort, and ye shall be removed from death, from evil'. In this way one ascends to the Sun, the Truth (*satyam, ibid.* I. 5), Sound (*svara*, ibid. III. 33): it is literally by the way of 'assonance' or 'tuning' that 'he who understands' (*evaṁvit*) is assimilated to the Source of Light; or—expressed in Christian terms—endues a Body of Glory. This is the metaphysical significance of all liturgical rites, and one may say also of all traditional arts, of which the last end is the realisation of the Absolute Beauty: and this is possible just because as Plotinus says, this music is 'an earthly representation of the music that there is in the realm of the ideal world',—Kabīr's 'unheard music',—and 'the crafts such as building and carpentry . . . take their principle from that realm and from the thinking there'. On this spiritual significance of 'rhythms' cf. E. Lebasquais, in *Le Voile d'Isis*, No. 184, 1935, p. 142, note 2, and René Guénon, *ibid.* No. 182, pp. 49–54. It may be observed, too, that the *Sāhitya Darpaṇa* III. 2–3 where the consummation of aesthetic experience is assimilated to the 'tasting of Brahman' (see my *Transformation of Nature in Art*, 1934, p. 49) is effectively a prolongation, restatement, or paraphrase of the Brāhmaṇa doctrine of sacrificial integration (*saṁskaraṇa*) as enunciated above in connection with the metres, and in the *Śatapatha Brāhmaṇa* in connection with the symbolism of the Fire-altar, the construction of which, like that of a cathedral, involves an eminent synthesis of all the arts.

7. Oldenberg, H. 'Die vedischen Wörter für Schön und Schönheit, und das vedischen Schonheitsgefühl', *Nahrichten v. d. K. Gesellschaftd. Wissenschaften zu Göttingen*, Berlin, 1918, Heft I, pp. 35–71; of which an English version appeared in *Rūpam*, No. 32, Calcutta, 1927, under the title 'Vedic words for the "beautiful" and "Beauty", and the Vedic sense of the Beautiful'. The discussion of *śrī*, where again there is a coincidence of the ideas of 'beauty' and 'light' is especially significant.

8. *Nī* is literally to lead or direct, and has a correlative in *ā-nī*, to lead towards oneself, or fetch. So *ā-nī* is used technically in connection with the act of imagination to denote the derivation of a specific form from an undifferentiated ground. For example, in a Buddhist *sādhana*, 'Thereupon our Blessed Lady (*bhagavatī*) is led forth (*ānīyate*) from the aetherial (*ākāśāt*) in her intelligible aspect (*jñāna-sattva-rūpa*) by means of the countless sheafs of rays by which the Three Worlds are enlightened', etc. The formal light is undefined by any specific form, but naturally emanates or projects (*nī*) in image-bearing rays; reciprocal (*avinâbhāva*) points of view; on the one hand, the image is a revelation, on the other a perception.

9. To the feminine *venā*, 'love', 'desire', 'darling', a designation of the Sun's bride Dawn (RV. I. 34.2)—cf. Ratī in relation to Kāmadeva, Śrī to Viṣṇu, and Psyche to Eros—corresponds to the Latin 'Venus'.

10. Hume has 'loveliness-uniter' for *saṁyad-vāmaḥ*. But *saṁyat*, like the Vedic *saṁgamana*, is rather 'meeting-place' than 'cause of meeting', 'union' or 'unity' rather than 'uniter'. The Ātman or Brahman is not the 'doer' of anything.

11. Sāyaṇa explains *dhīmahi* by *dhārayāma* and *labhāmahe*, 'may we hold, or get'. This value for *dhī* or dhyai, which means primarily to behold (speculatively, contemplatively) is most significant. It is precisely by speculation or contemplation that

things are known, found, done, made, and possessed; for example RV. x. 11.1 'Varuṇa knows all things speculatively' (*viśvam sa veda varuṇo yathā dhiyā*); IV. 1.10 'What the immortals have created by their speculation' (*dhiyā yad viśve amṛtā akṛṇvān*); x. 53.6 'Paths made by speculation' (*patho . . . dhiyā kṛtān*); *Kauṣītaki Up.* III. 6, 'He obtains whatever is intellectually visualised' (*manasāarvāṇi dhyānāny āpnoti*).

12. ἡ γὰρ σαφὴς φράσις πολὺ φως παρέχεται ταις των ἀκουόντων διανοίαις: 'clear expression floods with light the hearers' minds' and cf. σαφής, √sap in sap-iens, *Demetrius*, I. 17.

13. Cf. Dante, *Convivio*, III. 12. 'No object of sense in the whole world is more worthy to be made a type of God than the sun, which illumines first himself and then all other celestial and elemental bodies with celestial light'.

FIVE

Windows of the Soul

WHAT follows deals only with the power of vision; but it must be understood that whatever is said is applicable, *mutatis mutandis,* to the other powers of the soul, or internal senses and their physical organs. In the late Professor Bowman's discussion of the 'Person in the Eye'[1] there are many confusions.[2] He quotes Max Müller to the effect, 'the sun owes its origin to the eye', and asks 'whether it could really have been maintained in all seriousness that a minute organ of the human body can create an object of such cosmic proportions as the sun'; he tries to explain how this could have been imagined.

The misunderstanding is profound. It is true that in RV. x. 90.13 we find 'the sun was born of (his) sight' (*cakṣoḥ sūryo ajāyata*), and in AA. II. 1. 7 'by (his sight were emanated sky and sun' (*cakṣuṣā sṛṣṭau dyauś cādityaś ca*). But the visual power (*vibhūti*) referred to here is by no means that of the 'minute organ of the human body'; but that of the Primordial Person, God himself, whose eye is the Sun, or whose eyes are Sun and Moon, RV. *passim*. At the same time microocosmically, the eye does not originate the sun, but the Sun the eye. 'The Sun,[3] becoming vision, entered into the eyes' (*ādityaś ca cakṣur bhutvā akṣiṇī praviśat,* AĀ. II. 4.2).[4] 'The Self-originated (*svayambhū*)[5] pierced the gateways (*khāni,* of the senses)[6] outward, therefore looketh forth, not at the Inner Self' (KU. IV. 1). He who is hidden (*guhām praviśya*) within us[7] looketh forth in all creatures (KU. IV. 6, cf. AV. IV. 11.2); the only seer within us, himself is unseen (BU. III. 7.23). Accordingly, 'whoever sees, it is by *His* ray that he sees' (JUB. I. 28.8).

This is, indeed, the traditional theory of vision. So in Plato we find that 'of the organs, they (the Gods instructed by Zeus) constructed first light-bearing eyes . . . So whenever the stream of vision . . . flows out, like unto like . . . and) the fire from within collides with an obstructing object without . . . (it) brings about that sensation which we call "seeing"' (*Timaeus*, 45B).[8] And just as KU. IV. 1 goes on to point out that if we are to see the Seer, our seeing must be turned round (*āvṛtta cakṣus*), so Plato says that to apprehend the form or idea of the Good we ought to cultivate all those 'studies that compel the soul to turn its vision round towards the region wherein dwells the most eudaimonic part of reality, which it is imperative that I should look upon' (*Republic*, 526E).[9] If someone is looking out of a window, it becomes a matter of the simplest logic to point out that in order to see *him*, one must look in at the window.

But if the room is dark, and the external glare intense, we shall see nothing but our own reflection in the window. So it is when we look into another's eyes, and only see therein a tiny image of ourself, as if in a mirror. The material image and the optical mirror being coincident, the same name applies to both; and that we are dealing with a widely diffused and very ancient formula will be evident at once if we note that the 'apple' or 'pupil' (lat. *pupilla*, little girl) of the eye is not only in Skr. *kanīna* or *kanīnā*, *kanīnaka* or *kanīnakā* (mannikin or little girl) or *kumāraka* (little boy) but also in Gk. κôρη (maiden), in Hebrew *bath* (daughter) and *īyshōwn* (dim. of *īysh*, man), and in Chinese *t'ung* (Giles 12,308, a combination of the characters for 'eye' and 'child', m. ozf.). Chinese has also *mou* (Giles 8046)—proverbially, the *mou* of the eye is the best clew to character; it cannot deceive. Other connotations of the various words for 'child' are those of virginity or purity, and that of something 'darling', in which sense we say 'apple' (a corruption of *pupilla*?) of the eye.

In the traditional symbolism the 'pupil' of the eye, as reflected image, stands for what is best and highest and most intelligible in the seen, and for what is best and highest and most intelligent in the seer. We find this in Plato, *Alcibiades*, I. 132F—'the face of one who looks into another's eye is shown in the eye over against him, as if in a mirror, and we call this (mirror or reflection) the "pupil" (κόρη), because it is a sort of image (εἴδωλον) of the one who looks . . . So one eye looking at another, and at the most perfect part of it, with which it sees, will see itself . . . And if the soul, too, is to "know herself", she must surely look at soul, and at that region of the soul in particular in which the virtue of the soul subsists . . . the seat of knowledge and thought, the most divine part, that is the most like God; and whoever looks at this, and comes to know all that is divine, will best "know himself".'[10] Similarly Philo (I. 15)—God 'made man, and bestowed upon him the superior Mind (νοῦς),[11] the Soul of the soul, the pupil (κόρη) of the eye . . . the "eye of the eye".' In other words, 'l'oeil que, en se mirant dans un autre oeil, arrive à la connaissance de lui-même et en même temps à la connaissance de Dieu'.[12]

The eye, however, that does not 'know itself' will see nothing but itself (this man, So-and-so) and not the 'self's immortal Self' (MU. VI. 7), Philo's 'Soul of the soul'. The image actually seen in a physical mirror by the eye's intrinsic faculty is of my accidents, not of my essence.[13] Nevertheless, our self is a reflection of the Self in a likeness that, however imperfect, is perfectible. That the symbol must not be substituted for its referent is very clearly brought out in CU. VIII. 7 ff., where Prajāpati tells his pupils, Virocana and Indra, that 'the Person in the eye (*yo'kṣiṇi puruṣo dṛśyata, cākṣuṣaḥ puruṣa*) or in a mirror is 'the Self, the immortal, the fearless, Brahma'.[14] Told to look at themselves in a bowl of water,[15] Virocana is satisfied that the Self is this bodily self that is reflected, but Indra realises that this cannot have been Prajāpati's meaning; the perishing psycho-physical self seen in the looking-glass image cannot be the 'immortal' Self. He learns to distinguish this immortal from the bodily self and that 'where vision is lost in "space" (*ākāśam anuviṣaṇṇaṁ cakṣus*), that is the Person in the eye, (whose) means-of-vision is the eye . . . Mind (*manas* = νοῦς) is His divine eye, it is with that eye of mind, indeed, that he sees and determines values'.[16]

This will still be obscure unless we understand 'space' (*ākāśa*). In the context the immediate meaning, as rightly explained by Śaṅkara, is 'the black star' (*kṛṣṇa-tārā*), i.e. pupil of the eye, considered as a 'hole in the body' (*deha-chidram*). As such it corresponds to the opening or hole in the sky (*divaś chidram*), like the axle-hole (*yathā kham*) of a wheel (JUB. I. 3.6,7); the Sundoor, that is, normally concealed by his rays, but visible when these are withdrawn, as at death.[17] As one might see through the Sundoor into the Brahma-loka, so through the eye one might see the immanent Person whose outlook it is.[18]

More generally, *ākāśa* (or *kha*) as quintessence is the origin, locus and end of all phenomena (CU. I. 9.1 etc). All this universe was *ākāśa* in the beginning, and is so still; *ākāśa* is the Sun, because when he rises all this universe is shown (*ākāśate*); *ākāśa* is Indra, the seven-rayed Sun[19] and Person in the eye (JUB. I. 25.1, I. 28.2). The root, alike in *ākāśa* and in *cakṣus*, eye, is *kāś*, to shine or see. Thus *ākāśa* is rather image-bearing light than phsyical space as such; it is the *prima substantiarum*.[20] As αἰθήρ is distinguished from ἀήρ, so *ākāśa* from *vāyu*, the Gale (BG. XII. 6 etc.)—Ākāśa, indeed, as being light, is better rendered by 'aether' than by 'space'. Αἰθήρ is a principle that burns or shines, and just as it can be identified with God (Ζεύς ἐστιν αἰθήρ, Aeschylus Fr.65A), so *ākāśa*, or its equivalent *kham* ('vacuity', 'plenum')[21] is identified with Brahma (BU. VI; CU. III. 12.7, IV. 10.4) and all that is contained in this aether objectified is contained subjectively in the aether of the heart, the seat of Brahma (CU. VIII. 1.3).[22] So 'lost in "space"' means 'lost in God', in a light-space that cannot be traversed, and of which the objective realms of light are only a projection; His eye creating what it sees, and what 'we' also see by means of his light ray for which 'our' eyes are windows microcosmically, as the Sundoor is his window, macrocosmically.

It is not by looking at these eyes, but through them, that He can be seen; who is the Self that sees nothing but itself (BU. IV. 3.23), itself in all things, and all things in itself (BG. VI. 29); the Self of which nothing can be affirmed (*neti, neti*), and that 'never became anyone'. This is the distinction of the Sun whom 'not all know with the mind' from the sun 'whom all men see' (AV. X. 8.14), the distinction of Apollo from Helios. The natural man is spiritually blind. Hence it is a necessary part of the ritual of initiatory rebirth that his eyes should be anointed, so that he may see with the eye or eyes of the Sacrifice, the Sun, rather than with his own which he will only resume when, at the close of the sacrificial operation, he becomes again 'who he is', this man So-and-so.[23] 'His eye for mine, what a goodly recompense'! (Rūmī, *Mathnawī*, I. 922) The symbol participates in its referent.

Accordingly, the vision of ourselves that we see in another's eye is a symbol of the Self-seen Self in the Speculum Aeternum. The whole construction is not psychological, but metaphysical. The consummation is nowhere more magnificently formulated than in the

Mantiqu'ṭ-Tair, whereof the 'Birds' that reach their goal, and

ventured from the Dust to raise
Their Eyes—up to the Throne—into the Blaze,
And in the Centre of the Glory there
Beheld the Figure of—*Themselves*—as t'were
Transfigured—looking to Themselves, beheld
The Figure on the Throne en-miracled,
Until their Eyes themselves and *That* between
Did hesitate which *Sëer* was, which *Seen* . . .
and heard a Voice that said,
'The Sun of my Perfection is a Glass
Wherein from *Seeing* into *Being* pass
All who, reflecting as reflected see
Themselves in Me, and Me in Them . . .
Who in your Fraction of Myself behold
Myself within the Mirror Myself hold
To see Myself . . .
Come you lost Atoms, to your Centre draw,
And *be* the Eternal Mirror that you saw.'[25]

In Meister Eckhart's words, 'The eye with which I see God is the same eye with which God sees in me: my eye and God's eye, that is one eye and one vision, one knowledge and one love'.[26]

Professor Bowman is right in saying that the final conclusion is that the true Self is 'not the person *seen in* the eye, but the person who *sees with* the eye'. But I am not quite sure that he realises that this 'person' is the 'unseen Seer . . . other than whom there is no seer' (BU. III. 7.23) and of whom it is said that when the eye sees, when the mind thinks, and so on, 'These are only the names of *His* acts' (BU. I. 4.7),—not 'ours'.[27]

NOTES

1. A.A. Bowman, *Studies in the Philosophy of Religion*, London 1938, I, 250 ff.

2. For example, p.350, Ṛk and Sāman in CU I. 7.2 do not, as Bowman assumes, refer to the Ṛg- and Sama-Vedas as such, but are respectively the 'words' and 'music' of the incantations; the 'music' is solar, the 'words' its temporal support. Cf. my *Spiritual Authority and Temporal Power in the Indian Theory of Government*, 1942, p.51 and note 40.

It is of less importance that the transliteration of Skr. words is irregular and sometimes incorrect. It is undesirable to use the old system of Max Müller; but if this is done it should at least be realised that kh in the transliteration of Oriental languages represents a quite different sound from that of Max Müller's italicised *kh*, nowadays italicised *ch*. Similarly in other cases, e.g. Bowman's *g* for j, and *n* for ṇ.

3. In this context, of course, it is not the physical sun that is to be understood, but the pneumatic Sun (of RV. I. 115.1; Brahma, Prāna, etc) it is not the sun 'whom all men see' but the Sun 'whom not all know with the mind' (AV. X. 8.14), the 'Sun of the sun' of *Mahābhārata*, V. 46.3 that is meant; i.e. Apollo as distinguished from Helios (Plutarch, *Mor.* 393D, 400 C, D); the latter being what Plato calls a 'visible God', and the immanent Sun, our true Self (*ātman*) expressly invisible.

In all these contexts, the 'Sun' is Dante's 'Supernal Sun', Philo's 'Intelligible Sun' (νοητὸς ἥλιος), the 'archetypal brilliance' and 'Luciferous Deity' who emanates innumerable Rays, which are perceptible only to the Intellect, not by the sense (*De cher.* XXVIII. 97; *De ebrietate*, XI. 44).

4. 'The light of the body is the eye', Math. 6:22. Luke 11:34.

5. I.e. the Sun, Brahma, Prajāpati (ŚB. I. 9.3.10; TB. III. 12.3.1; BU. II. 6.3 etc).

6. To *kha*, space, void, aperture, gateway (of the rivers of sense perception), and to *dvāra*, door in the same sense (BG. VIII. 12) correspond Heb. *bāh bāh*, hollow as of a gateway, and 'apple (pupil) of the eye' (in Zech. II. 8), and Gk, πλη and θύρα as door or gateway of the senses, (Hermes Trismegistus *Lib.* I. 22, Philostratus 946, etc). Similarly Chinese *yen* (Giles 13, 129) is both eye, and hole or space, to be opened or shut.

7. In the 'cave' (*guhā*) or cella of the heart, the core of the mountain in which he is swallowed up, see my *Hinduism and Buddhism*, 1943, p. 8.

8. Similarly in Islamic psychology, cf. Rūmī, *Mathnawī*, I. 1126 (the light of the eye is derived from the light of the heart), and R. A. Nicholson's notes on *Mathnawī*, I. 676–7, and II. 1285–97. Chinese *yen* (Giles 13. 219); is eye, space, hole (cf. note 6); *kuang* (Giles 6389) is light, ray; and *k'ai* (Giles 5794) to open (as a door, road, or eye). Hence *yen kuang*, vision (lit. eye-ray, like *jih kuang*, sun ray, sunlight; *k'ai kuang* (lit. open light), to open eye. *Po* (Giles 9336) is wave, onflow; hence *yen po* (lit. eye-stream), glance (cf. Plato's 'visual stream').

9. Cf. *Symposium*, 219, *Philebus*, 61E, *Rep.* 518C, 519B, 526E, 532A, 533D. Rawson's attempt to oppose the Platonic view with that of KU. (in *The Kaṭha Upaniṣad*, 1924, p. 149) is grotesque. If 'the kingdom of heaven is within you', where else should we seek it? The 'inverted vision' of KU. is Ruysbroeck's *instärende* (*Book of Supreme Truth*, Ch. XIV)—'But those who turn outwards and find consolation in outward things, do not feel this, and if I should say much more of it, yet they would not understand'.

10. On what it means to 'know oneself' cf. my 'The "E" at Delphi', *Review of Religion*, Nov. 1941. [Rpr. SP2, pp. 43–5.]

11. For the two minds, lower and superior, unclean and clean, see my 'On Being in One's Right Mind', *Rev. of Religion*, Nov. 1942. [see chapter three of the present book.]

12. Hans Leisegang, 'Dieu au Miroir de l'Âme et de la Nature'. I have, unfortunately, lost the reference to the Journal in which this article appeared.

The image seen in a mirror (of whatever material) has always seemed to possess, as it were, a certain magical quality of revelation; compared with the corporeal object reflected, it is relatively immaterial and intangible, like the mental image by which the object is known mentally. Stress is always laid on the cleansing of the mirror; it must be free from dust. So, for example, *Paramārthasāra* XVI-A, 'Just as men in the world behold their bodily-form (*rūpam*) in an *uncontaminated* mirror (*ādarśe mala-rahite*), so the Self beholds itself in the pure intellect (*visudda-buddhau*)'.

13. Cf. 'The Traditional Conception of Ideal Portraiture' in my *Why Exhibit Works of Art*, 1943.

14. As also in CU. IV. 15.1. Cf. BU. II. 5.5 'This fiery immortal Person who is in the Sun, and subjectively (*adhyātmam*), this fiery immortal Person in the Eye, it is just he who is this Self', and IV. 4.1, where it is just this Person in the Eye who turns away back to his solar source when we die. Cf. *Kauṣ Up*. IV. 3 'in the Sun the "Great", in the mirror the reflection (*pratirūpaḥ*)'; and conversely *Kauṣ Up*. VI. 5 'as in the mirror, so in the Self'. The equivalence of 'eye' and 'mirror' is clear also in BU. III. 9.12, 15.

15. Cf. *Kalāmi Pīr*, Iwanow. p.65, where Adam's form (*ṣūrat*) is that of God as reflected in water. All things, indeed, are a mirror in which He is reflected; so 'To whatever side thou gaze, My form thou shalt enjoy' (Shams-i-Tabrīz, Ode XXV in Nicholson), and 'All mirror's in the universe, I hold, display Thy image with its radiant sheen' (Jāmi, *Lawā'ih* 26). Similarly Macrobius (*Com. ex Cicerone in Somnium Scipionis* I. 14), 'Unus fulgor illuminat, et in universis apparet in multis speculis'.

The 'form' is common to the *imago imaginans* and the *imago imaginata*. Hence the magical power of names (words, as Plato says, being images of things) and of portraits. We often say of a good portrait, 'That's me'; and if the portrait is 'ideal' this may be true in the higher sense. What Virocana overlooked is the distinction of nature in the reflected image.

16. *Kāmān paśyan ramate*, which *ramate* Śaṅkara explains by *viśinaṣṭi*.

17. For the Sundoor see my 'Svayamātṛṇṇā; Janua Coeli' in *Zalmoxis* II, 1939 [Rpr. SP1, pp. 465–520.]

18. As it were 'through the looking glass', not at it.

19. The Person in the eye is often identified with Indra, the immanent Breath, after whom the 'Breaths' (powers of the soul, vision etc) are called *indriyāṇi*. In several contexts (BU. IV. 4.3; ŚB. X. 5.2. 9–12) Indra is more specifically the Person in the right eye, and his 'wife' Virāj (Vāc), Indrāṇī the person in the left eye; their meeting place is in the heart-space (*hṛdyasya ākāśa*, cf. CU. VIII. 3), from which they ascend to pass through the Sundoor at our death.

20. Witelo, *Lib. de intelligentiis*, VIf.

21. On the significance of *kha* see note 6, and my '*Kha* and other Words denoting "Zero", in Connection with the Metaphysics of Space' in ESOS. VII. 1934. [Rpr. SP2, pp. 220–239.]

22. Cf. Bruce Codex I, XII, LIV 'He made himself to be Space (τόπος) . . . To the Spaces outside the Pleroma pierces the Light of his Eyes . . . Thy Will alone became Space for thee, because it is not possible for any to be Space for thee, in that of all, thou art the Space',—as in BG. IX. 4, 'Not I in them but they in Me'. Exodus 24:10 Elohim is rendered in LXX by τοπος.

23. TS. I. 2.1, II. 2. 9.3, II. 3.8.1, 2. II. 5.8.2, VI. 1.1.5, VI. 1.5.2; *Kāṭh. Ṣam*. II. 2: 1; ŚB. I. 6.3.38, 41, III. 1.3.11, 15; KB. VII. 4

24. 'Because for this he was manifested, till they saw Him who is indeed invisible' (Bruce Codex LI); 'They shall see eye to eye' (Isaiah, 52:8) = *sākṣāt aparokṣāt*, BU. III. 4.1, III. 5.1.

25. Edward Fitzgerald's version, Boston, 1899.

26. 'Dā inne ich got sihe, daz ist daz selbe ouge, dā inne mich got siht: mīn ouge

und gotes ouge daz ist ein ouge und ein gesicht und ein bebekennen und ein minnen' (*Meister Eckhart*, Pfeiffer p. 312, Evans I. 240).

27. 'By the only true God I deem nothing so shameful as to suppose that *I* understand or perceive. *My* mind responsible for its own activity, how could that be?' (Philo I. 78).

Throughout the present article we have been at pains to cite the parallels from other than Indian sources; since there is nothing more dispositive to misunderstanding than to suppose that a given doctrine, such as that of the Person in the Eye, is peculiar to the source in which we first encounter it.

SIX

The Coming to Birth of the Spirit

'You cannot dip your feet twice into the same waters, because fresh waters are ever flowing in upon you.' Heracleitus

THE present article embodies a part of the material which I have assembled during recent years towards a critical analysis of the Indian, and incidentally neo-Platonic and other doctrines of 'reincarnation', regeneration, and transmigration, as these terms are defined below.[1] These doctrines, often treated as one, appear to have been more profoundly misunderstood, if that is possible, than any other aspect of Indian metaphysics. The theses that will be proposed are that the Indian doctrine of palingenesis is correctly expressed by the Buddhist statement that in 'reincarnation' *nothing*[2] passes over from one embodiment to another, the continuity being only such as can be seen when one lamp is lighted from another: that the terms employed for 'rebirth' (e.g. *punar janma, punar bhava, punar apādana*) are used in at least three easily distinguishable senses: (1) with respect to the transmission of physical and psychic characteristics from father to son, i.e. with respect to palingenesis in a biological sense, defined by Webster as 'The reproduction of ancestral characters without change',[3] (2) with respect to a transition from one to another plane of consciousness effected in one and the same individual and generally one and the same life, viz. that kind of rebirth which is implied in the saying 'Except ye be born again' and of which the ultimate term is deification,[4] and (3) with respect to the motion or peregrination of the Spirit from one body-and-soul to another, which 'motion'[5] necessarily takes place whenever one such a compound vehicle dies or another is generated, just as water might be poured out of one vessel into the sea, and dipped out by another, being always 'water', but never, except in so far as the vessel seems to impose a temporary identity and shape on its contents, properly 'a water'; and thirdly, that no other doctrines of rebirth are taught in the Upanisads and *Bhagavad Gītā* than are already explicit and implicit in the *Ṛg Veda*.

'Spirit' we employ in the present introduction with reference to *ātman, brahman, mṛtyu, puruṣa,* etc., alike, but in the body of the article only as a rendering of *ātman,* assuming as usual a derivation from a root *an* or *vā* meaning to breathe or blow. But because the Spirit is really the whole of Being in all beings, which have no private essence but only a becoming, *ātman* is also used reflexively to mean the man himself as he conceives 'himself' (whether as body, or body-and-soul, or body-soul-and-spirit, or finally and properly only as Spirit),[6] and in such contexts we render *ātman* by 'self', or sometimes 'self, or spirit'. Capitals are employed whenever there seems to be a possibility of confusing the very Man or immanent God with the man 'himself'; but it must always be remembered that the distinction of spirit from Spirit and person from Person is 'only logical, and not real', in other words, a distinction without difference (*bhedābheda*). A sort of image of what may be implied by such a distinction (which is analogous to that of the Persons as envisaged in the Christian Trinity) can be formed if we remember that the Perfected are spoken of as 'rays' of the Supernal Sun, which rays are manifestly distinct if considered in their extension, but no less evidently indistinct if considered in their intension, i.e. at their source.

The Upanisads and *Bhagavad Gītā* are primarily concerned to bring about in the disciple a transference of self-reference, the feeling that 'I am', from oneself to the Spirit within us; and this with the purely practical purpose[7] in view of pointing out a Way (*mārga,* Buddhist *magga*)[8] that can be followed from darkness to light and from liability to pain and death to a state of deathless and timeless beatitude, attainable even here and now. In the Upanisads and early Buddhism it is clear that what had been an initiatory teaching transmitted in pupillary succession was now being openly published and in some measure adapted to the understanding of 'royal' and not merely 'sacerdotal' types of mentality, for example in the *Bhagavad Gītā.* On the other hand, it is equally clear that there existed widespread popular misunderstandings, based either on an ignorance of the traditional doctrines or on a too literal interpretation of what had been heard of them.[9] The internal evidence of the texts themselves with their questions and answers, definitions and refutations, is amply sufficient to show this. Hence, then, the necessity of those innumerable dialogues in which, alike in the Upanisads, the *Bhagavad Gītā*, and Buddhism, that which in 'us' is, and that which is not, the Spirit are sharply distinguished and contrasted; the Spirit being that which 'remains over'[10] when all other factors of the composite personality 'identity-and-appearance', or 'soul-and-body' have been eliminated. And furthermore, because 'That One that breathes yet does not breathe' (RV. x. 129.2) is not any what as opposed to any other what, It or He is described simultaneously by means of affirmations and denials, *per modum excellentiae et remotionis.*[11] The following analysis of the Supreme Identity (*tad ekam*), restricted to words derived from *an*, to 'breathe' or *vā*, to 'blow', may contribute to a better understanding of the texts:

Despirated Godhead.	*avātam, nirātmā, anātmya, nirvāṇa*, Pali *nibbāṇa*. Only negative definitions are possible.
Spirit, God, Sun, 'Knower of the field': King.	*ātman*, Pali *attā*. In motion, *vāyu, vāta*, 'Gale of the Spirit'; and *prāṇa*, 'Spiration', the 'Breath of Life' as imparted, not the breath empirically, but the 'ghost' that is given up when living creatures die.[12] Being 'One and many', transcendent and immanent, although without any interstice or discontinuity, the Spirit, whether as *ātman* or as *prāṇa* can be considered in the plural (*ātmanaḥ, prāṇah*), though only 'as if'. Form, as distinguished from substance: Intellect.
What-is-not-Spirit; Moon; the Field, World, Earth: the King's domain.	*anātman*, Pali *anattā*. The hylomorphic, physical and psychic, or lower-mental, vehicle of the Spirit, seemingly differentiated by its envelopes. Mortal substance as distinguished from its informing Forms.

These are not 'philosophical' categories, but categories of experience from our point of view, *sub rationem dicendi sive intelligendi*, rather than *secundum rem*.

We can scarcely argue here in detail what was really meant by the palingenesis, metempsychosis, or metasomatosis of the neo-Platonic tradition.[13] We shall only remark that in such texts as Plotinus, *Enneads* III, 4. 2 (Mackenna's version), where it is said that 'Those (i.e. of 'us'), that have maintained the human level are men once more. Those that have lived wholly to sense become animals . . . the spirit of the previous life pays the penalty',[14] it must be realised that it is a metempsychosis and metasomatosis (and not a transmigration of the real person) that is in question; it is a matter, in other words, of the direct or indirect inheritance of the psycho-physical characteristics of the deceased, which he does not take with him at death and which are not a part of his veritable essence, but only its temporary and most external vehicle. It is only in so far as we mistakenly identify 'ourselves' with these accidental garments of the transcendent personality, the mere properties of terrestrial human existence, that it can be said that 'we' are reincorporated in men or animals: it is not the 'spirit' that pays the penalty, but the animal or sensitive soul with which the disembodied spirit has no further concern.[15] The doctrine merely accounts for the reappearance of psycho-physical characteristics in the mortal sphere of temporal succession. The intention of the teaching is always that a man should have recognized 'himself' in the spirit, and not in the sensitive soul, before death, failing which 'he' can only be thought of as in a measure 'lost', or at any rate disintegrated. When, on the other hand, it is said that the 'Soul' is 'self-distributed' (cf. *ātmānaṁ vibhajya*, MU. VI, 26) and 'always the same thing present entire' (*ibid*, III, 4. 6), and that this '"Soul passes through the entire heavens in forms varying with the variety of place"[16]—the sensitive form, the reasoning form, even the vegetative form' (*ibid*, III, 4. 2) —it is evident that it is only as it were that there is any question of 'several Souls', and that what is described is not the translation of a private personality from one body to another, but much rather the peregrination of the Spirit (*ātman*) repeatedly described in the Upaniṣads as omnimodal and omnipresent, and therefore as occupying or rather animating body after body, which bodies or rather bodies and sensitive souls, follow one another in causally determinated series.[17]

All this is surely, too, what Eckhart (in whom the neo-Platonic tradition persists) must mean when he says 'Aught is suspended from the divine essence; its progression (i.e. vehicle) is matter, wherein the soul puts on new forms and puts off her old ones . . . the one she doffs she dies to, and the one she dons she lives in' (Evans ed. I, 379), almost identical with BG. II, 22 'As a man casting off worn-out garments, taketh other new ones, so the Body-dweller (*dehin* = *śarīra ātman*), casting off worn-out bodies, enters into new ones', cf. BU. IV, 4.4 'Just so this Spirit, striking down the body and driving off its nescience,[18] makes for itself some other new and fairer form'.

The three sections of Upanisads translated below begin with the question, 'What is most the Spirit'? That is to say, 'What is this "Self" that is not "myself"? What is this "Spirit" in "me", that is not "*my*" spirit'? It is the distinction that Philo is making in *Quaestiones . . . ad Genesis* II, 59 and *De Cherubim*, 113ff. (as cited by Goodenough, *By Light, Light*, 1941, pp.374–75) when he distinguishes 'us' from that in us which existed before 'our' birth and will still exist when 'we, who in our junction with our bodies,[19] are mixtures (σύγκριτοι) and have qualities, shall not exist, but shall be brought into the rebirth, by which, becoming joined to immaterial things, we shall become unmixed (ἀσύγκριτοι) and without qualities'. the 'rebirth' (παλιγγενεσία) is here certainly not an 'aggregation' or palingenesis in the biological sense, but a 'regeneration' (palingenesis as a being born again of and as the Spirit of Light), cf. Goodenough, p. 376, note 35.

'What is most the Self' or 'most the spirit'? As the late C. E. Rolt has said in another context (*Dionysius the Areopagite on the Divine Names and Mystical Theology*, 1920, p. 35), 'Pascal has a clear-cut answer: 'Il n'y a que l'Etre universel qui soit tel . . . Le Bien Universal est en nous, est nous mêmes et n'est pas nous'. This is exactly the Dionysian doctrine. Each must enter into himself and so find Something that is his true Self and yet is not his particular self . . . Something other than his individuality which (other) is within his soul and yet outside of him'.

'If any man come to me . . . and hate not his own soul (ἑαυτοῦ ψυχήν, Vulgate *animam suam*) he cannot be my disciple' (Luke, 15: 26). the English versions shrink from such a rendering, and have 'hate not his own life'. It is evidently, however, not merely 'life' that is meant, since those who are at the same time required to 'hate' their own relatives, if, on the contrary, they love them, may be willing to sacrifice even life for their sake: what is evidently meant is the lower soul, as regularly distinguished in the neo-Platonic tradition from the higher power of the soul which is that of the Spirit and not really a property of the soul but its royal guest.[20] It is again, then, precisely from this point of view that St. Paul says with a voice of thunder, 'For the word of God is quick and powerful, and sharper than any two-edged sword, piercing even to the dividing asunder of soul and spirit' (Heb. 4:12), and consistently with this that 'Whoever is joined unto the Lord is One Spirit (I Cor. 6:17, cf. 12:4–13).

With this may be compared, on the one hand, *Bhagavad Gītā*, VI, 6 'The Spirit is verily the foeman of and at war with what-is-not-the-Spirit' (*anātmanas tu śatrutve vartetātmaiva śatruvat*), where *anātman* = Buddhist *anattā*[21] all that, body-and-soul, of which one says *na me so attā*, 'This is not my spirit'; and on the other, with Eckhart's 'Yet the soul must relinquish her existence' (Evans ed. I, 274)[22] and, in the anonymous *Cloud of Unknowing*, Chap. XLIV, 'All men have matter of sorrow: but most specially he feeleth sorrow, that feeleth and wotteth that he is', and with Blake's 'I will go down unto Annihilation and Eternal Death, lest the Last Judgment come and find me unannihilate, and I be seiz'd and giv'n into the hands of my own Selfhood'. All scripture, and even all wisdom, truly, 'cries aloud for freedom from self'.

But if 'he feeleth sorrow that feeleth and wotteth that he is', he who is no longer anyone, and sees, not himself, but as our texts express it, only the Spirit, one and the same in immanence and transcendence, being what he sees, *geworden was er ist*, he feels no sorrow, he is beatified,—'One ruler, inward Spirit of all beings, who maketh manifold a single form! Men contemplative, seeing Him whose station is within you, and seeing with Him,—eternal happiness is theirs, none others' (KU. V, 12).[23]

An 'actual experience of Unknowing and of the Negative Path that leads to it' (Rolt, *ibid.*) is not easy to be had, unless for those who are perfectly mature, and like ripe fruits, about to fall from their branch. There are men still 'living', at least in India, for whom the funeral rites have been performed, as if to seal them 'dead and buried in the Godhead'. 'It is hard for us to forsake the familiar things around, and turn back to the old home whence we came.' (Hermes, *Lib.* IV, 9). But it can be said, even of those who are still self-conscious, and cannot bear the strongest meat, that he specially, if not yet most specially, 'feeleth joy', whose will has already fully consented to, though it may not yet have realised, an annihilation of the whole idea of any private property in being, and has thus, so to speak, foreseen and foretasted an ultimate renunciation of all his great possessions, whether physical or psychic. *Mors Janua vitæ.*

NOTES

1. See also my 'Vedic Exemplarism', *Harvard Journal of Asiatic Studies* I, 1936 [Rpr. SP2, pp.177–197.] and 'Rebirth and Omniscience in Pali Buddhism', *Indian Culture*, III, p. 19f. and p. 760; and René Guénon, *L'Erreur spirite*, Paris, 1930, Chap. 6.

2. *Mil.* 72, *na koci satto*, 'not any being'. Note that this expression is by no means necessarily exclusive of the Ātman as defined in the Upaniṣads by negation, of Basilides' οὐκ ὢν θεός, Eriugena's God who 'is not any what', Eckhart's 'non-existent' Godhead, Boehme's God who is 'no thing'.

3. In a number of important texts, rebirth is explicitly and categorically defined in terms of heredity, and this is probably the only sense in which the individual is thought of as returning to the plane of being from which he departs at death. It is expressly stated of the deceased that he is not seen again here (SB. XIII, 8. 4. 12, *etaj jīvā's ca pitaraś ca na saṁdrśyante*, and SB passim, *sakṛd parāñcah pitaraḥ*).

We have now RV. VI, 70.3. 'He is born forth in his progeny according to law' (*pra prajābhir jāyate dharmanas pari*); AB. VII, 13, 'The father enter the wife, the mother, becoming an embryo, and coming into being anew, is born again of her' (*jāyām praviśati, garbho bhūtvā, sa mātaram, tasyām punar navo bhūtvā jāyate*, cf. AV. XI, 4.20); AĀ. II, 5 'In that he both before and after birth maketh the son to become, (*sa yat kumāram . . . adhibhāvayati*), it is just himself as son that he maketh to become (*Kumāram . . . adhibhāvayaty ātmāname va*); CU. III, 17.5, 'That he has procreated, *that* is his rebirth' *aṣoṣṭeti punar-utpādanam*); BU. III, 9. 28, 'He (the deceased) has indeed been born, but he is not born again, for (being deceased) who is there to beget him again?' (*jāta eva na jāyate, ko nv enaṁ janayet punaḥ*). We have also BU. II, 2. 8 where filiation is rebirth 'in a likeness' (*pratirūpah*). It would be impossible to have a clearer definition of the ordinary meaning of 'reincarnation'. This filial Reincarnation is moreover precisely the ἀνταποκατάστασις or 'renewal of things by substitution' of Hermes, as explained by Scott (*Hermetica*, II, 322), 'The father lives again in his son; and though the individuals die and return no more, the race is perpetually renewed'.

It should be added that beside the natural fact of progenitive reincarnation there is also a formal communication and delegation of the father's nature and status in the world, made when the father is at the point of death. Thus in BU. I, 5. 17–20, when this 'All bequest' (*sampratti*) has been made, 'the son who has been thus induced (*anuśiṣṭaḥ*) is called the father's "mundane-representative"' (*lokyaḥ*), and so 'by means of the son the father is still-present-in (*prati-tiṣṭhati*) the world': and similarly in *Kauṣ Up.* II, 15 (10) where the 'All-bequest of the father to the son' (*Pitāputrīyaṁ sampradānam*) is described in greater detail, after which bequest if perchance the father should recover, he must either live under the lordship of the son or become a wandering religious (*parivāvrajet*, i.e. become a *parivrājaka* dead to the world at least in outward form).

4. Cf. my 'Indian doctrine of man's Last End', *Asia*, May 1937.

5. 'Motion' not a local motion, but an omni*presence*, and as we speak, although metaphorically, of a 'procession' *in divinis*. Not a local motion, but that of the Unmoved Mover, 'Motionless One, swifter than thought itself . . . who outgoeth others though they run' (*Īśā*. 4), 'Seated, He fares afar; reclining, goeth everywhere' (KU. II, 21), being 'Endless in all directions' (MU. VI, 17), and though 'He hath not come from anywhere' (KU. II, 18), still 'Perpetually differentiated and going everywhere' (*Muṇḍ*. I, 2.6) and 'Multifariously taking birth' (*bahudhā jāyamānah, Muṇḍ*, II, 2. 6).

6. Where we say 'Do not hurt me', meaning the body, or 'I know', or 'my soul' the very careful teacher would say 'Do not hurt this body', 'this mind knows', and 'the Spirit in "me"' or 'Body-dweller'.

7. Cf. Edgerton, 'The Upaniṣads, what do they seek and why?', JAOS. 51. 97; Dante, *Ep. ad Can. Grand.* §§15, 16. The Vedic tradition is neither philosophical, mystical, nor religious in the ordinary modern senses of these words. The tradition is metaphysical; 'mystical' only in the sense that it expounds a 'mystery', and in that of Dionysius, *Theologia Mystica*. The Indian position has been admirably defined by Satkari Mookerjee: '*Of course* the question of salvation is a problem of paramount importance and constitutes the justification and ultimate *raison d'être* of philosophical enquiry. Philosophy in India has never been a mere speculative interest irrespective of its bearing on life . . . The goal loomed large in the philosophical horizon, but it was recognised that there was no short cut or easy walk-over to it. The full price had to be paid in the shape of unfaltering philosophical *realisation* of the ultimate mysteries of existence achieved through a rigorous moral discipline; and mere academic and intellectual satisfaction accruing from philosophical studies was considered to be of value only in so far as it was calculated to bring about the happy consummation' (in *The Cultural Heritage of India*, Vol. III, pp. 409, 410, 1937; italics mine).

8. For the meaning of this word see my 'Nature of folklore and "popular art"' in *Quarterly Journal of the Mythic Society*, Bangalore, Vol. XXVII.

9. We do not say that a theory of reincarnation (re-embodiment of the very man and true personality of the deceased) has never been *believed* in India or elsewhere, but agree with René Guénon that 'it has never been *taught* in India, even by Buddhists and is essentially a modern European notion' and further 'that no authentic traditional doctrine has ever spoken of reincarnation' (*L'Erreur spirite*, pp. 47, 199).

It has been generally agreed by modern scholars that 'reincarnation' is not a Vedic doctrine, but one of popular or unknown origin adopted and taken for granted already in the Upanisads and Buddhism. Neglecting Buddhism for the moment, it may be pointed out that where we have to do with a fundamental and revolutionary thesis, and not the simple expansion of doctrines previously taught, it would be inconceivable from the orthodox and traditional Hindu point of view that what is not taught in one part of *śruti* could have been taught in another; in such a matter, one cannot imagine an orthodox Hindu 'choosing between' the RV. and Upanisads, as though one might be right and the other wrong.This difficulty disappears if we find that the theory of reincarnation (as distinguished from the doctrines of metempsychosis and transmigration) is not really taught in the Upanisads: in this connection we call particular attention to the statement of BU. IV, 3. 37 where, when a new entity is coming into being, the factorial elements of the new composite are made to say, *not* 'Here comes so-and-so' (previously deceased) but, 'HERE COMES BRAHMAN'. This is furthermore in full agreement with the Buddhist *Mil.* 72 where it is said categorically that no entity whatever passes over from one body to another, and it is merely that a new flame is lighted.

In differentiating reincarnation, as defined above, from metempsychosis and transmigration it may be added that what is meant by metempsychosis is the psychic aspect of palingenesis, or in other words psychic heredity, and that what is meant by transmigration is a change of state or level of reference excluding by definition the idea of a return to any state or level that has already been passed through. The transmigration of the 'individual' *ātman* (spirit) can only be distinguished as a particular case of the transmigration of the *paramātman* (Spirit, Brahman), for which last, however, it may be proved desirable to employ some such term as 'peregrination'; perigrination replacing transmigration when the state of the *kāmācārin* (Mover-at-will) has been attained.

There are doubtless many passages in the Upaniṣads, etc. which taken out of their whole context, seem to speak of a 'personal reincarnation', and have thus been misunderstood, alike in India and in Europe. Cf. Scott, *Hermetica*, II, pp. 193–194, note 6 ('he' in the first quoted sentence is the son of Valerius, and for our purposes 'so-and-so' or Everyman; the italics are mine): 'During his life on earth he was a distinct portion of πνεῦμα, marked off and divided from the rest; now, that portion of πνεῦμα, which was he, is blended with the whole mass of πνεῦμα in which the life of the universe resides. This is what the writer (Apollonius) *must* have meant, if he adhered to the doctrine laid down in the preceding part of the letter. But from this point onward, he speaks ambiguously, and uses phrases which, *to a reader who had not fully grasped the meaning of his doctrine*, might see to imply a survival of the man as a distinct and individual person.'

The modern mind, with its attachment to 'individuality' and its 'proofs of the survival of personality' is predisposed to misinterpret the traditional texts. We ought not to read into these texts what we should like or 'naturally' expect to find in them, but only to read in them what *they* mean: but 'it is hard for us to forsake the familiar things around us, and turn back to the old home whence we came' (Hermes, *Lib.* IV, 9).

Individuality, however we may hug its chains, is a partial and definite modality of being: 'I' is defined by what is 'not-I', and thus imprisoned. It is with a view to liberation from this prison and this partiality that our texts so repeatedly demonstrate that our vaunted individuality is neither uniformal nor constant, but composite and variable, pointing out that he is the wisest who can most say 'I am not now the man I was'. This is true in a measure of all *werdende* things; but the 'end of the road' (*adhvanaḥ pāram*) lies beyond 'manhood'. It is only of what is not individual, but universal (cosmic) that perduration can be predicated, and only of what is neither individual nor universal that an eternity, without before or after, can be affirmed.

10. KU. V, 4 *kim atra śiṣyate?* CU. VIII, 5 *atiśiṣyate . . . ātman*. Note that *tad śiṣyate* = Seṣa = Ananta = Brahman = Atman.

11. We have briefly discussed the Indian doctrine *de divinis nominibus* in JIH. XV, 84–92, 1936, and will only remark here that RV. V, 44. 6 *yādrg eva dadṛśe tādṛg ucyate*, 'As he is envisaged, so is he called' answers to St. Thomas, *Sum. Theol.* I, XIII.

12. *Prāna*, like Gk. πνεῦμα has the double value of *Spiritus* and *spiraculum vitæ* according to the context. 'It is as the Breath-of-life (*prāna*) that the Provident Spirit (*prajnātman*) grasps and erects the flesh' (*Kaus.* III, 3), cf. St. Thomas, *Sum. Theol.* III, 32. 1 'The power of the soul which is in the semen, through the spirit enclosed therein fashions the body', and Schiller, *Wallenstein*, III, 13 'Es ist der Geist der sich den Körper schart': and JUB. III, 32. 2. Whereas the divided *prāṇāh* are said to move within the vectors of channels (*naḍi, hita*) of the heart (see refs. Hume, *Upaniṣads*, ed. 2), in Hermes *Lib.* X, 13 and 17 the 'vital spirit' (πνεῦμα) traverses the veins and arteries 'with, but not as, the blood' and thus 'moves the body, and carries it like a burden . . . (and) controls the body'.

The Prāṇa is identified with the Prajñātman: as Prāna, 'life', as Prajñātman, 'immortality'; length of days in this world and immortality in the other are complementary. As distinguished from the Prāna, the divided *prāṇah* are the currents of perception by means of the sense organs and are prior to them. Hence as in KU. IV. i one says 'The Self-existent pierced the openings outward, thereby it is that one looks forth' (but must look in to see the Seer, see the discussion of this passage in JIH. XI, 571–8, 1935).

13. For many references, see Scott, *Hermetica*, II, 265ff.

14. Viz. of 'shameful transmigration into bodies of another kind', Hermes Trismegistus, *Asclepius* I, 12a, cf. BU. VI, 2. 16, CU. V, 10, 7–8, *Kaus.* I. 2. We understand that the result of a bestiality in 'us' is that bestial types are propagated: this is the reincarnation of character in our sense (1), and it is in this way that 'the sins of the fathers are visited upon their children'.

'Beasts', moreover, is a symbol, just as when we say 'Don't be a beast' or refer to some man as a 'worm' or some woman as a 'cat'. The Indian tradition regularly employs this sort of language, AĀ. II, 3. 8 (a *locus classicus*, cf. the definition of 'person' by Boethius, *Contra Evtychen*, II), for example, defining the spiritual man who 'knows what is and what is not mundane', etc. as a 'person' (*puruṣa*), and 'others' whose knowledge is merely an affection as 'cattle' (*paśu*).

15. In all these discussions it must be remembered that 'soul' (ψυχή *anima* without exact equivalent in Sanskrit, other than *nāma*, the name or 'form' of a thing by which its identity is established) is a two-fold value; the higher powers of the 'soul' coinciding with Spirit (πνεῦμα) and/or Intellect, (νοῦς ἡγεμών, or νοῦς), the lower with sensation (αἴσθησις) and opinion (δόξα). Hence the Gnostic hierarchy of animal, psychic, and spiritual men, the former destined to be lost, the intermediate capable of liberation, and the latter virtually free, and assured of liberation at death (Bruce Codex, etc.). By 'lost' understand 'unmade into the cosmos' (Hermes, *Lib.* IX, 6), and by 'liberated', wholly separated from the animal soul and thus become what the higher powers already are, divine. Render *ātman* by 'soul'. Observe that 'animal' is from *anima* = ψυχή 'soul', *animalia* = ἔμψυχα; hence Scott, *Hermetica*, I. 297 renders *Solum enim animal homo* by 'Man, and man alone of all beings that have soul'; it is by νοῦς and not by ψυχή that man is distinguished from animal (Hermes, *Lib.* VIII, 5). It may be noted that the Averroist doctrine of the Unity of the Intellect (for which 'monopsychism' seems a peculiarly inappropriate term) was repugnant to the Christian scholastic authors of a later age, precisely because of its incompatibility with a belief in personal immortality (cf. De Wulf, *Histoire . . .*, II, 361, 1936): on the other hand, imagination (*phantasmata*) and memory survive the death of the body not as they are in the passive intellect (Hermetic νόησις, Skr, *aśuddha manas*), but only as they are in the possible intellect (Hermetic νοῦς, Skr. *śuddha manas*) which 'is in act when it is identified with each thing as knowing it' (St. Thomas, *Sum. Theol.* I. 2. 67. 2c). Furthermore St. Thomas says that 'To say that the soul is of the Divine Substance involves a manifest improbability' (I, 90. 1), and Eckhart is continually speaking of the deaths and last death of the soul. It is clear at least that an immortality of the sensitive and reasoning 'soul' is out of the question, and that if the soul can in any sense be called 'immortal', it is with respect to the 'intellectual power of the soul' rather than with respect to the soul itself. Hermes' 'soul that is fastened to the body', *Lib.* XI, 24*a*, is no conceivably immortal principle, even supposing a temporary post-mortem cohesion of certain psycho-physical elements of the *bhūtātman*; neither can we equate the 'soul' that Christ asks us to 'hate' with 'man's immortal soul'. The quest of 'the modern man in search of a soul' is a very different one from that implied in Philo's 'soul of the soul'; one may say that modern psychology and æsthetics have in view only the lower or animal soul in man, and only the subconscious. What Philo (*Quis rerum divinarum*

Heres, 48, Goodenough's version, p. 378) says is that 'The word "soul" is used in two senses, with reference either to the soul as a whole or to its dominant (ἡγεμονικόν = Skr. *anataryāmin*) part, which latter is, properly speaking, the soul of the soul' (ψυχὴ ψυχῆς cf. in MU. III, 2 *bhūtātman* . . . *amrto' syātmā* 'elemental self . . *its* deathless Self'). The value of the European 'soul' has remained ambiguous ever since.

Hence in the analysis of neo-Platonic doctrines of rebirth, and also throughout the Christian tradition from the Gospels to Eckhart and the Flemish mystics, it is indispensable to know just what 'sort of soul' is being spoken of in a given context: and in translating from Sanskrit it is exceedingly dangerous, if not invariably misleading, to render *ātman* by 'soul'.

16. I do not know the source of this quotation; it is probably Platonic, but corresponds exactly to what is said in *Nirukta*, VII, 4, 'It is because of his great divisibility that they apply many names to Him . . . The other Gods, or Angels (*devāh*) are counter-members of the One Spirit. They originate in function (*karma*); Spirit (*ātman*) is their source . . . Spirit is the whole of what they are', and BD. I, 70–74 'Because of the vastness of the Spirit, a diversity of names is given . . . according to the distribution of the spheres. It is inasmuch as they are differentiations (*vibhutiḥ*, cf. BG. X. 40) that the names are innumerable . . . according to the spheres in which they are established'. Cf. MU. VI, 26 'Distributing himself He fills these worlds', and for further references my 'Vedic Monotheism' in JIH. XV. pp. 84–92, April, 1936. [Rpr. SP2. pp.166–167.

'Now there are diversities of gifts, but the same Spirit. And there are differences of administration, but the same Lord. And there are diversities of operations, but it is the same God that worketh in all . . . The members of that body, being many, are one body' (I Cor. 12:4–6 and 12).

17. For 'karma' (= 'adṛṣṭa') in Christian doctrine, cf. Augustine, *Gen. ad Lit.* VII, 24 (cited by St. Thomas, *Sum. Theol.* I, 91. 2) 'The human body pre-existed in the previous works in their causal virtues' and *De Trin*, III, 9 'As a mother is pregnant with the unborn offspring, so the world itself is pregnant with the causes of unborn things' (cf. St. Thomas, I, 115. 2 ad 4), and St. Thomas, I. 1103. 7 ad 2 'If God governed alone (and not also by means of mediate causes) things would be deprived of the perfection of causality'.

18. Hermes Trismegistus, *Lib.* X, 8*b*, κακία δὲ ψυχῆς ἀγνωσία . . . Τοὐναντίον δὲ ἀρετὴ ψυχῆς γνῶσις. ὅ γὰρ γνοὺς . . . ἤδη θεῖος, and XI, ii. 21 a 'But if you shut up your soul in your body and abase yourself, and say "I know nothing (Ουδιν νοω) . . .", then what have you to do with God?' *Ignorantia divisiva est errantium*, as Ulrich says in comment on Dionysius, *De div. Nom.* 'Agnostic' means 'ignoramus', or even *quis ignorare vult sive ignorantium diligit*. On the contrary, 'Think that for you too nothing is impossible' (Hermes, *Lib.* XI, ii. 20*b*), cf. 'Nothing shall be impossible to you' (Mat. 17: 20): 'Not till the soul knows all that there is to be known does she cross over to the unknown good' (Eckhart, Evans ed. I. 385); 'No despiration without omniscience' (SP. V, 74–5). Note that Hermes *Lib.* XI, ii. 20*b* 21*a* corresponds to CU. VIII. 1.

19. BG. XIII, 26 'Whatsoever is generated, whatever being (*kiṁcit sattvam*, cf. *Mil.* 72 *koci satto*, cited above) whether mobile or immobile, know that it is from the conjunction (*saṃyogāt*) of the Field with the Knower of the Field'. The 'Field' has been previously defined in XIII, 5–6; it embraces the whole of what we should call 'soul and body' and all that is felt or perceived by them.

20. Cf. Plutarch, *Obsolescence of Oracles*, 436F, where the soul of man is assigned to Prophecy (ἡ μαντικὴ here = προνοία, Providence as distinguished from 'compelling and natural causes') as its *material* support (ὕλην μεν ἀυτῇ τὴν ψυχὴν τοῦ ανθρώπου . . . ἀποδιδόντες); and BG. VI. 6 where the spirit is called the enemy of what is not the spirit (*anātmanas tu* . . . *ātmaiva śatruvat*).

'To be willing to lose (hate) our ψυχή must mean to forget ourselves entirely . . . to live no more my own life, but let my consciousness be possessed and suffused by the Infinite and Eternal life of the spirit' (Inge, *Personal Idealism and Mysticism*, p. 102 and James, *Varieties of Religious Experience*, p. 451).

21. μερισμοῦ ψυχῆς καὶ πνεύματος, cf. Hermes, *Lib.* x. 16 ὁ νοῦς τῆς ψυχῆς (χωρίξεται).

Anātman, similarly 'un-en-spired' (not 'despirated') in SB. II, 2. 2. 8 where gods and titans alike are originally 'un-en-spired' and 'mortal', and 'to be un-en-spired is the same as to be mortal' (*anātmā hi martyaḥ*); Agni alone is 'immortal' (*amartyaḥ*).

22. Compare the expressions used by St. Bernard, *deficere a se tota* and *a semetipsa liquescere* in *De diligendo Deo*; and as Gilson remarks, p. 156, 'Quelle difference y-a-t-il donc, a la limite, entre aimer Dieu et s'aimer soi-meme?'

23. *Eko vaśī sarva-bhūtāntarātmā ekaṁ rūpam bahudhā yaḥ karoti: Tam ātmastham ye'nupaśyanti dhīrās teṣāṁ sukhaṁ śāśvatam netareṣām.*

The force of *anu* in *anupaśyanti* we can only suggest by the repeated 'seeing . . . and seeing with'. It is lamented by the descending souls that 'Our eyes will have little room to take things in . . . and when we see heaven, our forefather, contracted to small compass, we shall never cease to moan. And even if we see, we shall not see outright' (Hermes, Stobaeus, *Exc.* XXIII, 36); 'For now we see through a glass, darkly; but then face to face: now I know in part; but then shall I know even as also I am known'. (I. Cor. 13: 12). Sight-of is perfected in sight-as, even as knowledge-of in knowledge-as (*adaequatio rei et intellectus*: to see Heaven 'outright' requires an eye of Heaven's width. *Dhīrāḥ*, 'contemplatives', those who see inwardly, not with the 'eye of the flesh' (*māṁsa cakṣus);* who see the Spirit 'above all to be seen' (*abhidhyāyeyam*, MU. I, 1), 'the Spirit that is yours and in all things, and than which all else is a wretchedness' (BU. III, 4. 2).

Note that *ekaṁ rūpam bahudhā yaḥ karoti* corresponds to S. II, 212 *eko'pi bahudhā homi*: and 'than which all else is a wretchedness' to the Buddhist *anicca, anattā, dukkha*.

SEVEN

Gradation and Evolution

DR. Ashley Montagu, in *Isis*, no. 96, p.364, distinguishes two explanations of the past and present existence of living creatures of different species as (1) Gradation, assuming a special creation of immutable species, and (2) Evolution, assuming the emergence of species in all their variety and mutability by the gradual operation of causes inherent in the species and their environment. He does not say and may not mean that these two explanations are incompatible; but the reader is likely to assume that the doctrine of a creation 'in the beginning' and that of the gradual development of new species are really irreconcilable propositions.

The two propositions are, doubtless, incompatible if the mythical account is to be interpreted historically. The serious mythologist, however, is well aware that to interpret myth as factual history is to mistake the genre; and that a myth can only be called 'true' when time and place are abstracted.[1] The object of the present note is to point out that if the doctrine of special creation is understood as it has generally been interpreted by Christian and other philosophers, then Gradation and Evolution are not irreconcilable alternatives, but only different ways, respectively ideal and historical, formal and figurative, algebraic and arithmetical, of describing one and the same thing.

In these philosophies causality is taken for granted; nothing happens by chance. The impossible never happens; what happens is always the realisation of a possibility. But we have to take account of two orders of causes, (1) a First Cause, in which the possibilities inhere, and (2) Mediate Causes, by which the conditions are provided in which the possible becomes the necessary. The First

Cause of the existence of things, or in other words their possibility, is often called 'God', but also 'Being', 'Life' or 'Nature' (*natura naturans*). This First Cause whether philosophically 'absolute' or mythically 'personified', is the direct cause of the being of things, but only indirectly of the manner of their being. The manner of their being (according to which they are distinguished as species) is determined by the Mediate Causes, known or unknown, of which the result is the production of the given species or individual at a given time or place. The category of Mediate Causes does not exclude any of those forces or tendencies or determining accidents on which the evolutionist relies as explanations of the observed series; if he differs from the philosopher in ignoring a First Cause, it is because he is not discussing the origin of life, but only its variety. Again: if by 'in the beginning' we understand an operation completed at a given moment, i.e. at the beginning of time itself, then, of course, Gradation and Evolution will be incompatible concepts. As to this 'beginning', it must, of course, be realized that (as St. Augustine says) the question, What was God doing *before* he created the world, is meaningless; or to say the same in other words, that a *succession* of events in the eternal now (of which empirical experience is impossible) is as inconceivable as the notion of a locomotion in the Infinite. What our philosophers actually understand by 'in the beginning' is a logical, and not a temporal priority. So Meister Eckhart, 'as I have often said, God is creating the whole world *now*, this instant' (Pfeiffer, p. 206); and Jacob Boehme, 'it is an everlasting beginning' (*Myst. Pansophicum*, IV. 9). Similarly in the *Ṛg Veda*: for, as Professor Keith very justly remarks, 'This creation cannot be regarded as a single definite act: it is regarded as ever proceeding' (*Harvard Oriental Series*, 18. CXXVI). This does not mean that it is unfinished *in principio* and *ex tempore*, but that it is apprehended by ourselves as a temporal sequence and *as if* cause and effect could be separated from one another by sensible periods. 'At that time, indeed, all things took place simultaneously . . . but a sequence was necessarily written into the narrative because of their subsequent generation from one another' (Philo, *De Opif. Mundi*, 67)—just as it is necessarily written into the evolutionist's narrative; what Gradation states *sub specie aeternitatis*, the Myth relates *sub specie aeviternitatis*, and History *sub specie temporis*. 'What is rooted in the nature of the All is [in the Myth] figuratively treated as coming into being by generation and creation: stage and sequence are transferred, for clarity of exposition, to things whose being and definite form are eternal' (Plotinus, *Enneads*, IV. 8.4). 'The beginning, which is thought, comes to an end in action; know that in such wise was the construction of the world in eternity' (Rūmī, *Mathnawī*, II. 970). And, finally (for present purposes): 'Nè prima nè poscia procedette lo discorrer di Dio sopra quest'acque' (Dante, *Paradiso*, XXIX. 20–1.

The concepts, then, on the one hand of an eternal and ideal pattern or 'intelligible world', unextended in space and time, and on the other of a temporal and 'sensible world' extended in space and time as an echo, reflection or imitation of the other, are not alternative, but correlative. Each implies the other; the uniformity of the intelligible world is in every way compatible with the multiformity of its manifestations. A real conflict of science with religion is unimaginable; the actual conflicts are always of scientists ignorant of religious philosophy with fundamentalists who maintain that the truth of their myth is historical. Neither of these can be really dangerous to anyone who is capable of thought on more then one level of reference; nor have we any intention to suggest that Dr. Ashley Montagu fits into either of these categories!

NOTE

1 'Mythology can never be converted into history' M. P. Nilsson, *Mycenean Origin of Greek Mythology*, 1932, p. 31. Cf. Lord Raglan, *The Hero*, 1936; E. Siecke, *Drachenkämpfe*, 1907, pp. 60–61.

EIGHT

Gradation and Evolution II

I HAVE shown in a former article[1] that the concepts implied by the terms 'Gradation' and 'Evolution' are not incompatible alternatives, respectively true and false, but only different ways of envisaging one and the same spectacle; or in other words, that the mythical notion of a creation of the world *in principio* and *ex tempore* is in no proper sense a contradiction of that of the succession and mutability of species in time. This proposition seems to demand, for its further clarification, at least a summary statement of the traditional doctrine of evolution, in which the emergence of an infinite variety of forms, past, present and future, is taken for granted.

In this doctrine, every one of the forms, every phenomenon, represents one of the 'possibilities of manifestation' of an 'ever-productive nature'[2] that may be called either the God, the Spirit, *Natura Naturans* or, as in the present context, the 'Life' according to which we speak of the forms of life as 'living'. This Life is the 'First Cause of lives; but the forms which these lives take is actually determined by the 'Second' or 'Mediate Causes' that are nowadays often called 'forces' or 'laws' notably that of heredity. No difficulty is presented here by the variability of the species; the shape that appears at any given time or place in the history of a 'genus', 'species', or 'individual' is *always* changing.[3] All the definitions of these categories are really, like 'round numbers', indefinite, because the reference is to 'things' that are always becoming and never stop to be, and that can only be called 'things' by a generalisation that ignores their variation over some longer or shorter, but always relatively short 'present'.[4] The traditional doctrine takes this flux for granted, and that every creature's 'life' is one of incessant death and regeneration (γένεσις, *bhava*, 'becoming'). There are no delimited and monads or egos, but only one unlimited.[5] Every form of life, the psychic included, is composite, and therefore mortal; only the beginningless Life, that wears these forms as garments are worn, and outworn, can be thought of as endless. There can be no immortality of anything that is not immortal now and was not immortal before our planet was, before the farthest galaxies began their travels. An immortality for 'myself' can only be postulated if we exclude from the concept of our Self all that is composite and variable, all that is subejct to persuasion;[6] and that is our 'end' (entelechy) and 'finish' (perfection) in more senses than one. 'Salvation' is from ourselves as we conceive them; and if it appears that 'nothing' remains, it is agreed that in fact no *thing* remains; in terms of the traditional philosophy, 'God' is properly called 'no thing', and knows not *what* he is, because he is not any 'what'.

From this point of view, which by no means excludes the facts of evolution as observed by the biologist, what we have called 'Life'—and this is only one of the names of 'God', according to his 'ever-productive nature'—seeks 'experience'.[7] 'Outward the Self-existent pierced the eyes, therefore creatures see';[8] which is to say that eyes have 'evolved' because the immanent Life desired to see, and so for all other powers of sensation, thought and action, which are all the names of his acts,[9] rather than 'ours'. Because of this desire or 'will of expression' there is a 'descent into matter' or 'origin of life', universally and locally,[10]—*La circular natura, che, è sugello alla cera mortal, fa ben sua arte, ma non distingue l'un dall'altro ostello,*[11]—*sadasad yonim āpadyate.*[12] The different forms of these births or inhabitations are determined by the mediate causes referred to above and which science also knows; nor can any beginning or end of their uniform operation be conceived.[13] When and whenever these causes converge to set up the temporal and spatial environment or context without which a given possibility could not be realised, the corresponding form emerges[14] or appears: a mammal, for example, could not have appeared in the Silurian, while it could not appear when the operation of natural causes had later on prepared the earth for the life of mammals. Every one of these transient forms of species and individuals reflects an archetypal possibility or pattern (*pater*, father) subsistent in what is called the 'intelligible' as distinguished from our 'sensible' world or *locus*

(Skr. *loka*) of compossibles. There is, for example, an 'intelligible Sun', 'Sun of the sun', or 'Sun that not all men know with their mind', other than, but represented by the physical sun; an Apollo other than Helios; and it is actually only of the invisible powers, and not of the 'visible gods' that images are made to be used as 'supports of contemplation'.[15] It is only to the extent that we think and speak of distinct 'species' and 'individuals' that we must also speak of their separate archetypal ideas; in reality, everything that flows (and πάντα ῥεῖ) is represented there in all its variety, although not in a temporal succession, but so that all can be seen at once:—'Contingency, the which extendeth not beyond the quadrangle of your matter, is all depicted in the eternal aspect'.[16]

The immediate motivations or purposes of life (*natura naturata*, man included) are those of the values established by choices made between the alternatives or contraries that everywhere present themselves, by which our behaviourism is conditioned, and in relation to which our procedure is passive. But the final purpose of life is to be, not a passive subject, but 'all in act', and this means to be liberated from the contrary 'pullings and haulings' of pleasure and pain and all other opposites; free to be as, when, and where we will, as Life is free, but lives are not.[17] The doctrine is animistic, of course, in that it presupposes a will that *nei cor mortaliè permotore*;[18] teleological, in that it is assumed that 'all things seek their ultimate perfection';[19] and solipsist, in that the 'world picture' is painted by the Spirit of Life on the 'walls' of its own awareness[20]—although not individually solipsist because, in the last analysis, there is only one Spectator, and what the 'individual' play-goer sees is merely a fraction of the synoptic spectacle; fatalistic, not in the arbitrary sense, but inasmuch as the careers of individuals are determined by a long heredity of causes,[21] at the same time, however that their 'Life' is an independent witness of, and not subjected to any fate; and optimistic, in that it lies within our power to rise above our fate by a verification of the identify of our Self with the Life that is never subjected nor ever becomes anyone, but is in the world and not of it. The doctrine is neither monistic nor dualistic, but of a reality that is both one and many, one in itself and many in its manifestations. And '*That* art thou'.

At the same time, in one important respect the scientific and metaphysical formulations differ; and necessarily, because the former is envisaging only a fragment of cosmic history, that of this earth, or that of this present universe at most; while the metaphysical cosmogony envisages the cosmic process in its entirety without beginning or end. In the scientific formulation, accordingly, evolution is thought of as proceeding in a straight line, or lines, of 'progress'; and from this point of view an involution can only be thought of as a regression, widdershins and counterclockwise; whence the feeling—hardly a thought—that finds expression in the notorious cliché: 'Yes: but you can't put back the hands of the clock', by which it is supposed that every re-former can be silenced for ever. In the metaphysical concept, however, involution is the natural complement and consummation, a continuation to fulfilment, and not a reversal of the 'forward' motion. And while it is true that involution logically 'follows' evolution, this does not mean that these apparently contrary motions of descent and ascent are only successive and not also coincident; on the contrary, the *Fons Vitae* is nowever 'fontal and inflowing'. Motion in time, as the years or aeons 'revolve', is that of a given point on the circumference of a wheel; and it needs no demonstration that the 'forward' movement of such a point is actually 'backward' with respect to opposite points, during a half of the period of time considered. Moreover, and still adhering to the pregnant symbolism of the circle, evolution and involution are not, for the metaphysician, exclusively temporal events, i.e., not merely peripheral motions, but also centrifugal and centripetal; and it follows that their course cannot be adequately represented by a straight line (even if taken to be a curve of however gigantic a radius), but only by spirals—or, if we are considering the whole course of Life, or of any separated life, only by the continuous double spiral of which the forms and adaptations are so widely distributed in the traditional arts.[22]

The traditional concept of 'Evolution' or 'Development of Self-realisation' is stated in general terms as follows:

> He who knows his Self[23] more manifested, attains to manifest Being. He knows the Self more manifest in herbs and trees, and in all kinds of animals. In herbs and trees there is, indeed, sap (moisture, protoplasm)—but intelligence in animals; in animals, assuredly, the Self's more manifest, for while there is also sap in them, there is no intelligence in the others. In man, again, there is a more manifest Self, for he is most endowed

> with prescience,[24] he speaks discriminately, sees discriminately (i.e. gives names to things and distinguishes their forms), he knows the morrow, he knows what is and is not mundane (material and immaterial), and by the mortal seeks to gain the immortal,—such is his endowment.[25]

Similarly, with reference to the Spirit (*rūḥ*) that has indwelt so many 'cities',[26] and the pilgrimage of Blake's 'Eternal Man'.[27] 'First he came into the realm of the inorganic . . . Long years dwelt he in the vegetable state . . . passed into the animal condition . . . From the animal condition towards humanity . . . Whence there is again a migration to be made'—which is an awakening from 'sleep' and 'Self-forgetfulness', for as Rūmī emphasizes, the Pilgrim does not clearly remember his former conditions until his goal is reached.[28]

Before proceeding, and to avoid any possible misconception, it must be emphasised, and cannot be over-emphasised, that this doctrine of a long development towards a perfect Self-awareness (in which a self-forgetfulness is necessarily implied) has nothing whatever in common with the notion of a 'reincarnation' of individual 'souls' inhabiting successive terrestrial bodies, whether vegetable, animal or human.[29] Our spiritual kinship with 'nature', for example, does not depend upon a possibility that in some animal or other, a relative of mine may have been reborn; but upon the recognition that every form of life, our own included, is animated by one and the same Life or Spiritual-Self, a Life that does not pick and choose among its habitations, but quickens one and all impartially.[30] This is, furthermore, the ultimate basis of an ethic of Self-love (*svakāma*) and in-nocence (*ahiṁsa*) that transcends the concepts of selfishness and altruism; for 'inasmuch as ye have done it unto one of these, ye have done it unto Me', and 'unto Me' means 'to your Self', if we know Who we are, and can say with St Paul, 'I live, yet not "I", but Christ in me'.

To continue: it is obvious that man's distinctive 'endowment' is not equally 'developed' in all men, however it may be latent in all, and that it can be attributed absolutely only to the 'Perfect Man', whose possible emergence is always predicted by the presupposition of a total, and therefore also human entelechy. Of such a Perfect Man, a Buddha ('Wake') or Christ, for example, we can better say what he is not than what he is—('Transumanar significar *per verba* non si poria'.[31] But of what can be attributed to him, nothing is more important in the present connection than the perfection of his Recollection; the Perfect Man is no longer, of the 'two that dwell together in us', the composite mortal individual, but this man's immortal part, or Life, and 'seeing that the Soul (our 'Life') is immortal and has been born many times, and has beheld all things both in this world and in the other, she has learnt all things, without exception; so that it is no wonder that she should be able to remember all that she knew before'.[32] In Vedic formulation, *Agni*, the Fire of Life, is necessarily 'omniscient of births' (*jātavedas*) and omniscient absolutely (*viśvavedas*), because apart from him there is no birth or coming to be; while in Buddhism, where also 'there is no individual-essence that passes over from one life to another', and it is absurd to ask 'Who was I?' in time past or 'Who shall *I* be?' in time to come, the highest value is nevertheless attached to the practical discipline of 'remembering past births' (*jātissaranam*) (87), occupied one after another until, as one who is Awake, he could exclaim, 'Never again, shalt thou, the builder of houses, build one for Me'. As Meister Eckhart also says, 'If I knew my Self as intimately as I ought, I should have perfect knowledge of all creatures', and it is 'not until the soul knows all that there is to be known that she can cross over to the Unknown Good'.[33]

In the light of these conceptions we are now at last in a position to understand the oracles and prophecyings of the Mythical Wanderers and illuminated Saints, *logoi* such as: Vāmadeva's, 'I am become Manu and the Sun, I am the priest and prophet Kakṣīvān; I gave the Aryan the earth, and to the sacrificer rain; I led forth the roaring waters, the Gods (Intelligences), ensure my banner. . . . Being in the womb, I know their every generation; a hundred iron cities held me fast, but forth I flew';[34] Māṇikka Vāçagar's, 'Grass, shrub was I, worm, tree, full many a kind of beast, bird, snake, stone man, demon. 'Midst Thy hosts I served. The form of mighty Asuras, ascetics, gods I bore. Within these mobile and immobile forms of life, in every species born, weary I've grown, Great Lord. . . . This day, I've gained release';[35] Amergin's, 'I am the wind that blows o'er the sea, I am the wave of the ocean . . . a beam of the sun . . . the God who creates in the head of the fire';[36] and Taliesin's, 'I have sung of what I passed through . . . I was in many a guise before I was disenchanted . . . I was the hero in trouble . . . I am old, I am young'.[37] All these are saying with Hermes Trismegistos' 'New born' son; 'Now that I see in Mind, I see myself to be the All. I am in heaven and on earth, in water and in air; I am in beasts and plants; I am a babe in the womb, and one that is not yet conceived, and one that has been born; I am present everywhere',[38] and have realized 'Pilgrim, Pilgrimage and Road, was but Myself toward Myself'.[39]

For, indeed, 'A man is born but once, but *I* have been born many times',[40] 'Before Abraham *I* am',[41] 'Never have I not been, and never hast thou not been, nor ever shall not be . . . Many a birth of mine and thine is past and gone, Arjuna: *I* know them all, but *thou* knowest not thine.'[42]

It is just because the One-and-Many is thus 'the single "form" of many different things' that 'God' is so uniformly described as Omniform or Protean (*viśvarūpa, sarvamaya,* παντόμορφος, etc.), and thought of as a wandering juggler or magician forever appearing in some new disguise. No wonder that the forms of life melt into one another and cannot be defined (however inconvenient that may be for systematic purposes), for all are strung on one and the same thread.

In conclusion, I can only reaffirm that in the traditional doctrine of evolution and involution as one of progress towards an intelligible and attractive goal there is nothing whatever inconsistent with, but much rather inclusive of and explanatory of all the facts of evolution as found by the biologist and geologist. What these facts reveal to a metaphysician is not a refutation of his axiology but that the Ever-productive Nature moves in an even more mysterious way than had hitherto been supposed. At one time, indeed, the naturalist himself used to think of his investigation as a finding out of the 'wonderful ways of God', and no one supposes that he was for that reason any the less able to 'observe' phenomena. The theologian who is altogether ignorant of biology, if he sometimes forgets that 'the invisible things of God are known by the things which were made', if for example he knows of the 'Divine Sport' but nothing of 'Mendelian sports', is no doubt missing something. But the scientist, if he is altogether ignorant of, or, much worse, misinformed about, the real nature of the traditional doctrines, and therefore fears them, is even more unfortunate; since, however great his knowledge or skill may be, for so long as the facts are held to be 'meaningless' and judgment is suspended, their discoverer is taking no responsibility for their good use and will always leave them to be exploited at will by the devourers of humanity—and these he will in their turn, from the security of his ivory tower, 'observe' without daring to criticise. We overlook that 'science' is no more than 'art' or 'ethics' an end in itself; all these techniques are means to a good life.

Can they be used as such if we deny that life has any purpose? The 'purely objective' point of view, however valid it may be in the laboratory, is humanly speaking far more unpractical than the traditional philosophy, which it is not even supposed that a man can really understand unless he lives accordingly.

The jargon of the Perennial Philosophy has been called the only perfectly intelligible language; but it must not be overlooked that it is as much a technical language as is the jargon of Chemistry. Whoever would understand Chemistry must learn to think in the terms of its formulae and iconography; and in the same way whoever would understand the Perennial Philosophy must learn, or rather relearn, to think in its terms, both verbal and visual. These are, moreover, those of the only universal language of culture, the language that was spoken at the Round Table before the 'confusion of tongues', and that of which the 'ghost' survive in our daily conversation, which is full of 'super-stitions', i.e., figures of speech that were originally figures of thought, but have, like 'art-forms', been more or less emptied of meaning on their way down to us. Whoever cannot use this language is excluded from the ancient and common universe of discourse of which it is the *lingua franca*, and will have to confess that the history of literature and art, and the cultures of innumerable peoples, past and present, must remain for him closed books, however long and patiently he may read in them. It is precisely in this sense that it has been so well said that 'the greater the ignorance of modern times, the deeper grows the darkness of the Middle Ages'.

It may be that no one should receive a degree in Divinity who has not also some working knowledge of Biology; and that no one should be given a degree in science who has not had at least so much training in Philosophy as to be able to understand what a mythologist, theologian or metaphysician is talking about. I have never been able to understand how anyone having an adequate knowledge of physics *and* metaphysics can imagine or attempt to demonstrate a conflict of reason with revelation, or recognise a schism between the active life of research and the visionary life of the contemplative philosopher. I would rather say, on the contrary, that whoever cannot or will not, at least to some degree, follow both these trades—literally, 'paths', *viae*—is not in full possession of all his faculties; and that no one can be at peace with himself or with his environment, no one can be really happy, who cannot recover the once universal concept of a coincidence of efficiency and meaning both in 'nature' and in his own 'creations', in so far as the latter have been well and truly made; whatever is not significant is, from any other than a most crudely utilitarian point of view, insignificant, or in other words, negligible. All this amounts to saying that in any superior social order, with really high standards of *living*—and that means, 'not by bread alone', however soft or bun-like it may be—there is no place for a distinction of sacred or profane, *facere* from *sacra facere*. Such a condition has obtained in many past and persists in some precariously surviving cultures; but it will be out of our reach until Bellerophon has dragged into the light of day and exposed the chimera of an inevitable conflict of science with religion. The whole affair is actually a sham battle in which neither side is attacking or defending real issues.[43]

NOTES

1. 'Gradation and Evolution', [See preceeding essay].

2. Plato's ἀειγενὴς φύσις, *Laws*, 773E, cf. Stasinus as cited in *Euthyphro*, 12A, and φύσις ἁπλή in Philo, LA. 2.2. Gk. φύω = Skr. *bhū*, to become or make become; φύσις from φύω may be compared with Brahma, from *bṛh*, to grow or make grow. The word Prāṇa, spiration or breath, and designating the Spirit (*ātman*) present as the vital principle in living things, is often translated as 'life'.

3. It is too often overlooked that 'individual' is as much a generalisation as 'species'; in relation to such 'universals', or much rather, 'abstractions', the realist becomes a nominalist. 'Nobody remains one, nor "is" one; but we become (γιγνόμεθα = *bhavanti*) many . . . and if he is not the same, we cannot say that "he is", but only that he is being transformed as one self comes into being from the other . . . "shall be" and "has been", when they are spoken, are of themselves a confession of "not being", and it is only of God, in whose "now" there is neither future nor past, nor older nor younger, that we can say that "He is"' (Plutarch, *Moralia*, 392D-393B); for which innumerable parallels could be cited from traditional sources. The word 'phenomenon' implies an 'of what?', and an answer to this question can only be made in terms of metaphysics; of the phenomena themselves, which are by definition the proper field of an empirical and statistical science, which observes their succession, and predicts accordingly, we cannot say that they *are*, but only that they *appear*.

4. It is obvious that 'we', whose only experience is always in terms of past and

present, cannot have an empirical experience of a 'now without duration', or 'eternity'; our so called 'present' is not a 'now' but only a 'nowadays'.

5. As personalists and individualists we use the expression 'I' only for convenience, but do so unconsciously; the Buddhist, or any other of the metaphysicians who maintain that to say 'I' belongs only to God, likewise use the pronoun only for convenience, but do this consciously.

6. This *via remotionis* is the recognized technique of self-naughting and Self-realisation; for example, in Buddhism, where my body, feelings, thoughts, etc., all 'that is not my Self', and in the same way for Walt Whitman, 'not Me, myself'. Modern psychology is an analysis of 'what is not myself' rather than a technique of Self-realisation.

7. *Maitri Up.* II. 6, and related Brāhmaṇa texts.

8. *Kaṭha Up.* IV. 1, with the corollary that, to see our Self, the direction of vision must be reversed. Similarly for Plato (*Phaedo*, 83B, *Republic*, 526E. *Symposium*, 129).

9. *Bṛhadāraṇyaka Up.* I. 4.7. Similarly for Philo, and in Islam.

10. It should be observed that 'life' is attributed to minerals as well as to higher organisms; the problem of an 'origin of life' preceding that of the transition from inorganic to organic forms.

11. Dante, *Paradiso*, VIII. 127–9. The *circular natura* is that of the Unmoved Mover who from his station at the centre of the Wheel of Life is its motive power and that of each of its living wheels within wheels.

12. 'Proceeds to aughty or naughty (i.e., good or evil) wombs', *Maitri Up.* III. 1. Similarly Matt. 13:3–9 and 27: 'Some fell upon stony places . . . other fell into good ground . . . the field is the world.' For the metaphor of sowing cf. *Timaeus*, 41 and 69. Naught-y = evil, because *ens et bonum convertuntur*; cf. G. Unthat = Skr. *akṛtam*, sin being always of omission, a getting nothing done.

13. 'The world is pregnant with the causes of things as yet unborn' (St Augustine, *De trin.* 3.9, quoted with approval by St Th. Aquinas). Man is the product and heir of past doings (*Aitareya Āraṇyaka*, II. 1.3, and Buddhism, *passim*). Cf. Walt Whitman, 'Before I was born out of my mother, generations guided me', and William Blake, 'Man is born like a garden, ready planted and sown'.

14. 'Emerges', i.e. from its prior state of being 'in potentia', No reference is intended to the 'emergent evolution' or 'emergent mentalism' of S. Alexander and Lloyd Morgan, Cf. My *Time and Eternity*, 1947, p. 19, note 21.

15. Plato, *Laws*, 931A The indication is important for the theory of iconography and 'imitation' generally. Abstraction ('taking away') eliminates qualities, and this is the technique of the 'negative theology', or in other words of iconoclasm. Iconography or 'adequate symbolism', verbal or visual, attributes qualities, and is the method of the 'affirmative theology'; the presumption being that a reality on any level of reference (e.g., in the intelligible world, in heaven) is represented by an analogous reality on any other (e.g., in the sensible world, on earth). There are, accordingly, objective adequacies or correlatives; the traditional symbolism, verbal or visual, is not a matter of forms arbitrarily determined by psychological association and thereafter accepted by 'convention'. The reference of such symbols to an individual poetic or artistic fancy reflects a wholly modern conception of originality, and to suppose that a serious student of symbolism (verbal or visual semantics or hermeneutics) is 'reading meanings into them' is only another aspect of the same pathetic fallacy.

For example, spirit is represented by the quickening wind that 'raises' waves or dust, and possibility by still waters or the maternal earth; or respectively by the warp and woof threads of which the 'tissue' of the universe is woven. The meaning of particular symbols is often partly determined by their context, but always consistent;

for example, when the material of the cosmos is called a 'wood' (ὕλη, Skr. *vana*) the power by which all things are made is necessarily an 'architect' or 'carpenter' and works by his 'art'. When we call the early Ionian philosophers 'naturalists' we generally overlook that 'nature' was for them a creative power (cf. Note 2) rather than an environment, as it was still for Philo (*De sacr.* 75, 98 and *Quis heres* 116) and in Scholastic philosophy ('Natura naturans, Creatrix universalis, Deus').

16. Dante, *Paradiso*, XVII. 37.

17. See my 'Symplegades' in *Studies and Essays in the History of Science and Learning offered in Homage to George Sarton on the Occasion of his Sixtieth Birthday*, ed. M. F. Ashley Montagu, N.Y. 1947. pp. 463–488.

18. Dante, *Paradiso*, I. 116. Cf. *Maitri Up.* II. 6, *hṛdantarāt . . . pracodayitṛ*, 'from within the heart . . . the impeller'.

19. Meister Eckhart. 'All the past Imams agree in regarding as the goal of everything its attainment of ultimate perfection' (*Kalāmi Pīr*, 63).

20. Śaṅkarācārya, *Svātmanirūpaṇam*, 95.

21. Man is the product and heir of past doings (*Aitareya Āraṇyaka*, II. 1.3 and Pali Buddhism, *passim*). 'The world is pregnant with the causes of things as yet unborn' (St Augustine, *De trin.* 3.9, endorsed by St Thomas Aquinas); 'Nothing in the world happens by chance' (St Augustine, QQ. CXXXIII. 34). 'Before I was born out of my mother, generations guided me' (Walt Whitman).

22. "Der Abendländer (i.e., the modern mind) denkt linienhaft in die Ferne, darum mechanisch, areligios, faustich . . . Das Morgenland und die Bible denken nicht linienhaft, sondern zeitraumlich, spiralisch, kreislaufig. Das Welgeschehen geht in Spiralen, die sich bis in die Volendung fortsetzen' (Alfred Jeremias, *Der Antichrist in Geschichte und Gegenwart*, 1930, p.4). On spirals and double spirals see also my 'Iconography of Dürer's "Knots" and Leonardo's "Concatenation"' in *Art Quarterly*, Spring 1944. Meister Eckhart's 'fontal and inflowing' is paralleled by *Jaiminīya Upaniṣad Brāhmana* I. 2. 7 parācīr . . . nivesṭamānāḥ, 'proceeding and inwinding', cf. the 'enigma' of RV. V. 47.5 that 'while the rivers flow, the waters are at rest'.

Cf. E. R. Dodds, 'procession and reversion together constitute a single movement, the diastole-systole which is the life of the universe. . . . Being, which becomes Life by procession, becomes Intelligence by reversion' (*Proclus, The Elements of Theology*, 1933, pp. 219, 222). 'Diastole-systole' corresponds to the Indian concept of *prāna*, Spiration, Life, which in living things *prāṇa-bhṛtaḥ)* becomes *prāṇipīnau*, inspiration-and-expiration. For the parallel in Hebrew metaphysics see G. G. Scholem, *Major Trends in Jewish Mysticism*, 1941, p. 260, on *hithpashtuth* and *histalkuth*, 'egression' and 'regression'.

23. 'Knows him-Self' (*tasya . . . ātmānam veda*)—not this mortal and composite individuality, but 'its, or his immortal Self' (*amrto'sya ātman . . . ātmano'tmā netà'mṛtaḥ, Maitri Up.* III.2 and VI.7); 'the Self of all beings' (*Satapatha Brāhmaṇa* X.4.2.27) or 'Being of beings' (*Atharva Veda*, IV.8.1), Philo's ψυχὴ ψυχῆς, Islamic *jān-i-jān*, and what, in the present article, we have spoken of as 'Life'.

24. *Prajñā*, πρoνοία, pro-gnosis; à priori, intuitive knowledge.

25. *Aitareya Āraṇyaka* II. 3.2. As pointed out by A. B. Keith, this is *not* a doctrine of the rebirths of individual souls (*Aitereya Āraṇyaka*, 1909, p. 217, note 2).

26. 'Cities', i.e. constitutions or forms of life; in Nicholson's words, 'phases of experience through which the soul must pass in its journeys *from* and *to* God before it can attain to gnosis'. Cf. Skr. *puruṣa*, explained as *purisaya*, 'citizen', in the same sense.

27. 'Man', or more literally 'human nature' (*khalqat ādmi*). *Ādmi* is 'Adam', ἄνθρωπος, *puruṣa*, *homo* rather than *mard*, ἀνήρ, *nara*.

28. Rūmī, *Mathnawī*, 4.3632–55, condensed; see also I.3165–8 and 3873–4, and

VI.126–8, with R. A. Nicholson's commentaries on these passages (text, translations and commentaries all in the Gibb Memorial Series).

29. Even when Rūmī speaks of the possibility of a 'transportation from rationality to the grade of animals' no doctrine of reincarnation is involved; cf. Nicholson's commentary on this passage (I.3320 and IV.3657f). In the same way in Christian contexts, when St Thomas Aquinas says that 'the human body pre-existed in the previous works in their causal virtues' (*Sum. Theol.* I.91.2 ad 4) and Meister Eckhart that 'Aught is suspended from the divine essence; its progression is matter, wherein the soul puts on new forms and puts off her old ones. The change from one into the other is her death; the one she doffs she dies to, and the one she dons she lives in' (Pfeiffer p.530)—an almost verbal equivalent of *Bhagavad Gītā*, II.22–these are, indeed, doctrines of karma (as causality) and of bhava (becoming), but not of a reincarnation. The same applies to even so late an Indian text as that of the *Garuḍa Purāṇa*, VI.40, 'after hundreds of births the condition of humanity on earth is attained' (*jātisateṣu labhate bhuvi mānuṣatvam*): the reference is to a transmigrant principle, not to reincarnating individuals. The subject is treated at some length in my 'One and Only Transmigrant', *JAOS*, Supplement No. 3, 1944, [Rpr. SP2, pp.66–87.] but it could be even more conclusively demonstrated that 'reincarnation' is not a doctrine of the Perennial Philosophy. The language of the texts is symbolic, and can be misinterpreted; but it is just as when we call a man an 'ass', and mean that he is 'asinine' rather than that he has four legs; while it is in the same sense, and no other, that it can properly be said of the stupid or sensual man, whose character is normally 'reborn' in his children, that 'he becomes an ass in a future life'.

Compare *Manu*, II.201 as translated by G. Bühler: 'By censuring (his teacher), he will become (in his next birth) an ass'. Here the present *bhavati*, 'becomes', is rendered by the future, and the words 'in his next birth' are inserted by the translator himself, and correspond to nothing in the text!

30. 'God' endowing all things with their life, but leaving the manner of their existence to the operation of mediate causes, with which he does not interfere; as in an organ one blower is the first cause and *sine qua non* of sound, but the various sounds produced are determined by the qualities of the pipes. In Islam, for example, the whole of the divine fiat is contained in the single word 'Be!' (*kun*), or more correctly, 'Become' (Cf. A. M. Goichon, *La philosophie d'Avicenne*, Paris, 1944, p. 62). Similarly in Genesis, 'Let there be light'; but 'colour' (individuality, caste); is determined by the nature of the illuminated surfaces. Otherwise expressed, all things drink of one 'milk', but this is the nourishment of different qualities in each (*Atharva Veda*, VIII.10.22–29).

31. Dante, *Paradiso*, I. 71.

32. Plato, *Meno*, 82 C.

33. For all this material, and further references, see my 'Recollection, Indian and Platonic', *JAOS*, Supplement 3, 1944.

34. *Ṛg Veda*, IV.4.10. For Vāmadeva (Indra, Breath, immanent Life) see *Aitareya Āraṇyaka* II.2.1, 2 and 2.5, and my 'One and Only Transmigrant', *passim*.

35. G. U. Pope, *Tiruvāçagam*, 1900, p. 3.

36. Amergin, *Oxford Book of English Mystical Verse*, p. 1.

37. Taliesin, J. G. Evans, *Poems from the Book of Taliesin*, 1915; R. D. Scott, *The Thumb of Knowledge*, 1930, pp. 124f.

38. Hermes Trismegistos, *Lib.* XIII.11 B, cf. II.2.20 B. Like *Atharva Veda*, II.4 on the Breath (*prāna*, 'Life'); in 14, where the Purusa, 'Man', is born again (*jāyate punah*) 'when thou, O Breath, giv'st life' (*jinvasi*). Whitney's 'A man . . . is born again' completely distorts the meaning (all scholars are agreed that 'reincarnation' is unknown to the Samhitās), and this is a good example of the way in which even much

later texts are commonly mistranslated and made to imply a doctrine of reincarnation, where nothing of the sort was intended.

As remarked by G. G. Scholem, appropros of the Kabbalistic ('traditional') doctrine of 'transmigration' (*gilgul* = Ar. *tanazzul*): 'If Adam contained the entire soul of humanity, which is now diffused among the whole genus in innumerable modifications and individual appearances, all transmigrations of souls are in the last resort only *migrations of the one soul* whose exile atones for its fall' (*Major Trends in Jewish Mysticism*, 1941, p. 278, italics mine). Hence, 'to know the stages of the creative process is also to know the stages of one's own return to the root of all existence' (ibid. p. 20).

39. Farīdu'd-dīn'Aṭṭar, *Manṭiqu't-Tair*, tr. Fitzgerald. In these few words and the preceding statements are condensed the essence of 'mystic' or 'perfect' experience, in so far as it can be communicated in words. The experience is 'self-authenticating'; its validity can neither be proved nor disproved in the class-room. On the other hand, to have had, or to believe in the reality of such experience is in no sense contradictory of the 'facts of science'. The scientist may at will ignore, but cannot quarrel with the traditional metaphysics without stultifying his own position.

40. Shams-i-Tabrīz, in Nicholson, *Diwān of Shams-i-Tabrīz*, 1898, p. 332. the text continues, 'I am the theft of rogues, I am the pain of the sick, I am both cloud and rain, I have rained in the meadows . . .' For 'rain' in this sense cf. *Ṛg Veda*, IV, 26.2 and *Atharva Veda* II.4.5.

41. John 8.58; cf. *Saddharma Puṇḍarīka*, XV.1 and *Shams-i-Tabrīz*, XVII (Nicholson, l.c.) 'I was on the day when the Names were not'. For 'names' in this sense cf. Murray Fowler, 'Polarity in the Rig-Veda', *Review of Religion*, Jan. 1943.

42. *Bhagavad Gītā*, II.12 and IV.5.

43. A long time having elapsed between the preparation and the publication of the present article, I could now have improved and added to it. For further material on the same theme the reader is asked to refer to my 'Gradation, Evolution, and Reincarnation' in *Am I My Brother's Keeper?* (New York, 1947, pp.104–110), apropos of notes 33–8 above, and Erwin Schrödinger's 'Consciousness is a singular of which the plural is unknown'; and *Time and Eternity* (Ascona, 1947), emphasising that, in all traditional doctrine, Eternity is not ever-*lasting*, but always *Now*, and that Gradation implies the creation of all things not merely in a 'beginning' but in this Now of Eternity, so that, as Philo says, 'there is an end of the notion that the universe came into being "in six days"', and while 'we must think of God as doing all things at once', 'a sequence was necessarily written into the narrative because of their subsequent generation from one another' (*Opif.* 13 and 67 + *LA* I.20)—which subsequent generation corresponds to what we now call 'evolution'.

NINE

Fate, Foresight, and Free-will

NO event can be thought of as taking place apart from a logically antecedent and actually imminent possibility of its taking place; and in this sense, every new individual is the forthcoming of an antenatal potentiality, which dies as a potentiality in the first place at the creature's first conception and thereafter throughout life as the various aspects of this potentiality are reduced to act, in accordance with a partly conscious and partly unconscious will that ever seeks to realise itself. We can express the same in other words by saying that the individual comes into the world to accomplish certain ends or purposes peculiar to itself. Birth is an opportunity.

The field of procedure from potentiality to act is that of the individual's liberty; the 'free-will' of the theologian is, in accordance with the parable of the talents, a freedom to make use of or to neglect the opportunity to become what one can become under the circumstances into which one is born; these 'circumstances' of the born being consisting of its own soul-and-body and the rest of its environment, or world, defined as a specific ensemble of possibilities.

The liberty of the individual is evidently not unlimited; he cannot accomplish the impossible, i.e. what is impossible for him, though it might be a possible in some other 'world' as above defined. Notably, he cannot have been born otherwise than as he was actually born, or possessed of other possibilities than those which he is naturally (by nativity) endowed; he cannot realise ambitions for the realisation of which there exists no provision in his own nature; he is himself, and no one else. Certain specific and partly unique possibilities are open to him, and certain other possibilities, usually vastly more numerous, are closed to him; he cannot, as a finite being, be at the same time a man in London and a lion in Africa. These possibilities and impossibilities which are those of and predetermined by his own nature and cannot be thought of as having been arbitrarily imposed upon him, but only as the definition of his own nature, represent what we call the individual's fate or destiny; whatever happens to the individual being merely the reduction of a given possibility to act when the occasion presents itself, while whatever does not happen was not really a possibility, but only ignorantly conceived to have been so.

Freedom of individual will is then the freedom to do what the individual can do, or to refrain from doing it. Whatever one actually does under given circumstances is what one wills to do under those circumstances: to be forced to act or suffer against one's will is not a coercion of the will, but of its implements, and only in appearance a coercion of the individual himself to the extent that he identifies 'himself' with his implements. Furthermore, the destiny of the individual, what he will do of himself under given circumstances, is not altogether obscure to him, but rather manifest to the extent that he really knows himself and understands his own nature. It is noteworthy that this measure of foresight (providence) by no means interferes with his sense of liberty; one merely thinks of the future decision as a present to resolve. There is in fact a coincidence of foresight and freewill. In the same way, but to the limited extent that one can really know another's essence, one can foresee its peculiar destiny; which foresight in no way governs that creature's conduct. And finally, if we assume an omniscient providence in God, who from his position at the centre of the wheel inevitably views the past and future *now*, which 'now' will be the same tomorrow as it was yesterday, this in no way interferes with the freedom of any creature in its own sphere. As Dante expresses it, 'Contingency . . . is all depicted in the eternal aspect; though it takes not its necessity therefrom' (*Paradiso*, XVI. 37f). Our difficulties here arise only because we think of providence as a foresight in the temporal sense, as if one saw today what must happen tomorrow. Far from being a foresight in this temporal sense, divine providence is a vision always contemporary with the event. To think of God as looking forward to a future or backwards to a past event is as meaningless as it would be to ask what was He doing 'before' he made the world.

Not that it is by any means impossible to shrink from a foreseen destiny. Destiny is for those who have eaten of the Tree, and this includes both that 'fraction' (*pada, amsa*) of the Spirit that enters into all born beings, and seems to suffer with them, and these created things themselves, in so far as they identify 'themselves' with the body-and-soul. Destiny is necessarily a passion of good and evil; it is as such that it presents itself to us as something that we could either welcome or avoid, at the same time we cannot refuse it, without becoming other than we are. This acceptance we explain to ourselves in terms of ambition, courage, altruism, or resignation as the case may be. In any case, it is one's own nature that compels us to pursue a destiny of which we are forewarned, however fatal the result expected. The futility of warnings is a characteristic theme of heroic literature; not that the warnings are discredited, but that the hero's honour requires him to continue as he has begun; or because at the critical moment the warning is forgotten. We call the man 'fey'.

A poignant example of shrinking from and yet accepting a foreseen destiny can be cited in the 'hesitation' of a Messiah. It is thus that in *Ṛg Veda*, x. 51 Agni fears his destiny as sacrificial priest and cosmic charioteer, and must be persuaded; thus the Buddha 'apprehensive of injury' is overpersuaded by Brahma (*Saṃyutta-Nikāyha*, I. 138 and *Dīgha-Nikāya* II. 33); and thus that Jesus prays 'Father . . . take away this cup from me; yet not as I will, but as Thou wilt' (Mark, 14: 36), and 'Father, save me from this hour; but for this cause came I unto this hour' (John, 12: 27).

Desire must not be confused with regret. Desire presupposes a possibility which is either actually such, or imagined to be such. We cannot desire the impossible, but only regret the impossibility. Regret may be felt for what has happened, but this is not a desire that it had not happened; it is a regret that it 'had to happen' as it did; for nothing happens unless by necessity. If there is one doctrine that science and theology are perfectly agreed upon, it is that the course of events is causally determined; as St. Thomas says, 'If God governed alone (and not also by means of mediate causes) the world would be deprived of the perfection of causality. . . . All things (appertaining to the chain of fate) . . . are done by God by means of second causes' (*Sum. Theol.* I. 103. 7 ad 2, and 116. 4 ad 1).

The *Śvetāsvatra Upaniṣad* (I. 1–3) distinguishes in a similar manner Brahman, Spirit of God, the One, as over-standing[1] cause, from his Power or Means-of-operation (*śakti* = *māyā*, etc.). known as such to contemplatives, but 'considered' (*cintyam*) as a plurality of 'causal combinations of time, etc., with the passible spirit' (*kāranāni kālatmayuktāni*), which latter, 'because it is not a combination of the series, time, etc.,' is not the master of its own fate, so long as it remains oblivious of its own identity with the transcendental Spirit. In the same way again, Śaṇkarācarya explains that Brahman does not operate arbitrarily, but in accordance with the varying properties inherent in the characters of things as they are themselves, which things owe their being to Brahman, but are individually responsible for their modalities of being. This is, of course, the traditionally orthodox view; as Plotinus expresses it (VI. 4.3) 'all is offered, but the recipient is able to take only so much', and Boehme 'as is the harmony, viz. the life's form, in each thing, so is also the sound of the eternal voice therein; in the holy, holy, in the perverse, perverse . . . therefore no creature can blame its creator, as if he made it evil' (*Sig. Rerum*, XVI. 6, 7 and *Forty Questions*, VIII. 14).

NOTE

1. *Yah . . . adhitisthati*, in verse 3. Both meanings are implied, viz. 'He over-rules' and 'He takes his stand upon'. The corresponding object is *adhiṣthānam*; as in *Ṛg Veda*, X. 81. 2. where the question is asked 'What is his standing ground?' (*kim . . . adhiṣthānam*) of 'the immortal incorporeal Spirit' is the mortal body (*sárīra*) that is in the power of Death 'standing ground' being thus synonymous with 'field' (*kṣetra*) in the *Bhagavad Gītā*, XIII. 2, where again it is the 'body' that is thus referred to.

TEN

Mahātmā

THE term 'Mahātmā' has been much abused but has precise and intelligible meanings and a long history. Like so many other of the technical terms of Indian metaphysics, the word is difficult to explain and seems to have a vague or sentimental connotation mainly because of our general ignorance of Christian and all other traditional philosophies, so that, for example, we are no longer able to distinguish spirit from soul or essence from existence; and because of the absolute values we mistakenly attach to 'personality', or rather, individuality.

At a point already far from the beginning we find in a Buddhist Sutta the distinction drawn between the Greater and the Lesser 'selves' of a man, respectively *mahātmā* and *alpātmā*,* these 'selves' corresponding to St. Bernard's *esse* and *proprium*, 'being' and 'property', i.e. the psycho-physical qualities by which one individual is distinguished from another. These two 'selves' are, again, the 'lives' of John, 12:25, 'He that would save his life, let him lose it', and one of them is that 'life' that a man 'must hate if he would be my disciple' (Luke, 14:26); in these texts the words which have been rendered by 'life', here and in Luke, 9:24, 'Whosever shall lose his life for my sake', are Latin *anima* and Greek *psyche*, implying (1) self as a psychological entity, all in fact that is implied by *psyche* in our 'psychology' and (2) the spiritual 'self'.

In Mahātmā, *maha* is simply 'great', 'higher', or 'superior': *ātman*, like Greek *pneuma*, is primarily 'spirit'. But because the spirit is the

* These terms are given in their Sanskrit, rather than in their Pali forms, to avoid confusion. The distinction is the same as that of the 'fair' (*kalyāna*) from the 'foul' (*pāpa*) self, as drawn in *Aṅguttara-Nikāya*, I. 149.

real being of the man, as distinguished from the accidents of this being by which the individual is known as So-and-so and is possessed of particular qualities or properties, *ātman* in reflexive usage acquires the value of 'self', whatever may be our opinion as to the nature of this 'self' whether physical, psychic, or spiritual. In this sense it can be used to denote either of the 'lives' referred to in the texts cited above. But it is precisely at this point that the fundamental importance of the traditional and often repeated injunction 'Know thyself' emerges: for the 'reasoning and mortal man' 'has forgotten who he is' (Boethius), and to those who have thus forgotten are applied the words of the Song of Songs, 'if thou knowest not thyself, depart'. The word of God, as St. Paul so trenchantly expresses it, is 'sharper than any two-edged sword, piercing even to the dividing asunder of soul and spirit' (Heb. 4: 12); as it must, if the way of return to God is to be stated; for if it be true that 'whoever is joined unto the Lord, is one spirit' (1 Cor. 6: 17), this can only be by 'an elimination of all otherness' (Nicolas of Cusa). Therefore, as Eckhart says, 'All scripture cries aloud for freedom from self', and here the word 'all' must be taken in its widest possible sense, for this is the burden as much of Brahmanical, Buddhist and Islamic scripture as it is of Christian. It must be observed, however, that this is much rather a metaphysical than an ethical doctrine, and that 'freedom from self', means very much more than it conveyed by our word 'unselfishness': 'selfless conduct' will be merely symptomatic of the man whose self has been 'naughted' and whose works are 'those of the Holy Ghost (*spiritus, pneuma, ruaḥ, ātman*) rather than his own' (St. Thomas Aquinas, based on 2 Cor. 3:17 and Gal. 5:18). The altruist does as 'he' would be done by: the acts of one who is altogether 'in the spirit' are unmotivated, whether for good or evil, they are simply manifestations of the Truth apart from which 'he' no longer exists; it is only conventionally and logically, and for practical convenience, and not really, that he can speak of himself as 'I' or of anything as 'mine'; in reality 'I live, yet not "I", but Christ liveth in me' (Gal. 2:20), 'I wander in the world and am not anyone' (*akimcano carāmi lokl,* Buddhist).

The term Mahātmā is primarily a designation of the 'Great Unborn Spirit' (*mahān aja ātmā,* BU. IV. 4.22; *ātmā mahān,* KU.III.10), the Supernal Son (MU.VII.11.8), the spiritual-essence (*ātman*) of all that is (RV.1.115.1) at once the Giver of Life and Death the Ender (*mahātmā* in KU.1.16): a designation, that is to say, of the spirant God as distinguished from the despirated Godhead, which distinction is superseded only in the Supreme Identity of the Person (*puruṣa*), That One (*tad ekam*). The Spirit as described in Indian scripture is thus the Light of lights, and the only free agent in all things; for in this 'eternal philosophy' it is not 'we' who see, hear, act and so forth, but the immanent Spirit that sees, hears and acts in us.

If now the fundamental question is asked in the Upaniṣads and Buddhism, 'By which self' is freedom attainable, the answer is evidently 'by the spiritual self', and not by the individual, psycho-physical ego. The possibility of a salvation from pain, fear and death and all that we mean by 'evil' is the possibility of transposing our consciousness of being (valid in itself but not to be confused with our concept of being So-and-so) from the human ego to the immanent Spirit which lends itself to every individuality impartially without ever itself becoming anyone; the possibility, that is to say, of transferring our consciousness of being from the lesser to the greater self; the possibility, of becoming a 'Mahātmā', or as St. Paul would express it, of 'being in the spirit'. To call a man Mahātmā is then as much as to say 'Great Spirit', 'Sun', 'Great Light'; it is more than to call him a saint, it is to call him a Son of God and a shaft of the Uncreated Light. It implies, indeed, that the man so called is no longer in the common sense 'himself', no longer 'all-too-human', but being 'joined to God, is one spirit' (1 Cor. 6:17).

This is not a claim that any man would make for himself; he cannot make it as a man, nor is it one that could be proven. If a man has really here and now 'become what he is' (*geworden was er ist*), a blast of the Spirit (for 'That *art* thou'), 'free in this life' (*jivan-mukta*), or as Rūmī expresses it, 'a dead man walking, one whose spirit hath a dwelling place on high at this moment', all this is strictly speaking a secret between himself and God. The reader may not believe that the state of perfection 'even as your Father in heaven is perfect' implied by the epithet Mahātmā can be realised, or may not believe that it has been realised in the man of whom we can still speak as Mohandas Gandhi. My only object has been to explain the real meaning of the term Mahātmā which has been applied to Gandhi by those who regard him as a Messiah, and which has become inseparably connected with his name.

I conclude with the definition of the Mahātmā given in the Buddhist Sutta (*Aṅguttara-Nikāya,* I. 249) cited at the beginning of the second paragraph of this article. The Mahātmā 'is of full-grown body, will and foreknowledge; he is not emptied out, but a Great Spirit whose behaviour is incalculable'.

ELEVEN

*On Hares and Dreams**

'The Hare hath swallowed up the imminent blade'
Ṛg Veda, x 28.9.

'Whom the great Dog pursues in an unending race'
Aratos, *Phainomena—678.*

DR. LAYARD, author of *The Stone Men of Malekula*, is a well-known anthropologist, and has since become a psycho-analyst. Dr. Laynard's new book falls into two parts: the first an annotated case history of a patient's problems, with special reference to her dream of a hare which she was required to sacrifice, the victim being at the same time perfectly willing; and the second summarising the Egyptian, Classical, European, Indian, Chinese and American mythological significance of the archetypal symbolism of the Hare.

The case history will be of particular interest to anyone who, like the reviewer, is thoroughly distrustful of psycho-analysis, Freud and Jung; I think that Dr. Layard owes much less than he supposes to Jung, and much more than he supposes to his faith in supra-personal spiritual forces. His procedure in a case in which any false step would have produced disastrous results is extremely sagacious throughout: and while his knowledge of archetypal symbols seems to have come to him primarily from psycho-analytic sources, it is evident that his successful interpretations, inductions and applications *ad hominem* are to be accounted for partly by his anthropological background, but still more by his profound conviction of the reality of religious experience. It is surely his belief in spiritual—as distinct from merely somatic and psychic—forces that enabled him to avoid the pitfalls of a too personal interpretation of the dream symbols and to stress their impersonal and religious significance.

Dr. Layard recognises that the sacrifice of the willing Hare is really

* With special reference to *The Lady of the Hare; a Study in the Healing Power of Dreams*: by John Layard. London, Faber and Faber, 1945, pp. 277 and 22 illustrations.

that of the outer man, or self of uncontrolled instinct, to the inner man or 'Soul of the soul', the 'self's immortal Self and Leader' of the Upaniṣads. He uses, of course, not these, but the technical terms of psycho-analysis, 'shadow', and 'animus' or 'anima'; by which I understand the psycho-physical and spiritual 'selves' respectively; it is of the first of these that Meister Eckhart says that 'the soul must put itself to death'. For the end of self-integration which the healer of souls has in view it seems to me better and simpler to adhere to the traditional psychology (*e.g.* that of Plato, Philo, the Vedic and earlier Christian) according to which, in the words of St. Thomas Aquinas, *duo sunt in homine*, a fact that our everyday speech acknowledges whenever we speak of 'taking counsel with ourselves', or of 'con-science', or think of 'being true to oneself' or even when we say to someone who is misbehaving, 'Be yourself'. Using these equally Platonic and Indian terms, we say that our internal conflicts, which are essentially a matter of waiting to act in one way and knowing that we ought to act in another, remain unresolved until an agreement has been reached as to which shall rule, our worse or better self. The sacrifice of the hare represents in these terms an *ātma-yajña*, or sacrifice of the self to the Self, having this result, that the man who has made his sacrifice is now 'at peace with himself'; the very word for 'peace' (*śānti*) corresponding to the fact that a victim has been 'given its quietus' (*śānta*).

The world recoils from such an approach and justifies itself on the ground that 'desires *suppressed* breed pestilence'—a truth that psycho-analysis has rediscovered. In fact, however, there is no question of a suppression of the outer man, but only of integration, only of the substitution of autonomy for the subjection to his ruling *passions* that *l'homme* moyen sensuel *suffers* from. When the peace has been made, friendship and co-operation replace conflict; and as the *Aitareya Āraṇyaka*, (II. 3. 7) says of the man who has recognised, and identified himself with (in the Pauline sense, so that 'I live, yet not I but Christ in me'), the Lord of the powers-of-the-soul (*bhūtānām adhipati*, immanent Breath, Spiritus) and as one 'unfettered' (*visrasā*) leaves this world, 'This self lends itself to that Self, and that Self to this self; they coalesce (*tāv anyonyaṃ abhisambhavantah*). With this aspect (*rūpa*) he is united with (*abhisambhavati*) yonder world, and with that aspect he is united with this world.'

The two 'aspects' correspond, of course, to the two natures or aspects (*rūpa*) of Brahma, respectively morphic and amorphic, mortal and immortal with which he experiences both the real (yonder world) and the unreal (this world) (*Bṛhadāraṇyaka Up.* III. 3. 1, *Maitri Up.* VIII. 11. 8)—or, if we call this world real, then both this reality and the 'reality of the reality', or, again, in Platonic terms, both the sensible and the intelligible worlds. The man who has thus 'put himself together again' (*ātmānaṁ saṁdhā*) and is accordingly 'synthesised' (*samāhita*, in *samādhi*) is at the same time unloosed or untied (*visrasā*), an expression used with reference both to his 'death' (as in *Bṛhadāraṇyaka Up.* III. 7. 2, *Kaṭha Up.* V. 14, compare *Ṛg Veda*, VIII. 48. 5 and Plato, *Timaeus*, 81D, E) and (notably in the *Aitareya Āraṇyaka* context) to the 'undoing of all the knots of the heart' (*Kaṭha Up.* VI. 15) or of the 'fetters of death' with which the powers of soul are infected at birth and from which the Sacrifice is a means of liberation (*Jaiminīya Upaniṣad Brāhmaṇa*, IV. 9 and 10); expressed in the terms of psycho-analysis, the man thus liberated and regenerated is now 'uninhabited'; applicable to him are the words of St. Augustine, 'Love God, and do what you will', and Dante's 'Now take thine own will for thy guide . . . above thyself I crown and mitre thee'.

The language of the *Āraṇyaka* passage is pregnant, and can also be interpreted in terms of death and rebirth, as in John, 3: 3, for 'in so far as a man has not sacrificed, he is still unborn' (*Jaiminīya Up. Brāhmaṇa*, III. 14. 8). In this connection it should not be overlooked that in the exegesis of the Vedic sacrifice it is emphasized that the willing victim represents the sacrificer himself, and that the sacrificial Fire 'knows that he has come to give himself up to me'; and furthermore, that the true Sacrifice is enacted within you, day by day. The language of the *Āraṇyaka* can also be interpreted in terms of the 'sacred marriage' of heaven and earth, sacerdotium and regnum. Dr. Layard is quite aware of these implications (p. 69); but I mention them here because the traditional concept avoids the confusing distinction of *animus* from *anima*; *animus* in psycho-analysis representing the higher principle as envisaged by women, and *anima* the higher principle as envisaged by men. The Central Breath or principle of Life ('*Spiritus est qui vivificat, caro non prodest*') is 'neither male nor female or neuter', but in terms of the 'sacred marriage' it is always, and equally for women and for men, the 'Bridegroom'; for alike in Christian and Indian thought, 'all creation is feminine to God'. It is in this connection, indeed, that we have to understand the doctrine of 'rebirth as a man' as a condition of salvation: this does not mean at all that 'men' are salvable and 'women' are lost, but has to do with the respectively virile or noetic and feminine or sensitive natures that coexist in every man and woman, as they did in Adam; it is just as possible for the woman to play the manly part as it is for a man to be 'womanish' for example, modern 'aesthetics', to which so many 'men' have devoted their energies, is essentially and as the word itself implies a *sentimental* science, contrasting in this respect with the older and more virile theories which correlated art with cognition rather than with mere feeling. The Man in 'this man' so-and-so is just as much the Man in 'this woman' so-and-so; and it is of this 'Common Man', Heracleitus' 'Common Reason' and Philo's 'Man in the image of God' that the outer self of any man or woman is only a reflection or shadow and, strictly speaking, only the temporary mortal vehicle. *Anima* in any case is a poor word for the higher principle, since this is really the name of the carnal or animal 'soul' (*nefeṣ, bhūtātman*), while the immanent Daimon (Yakṣa) who is the Guide or Duke (*hēgemōn, neį*) of the soul is the 'Spirit' (*ruaḥ, paramātman*). Symbols (*rūpa, śilpa*) are properly speaking 'supports of contemplation' (*dhiyālamba*); and their use (*prayojana*) in the case of those for whom they *are* symbols and not merely 'art forms' is 'to open the doors of the spiritual world and to enable the Spirit to pervade both body and soul' (W. Andræ, *Die ionische Säule, Bauform oder Symbol*, 1933, p. 67)—although, as Andræ also says, 'they have been more and more emptied of their content on their way down to us'.

The second part of the book is an extensive, although not exhaustive, exposition of the meaning of the Hare in the world's mythologies. I am surprised and delighted to find it boldly stated in an 'Introductory' (p. 105) that 'it is a truism that no symbol has ever been invented; that is to say that no one has ever successfully "thought out" a symbol and used it to express a truth. Such artificial efforts are doomed to failure, and never succeed in drawing to themselves the power of real symbols, since they are no more than similes based on a mental process that never touches the depths of human personality. Such are the "didactic" similes we know so well and react against so wisely. True symbols, on the other hand, are those that leap to mind without conscious effort'. In other words, they are 'given' or 'revealed', and neither 'conventional' nor, indeed, unconventional. The traditional symbols are, in fact, the technical terms of the Philosophia Perennis, and they form the vocabulary and idiom of a common universe of discourse; one from which, [text missing in original] and so from all real understanding of myths, whoever is no longer able to use these 'figures of thought' or, like the modern 'symbolists', only resorts to analogies based on private associations of ideas, is automatically excluded. Dr. Layard's position is like that of the Assyriologist Walter Andræ, 'He who find it marvellous that the shapes of symbols not only persist for millennia, but even, as will yet be seen, come to life again after an interruption lasting for thousands of years, should say to himself that the power that proceeds from the spiritual world and that forms one part of the symbol, is eternal . . . It is the spiritual power that here knows and wills, and reveals itself when its time comes' (*Die ionische Säule, Bauform oder Symbol*, 1933, p. 66).

Had Dr. Layard known Karl von Spiess' important work on 'Die Hasenjagd' published in *Marksteine der Volkskunt*, i.e. the *Jahrbuch für historische Volkskunde*, V, VI Bd. 1937, pp.243–267, he might have penetrated even more deeply than he has the significance of the Hare. More especially in connection with the contraries, or pairs of opposites, which he discusses on pages 46 to 69 and alludes to elsewhere. For the symbolism of the Hare is very closely connected with that of Symplegades, an archetypal motive of world-wide distribution and notably American, Celtic and Indian as well as Greek. It has long been recognised that the Symplegades, or 'Clashing Rocks', are the jambs of the Janua Coeli, the Sundoor and World-door of the *Chāndogya* (VIII. 6, 5, 6) and *Maitri* (VI. 30) *Upaniṣads*, where these Gates are an entrance for the wise but a barrier to the foolish. In the words of Karl von Spiess, 'Beyond the Clapping Rocks, in the Other-world, is the Wonder of Beauty, the Plant and the Water of life', and in those of Whitman, 'All waits undreamed of in that region, that inaccessible Land' a Land from which there is 'no return' by any necessity or operation of mediate causes (*anānkē, karma*) but only as 'Movers-at-will' (*kāmacārin*).

The jambs of the door, which are also the self-operating, automatic Jaws of Death, are the pairs of the opposites, or contraries (*enantīa, dvandvau*) to which our likes attract us or from which our dislikes repel us and from the tyranny of which the pilgrim seeks to escape (*dvandvair vimuktāh sukhaduḥkhair-sañjñai gacchanti padam avyayam, Bhagavad Gītā*, xv. 5). It is of these contraries, as Nicolas of Cusa says, that the *wall* of Paradise is built; whoever would enter must pass by the doorway of the highest spirit of reason ('I am the door of the sheep; by me . . .'), that is to say between the Clashing Rocks, for in the words of an Upaniṣad, 'there is no side-door here in the world'. This is also why so many rites are performed at dawn or dusk 'when it is neither night nor day', and with means that are non-descript, for example 'neither wet nor dry'. It is, in fact, from this point of view alone that it can be understood why the Indian word for theosis, deification (*brahma-bhūti*, literally 'becoming Brahma'; in Buddhism, synonymous with the attainment of Buddhahood, the state of the 'Wide-awake') is also a denotation of twilight (*saṁdhi*, literally 'synthesis', or state of being 'in *samādhi*'). The danger of being crushed by the contraries, again is the reason of carrying the bride across the threshold of the new home, the Bridegroom corresponding to the Psychopomp who carries the soul across the threshold of the other world where both are to 'live happily ever after'. The way is 'strait' indeed just because the contraries 'clash', making immediate and incessant contact. For example if we consider the contraries past and future, the way lies evidently through the eternal now without duration, a moment of which empirical experience is impossible and that gives us *no time* in which to get by; or using spatial symbols, the way lies through the undimensioned point that separates every here from there, and that leaves us *no room* through which to pass; or if the terms are ethical, then the way is one that demands a spontaneity and innocence transcending the 'knowledge of good and evil' and that cannot be defined in the terms of the values of virtue and vice that apply to all human behaviour. Thus he alone is qualified to pass through the midst of the Sun who is virtually already past; logically and humanly speaking the way is an impasse; and it is no wonder that all traditions speak of a Way-god, Door-god and Psychopomp who leads the way and opens the door for those who are willing to follow.

In all the stories of that the folklorists term the 'Active Door', whether Eskimo, Celtic or Greek, we find that a part, the *hinder* part, or appendage, of the person or vehicle, ship or horse in which the journey is made, is cut off and left behind. Thus, in the case of the

Irish heroes, the portcullis of the Otherworld Castle falls so swiftly that it cuts the clothing and spurs from the rider's back and feet and halves his horse, of which the hinder part is lost; and since the way in is to what is both Immortal and Unknown, it is clear that what is cut off is the entrant's mortal part, the known self or personality that never was, because it was for ever changing and had never known a now or escaped from the logical net of the polar alternatives.

Dr. Layard rightly emphasises that the Hare is a sacrificial animal and typically meets a fiery death, of which he cites the Bodhisattva's leap into the fire as a pertinent example; and, in fact, the passage of the Sundoor is, like the ritual Sacrificer's symbolic self-immolation, an ordeal by fire in some sense 'all resurrection is from ashes'. If, as it seems, there is some slight foundation in actual fact for the fiery self-immolation of Hares (pp.105–6), this is only another illustration of what Philo calls the 'laws of analogy', the exegetical principle that anagogic meanings are contained in, and not 'read into' the literal sense.

The Hare is one of the many types of the Grail winner or Hero of the Life-quest, and its proper association with Soma and the Food of Immortality is admirably illustrated in the Tang mirror of Dr. Layard's Fig. 6, 'showing the Hare pounding the Herb of Immortality in the Moon'. The Dog, on the other hand, is one of the many types of the Defender of the Tree or Plant of Life. The drama is enacted every day when the farmer's dog chases the hare that has come through a gap in the fence to steal his cabbages or lettuces, just as it is in other terms when the farmer himself with his bow and arrow or gun protects his orchard against predatory birds; it is only, indeed by means of such homely parables as these that spiritual truths can be expressed. All expression is really figurative; except for the æsthetic, the figures are figures of thought and by no means meaningless tropes, and the same holds good for such dreams and visions as are significant; to ignore the content and consider only the aesthetic surfaces of any of these pictures is to 'add to the sum of our mortality'. The figures are Janus-faced, and whoever looks at only one of their faces, overlooking that in the symbol there subsists a 'polar balance of physical and metaphysical' is living a one-sided life, not altogether human but by 'bread alone', 'the husks that the swine did eat'. The senses referred to above underlie also the 'decorative', that is to say 'appropriate' motive of the hunted Hare in art,[1] and even the still surviving sport of Hare and Hounds and the Paper-chase, although here, just as in the case of other traditional ornaments and sports the sense has been forgotten and only the amusement or exercise remains; which is a part of what some philosophers intend when they speak of the modern world as one of 'impoverished reality'. Like all other symbols, the sense of the Hare depends in part on the context: but in the sense that the Hare, like Christ and like the soul that 'puts itself to death' is at once a willing Sacrifice and the winner of the Quest of Life, the meaning of the symbolism can hardly be better stated than in the words of Karl von Spiess: 'This is the situation, viz. that the Hare has run into another world to fetch something—the Plant of Immortality. Thereupon the guardian Dog, pursuing the Hare, is hard upon it. But just where both worlds meet, and where the Dog's domain ends, it is only able to bite off the Hare's tail, so that the Hare returns to its own world docked. In this case the Dog's jaws are the "Clapping Rocks". This story of the Hare is usually told in the form of an ætiological myth explaining the reason of its stumpy tail.'

Many other fascinating problems are either touched upon, or in some cases neglected, by the author. Here I shall only refer very briefly to two of these. The story of the Hare (p. 161) taken from African (Banyanja) sources is a particularly interesting version of the 'rope-trick' which, as elsewhere, can only be understood in terms of the widely-distributed 'thread-spirit' (*sūtrātman*)[2] doctrine, according to which all things under the Sun are and remain connected with him as their source, or otherwise would be scattered and lost like the beads of a necklace when the string is broken; it is by way of this luminous pneumatic thread or golden chain that as if by a ladder that the spirit returns to its proper home when the burden of material attachments has been discarded. In the African story the Man plays the part of the Dog; the opposition is of reason to intuition. Comparison may be made with the Irish version of the Rope-trick as performed by Manannan mac Lir, the master magician and trickster who in Celtic mythology corresponds to Indra who by his jugglery (*indrajāla*) as it were 'pulls this world out of his hat'. Mannannan in the story of the Gilla Decair or O'Donnel's Kern[3] casts up his thread, which attaches itself to a cloud in the air, and produced a Hare and a Hound from his bag of tricks; the Hare runs up the thread and the Hound pursues it; when the magician pulls down the thread again, the Hound is picking the hare's bones. From Dr. Layard's point of view this would represent the destruction of intuition by logic, as in the case of the slaughter of the Hare's mother by the man in the African version.

In another Irish story[4] that would have interested Dr. Layard, one O'Cronagan starts a Hare and slips a pair of his hounds after it; the Hare doubles, and when the hounds are close upon it it jumps into O' Cronagan's lap with a cry of 'Sanctuary!', at the same time turning into a beautiful young woman; she takes him home with her into a *sidh* which is as much as to say that she is really a fairy. Thereafter she returns with O'Cronagan to the world and lives with him as his wife, and he prospers greatly; his former and human wife has disappeared. Dr. Layard is undoubtedly right in regarding the Hare as an essentially feminine principle, and perhaps the surviving emblem of a Goddess (Fig. 14) of Dawn and Fertility or Love, alike in the literal and the spiritual senses of the forms; and the Dog as essentially masculine (pp. 176, 186, 197). This is supported not only by the transformations of women (amongst others, witches, who may have been originally priestesses and healers whose rites degenerated only when they fell from grace in the same way that the Gods of an older religion become the Devils of one that supersedes it) into Hares,[5] but even more by the fact that it is the Hare that fetches or prepares the Water of Life. To prepare and offer the Elixir by which the God or Hero is enthused is always a feminine function; as in *Ṛg Veda,* VIII. 91 where Apālā prepares Soma for Indra by chewing (as Kava is prepared by women in the South Sea Islands) and is to be equated with 'Faith, the daughter (and bride) of the Sun' to whose power is attributed in the *Satapatha Brāhmaṇa* (XII. 7. 3. 11) the transubstantiation of the ritual substitutes for the true Elixir that none on Earth partakes of. That the hare is 'a symbol of the Repentant Sinner' (p. 205) is significant in the same connection; for the self or soul is always feminine and, as I have shown in a paper on self-sacrifice[6] her sensitive powers can be equated with the Soma-shoots from which the true Elixir is strained in order that it may be daily offered up on the fire-altar of the heart. Nor will it be overlooked that Wisdom, Hochma, Sophia, *Māyā*, Natura naturans, the Mother of God and of all living is a 'woman'; and the mysterious problem of 'Easter Eggs' may be related to that of Leda and her impregnation by Zeus in the form of a swan. All these considerations go far to explain at the same time the Hare's elusive and truly feminine ambiguity: the soul may be our most dangerous enemy or dearest friend: 'he that would save it, let him lose it', that is sacrifice it.

I have only one specific criticism to offer. Dr. Layard rightly connects German *Hasen* and English 'hare' with Sanskrit *śaśa*, literally the 'leaper'. But he also tries to connect Greek *lagos* with Sanskrit *laṅgh*, to 'leap' (and so with *laghu*, 'light'). This seems to be impossible; because for any cognate of *laṅgh* one would expect in Greek the presence of *chi* rather than *gamma*. The proper connection of *lagos* is with *v'lag*, 'adhere', 'cling', 'clasp', the implication being erotic.

The material available, of which Dr. Layard has collected so much, is inexhaustible. But perhaps I have said enough to show that, as Professor Mircea Eliade has so well said 'the memory of the people preserves above all those symbols which refer to "theories", even when these theories are no longer understood', and to show that these symbols, which the psycho-analyst is rediscovering, can be not only understood but made effective use of in that work of the healing of souls to which the traditional philosophies have always been directed.

ADDENDUM

Since the above was written, I have collected the following material:

The connections of the Hare with the Moon and the Dog are notably stated in the *Śatapatha Brāhmaṇa*, XI. 1.5.1, 2. 'The Moon is that celestial Dog; he overlooks (with an evil eye) the sacrificer's cattle, and that is to their hurt, unless an expiation (*prāyaścitta*) be made. That is why men fear the moon's down-shining, and slip away into the shade. So they call that fever (*upatapat*, caused by the moonstroke) a "being bitten by the Dog" (*śvālucitam*), and this [here probably deictically, making an appropriate gesture], the "Hare in the Moon"—after which the Moon is *śaśāṅka*, "Hare-marked". The Moon is verily Soma the (ambrosial food of the Gods.' Another reference to the 'Hare in the Moon' occurs in the *Jaiminīya Brāhmaṇa*.'[7] Here the Hare is *śaśa* inasmuch as it 'instructs'—*śāsti*—all this world; and Yama, Death, is [the Man] 'in the Moon' who 'restrains'—*yamati*—all things, and he is called the 'Eater'—*atsyan*, more literally, 'he who intends to eat', no doubt with reference to the Hare as his prospective food; only when he has been 'pacified'—*śamayitvā*—by sacrificial-offerings does it [the Hare] 'win the life-sap (*ūrjam*, 'urge' or activating energy) of the worlds'; and the Comprehensor of this doctrine who offers the Angihotra—sacrifice, ritually of a victim and subjectively of self to Fire—rises unto companionship in their world with the Gods and Yama.

A story of Hares and the Moon is related in the *Pañcatantra*. A herd of elephants resorts to the cool waters of the Moonlake, but in their coming and going cause the death of many hares living on its shores. The Hare-king Stone-face accepts the proposal of the Hare 'Victory'. The latter, pretending to be the ambassador of My Lord the Moon, persuades the Elephant-king that he has annoyed the Moon, after which the elephants withdraw and leave the lake in peace. In the same collection there occurs the story of the Hare and the Lion; the latter has been destroying all the animals recklessly; until an agreement is made that he shall be given one creature daily for his food, chosen by lot. When the time comes for a Hare to be given, the latter devises a stratagem. The Hare arrives late and explains that he has been delayed by another Lion. The Lion-king is infuriated, and proposes to destroy his rival. The Hare conducts him to a well of clear water, at the bottom of which the Lion-king sees his own reflection, and supposes that this is his rival; he leaps at the reflection, and is drowned. Thus the Hare saves both himself and all the other forest-dwelling creatures.[8]

These two stories are again related, and interpreted, by Jalālu'd-Din Rūmī in the *Mathnawī*. In the first case Rūmī takes the Elephant to be the type of the timid soul, and the Hare as a deceiver who prevents the soul from obtaining the Water of Life; even so, it is noteworthy that there is still preserved the close connection of the Hare with the Moon and with the Water of Life. In the second case the Hare is the type of the rational soul proceeding with deliberation and foresight, and triumphing over death, represented by the Lion as the type of the carnal soul. In annotation, Nicholson quotes Damiri, who says that the Hare 'sleeps with its eyes open'.[9]

In *Jātaka*, IV. 84 a king has two sons, and is distracted by grief when one dies. To cure him of this excessive grief the other son feigns madness, and goes about the city demanding a hare. He refuses all those that are offered to him, saying 'I crave no hare of earthly kind, but only the Hare in the Moon'. This is an expression for the impossible, or unattainable, like our modern 'crying for the moon'. To avoid the incidence of death is equally impossible; and as usual, the bereaved king is consoled by his consequent realisation of the universality and inevitability of such losses as have befallen him.

In the *Dhammapada*, 342 we have the simile of the Hare caught in a trap:

> Men foregone by fear and longing wriggle this way and that like a hare ensnared;
> Held by the bonds of their attachments, again and again they undergo long miseries.

The moral is obvious; avoid the snare.

A design of three rabbits having in all only three ears (so that each of the two ears of any one forms one of the ears of another) represents the Christian Trinity.[10]

The connection of the Hare, as a Promethean symbol, with fire—discussed by Dr. Layard, p.193—makes her a dangerous animal, and this is well illustrated by the *Atharva Veda*, v. 17.4: 'the misfortune that falls upon the village, of which they say "It is a comet" [literally, star with streaming hair] as such, the Brahman's wife burns up the kingdom wherein the Hare hath come forth together with meteors.' I do not know why Whitney queries *śaśa* here—probably because of his notable ignorance of the traditional symbolism; but he says rightly that 'such apparent portents are really the woman, that has been misused'. That the 'woman' in this case is the Sacerdotal 'Word' (*vāc, vox*) usurped by the Regnum makes no difference in principle. In another AV. passage, IV. 3.6, we find the expression 'Down with the śaśayū!' and this, in a context of spells directed against tigers and other wild animals, may mean 'chaser of hares', perhaps a wild dog.

There are some illustrations of the Hare or Rabbit escaping from the jaws of a monster, Chinese and Mexican, in G. Hentze's *Sakralbronzen und ihre Bedentung ind en fr hchinesischen Kulturen,* Antwerp 1941, Tafelband I. Abb. 134 and II Abb. 51 and 53, Textband pp.73, 139. Hentze equates the Hare with the young Moon itself; i.e. with the Soma that it carries off. Where the Hare is not merely *in*, but identified with the Moon, the dragon would be Rāhu.

In South America, the enemy of the Moon is frequently not a snake but a Jaguar. Thus in A. Mètraux, *Myths of the Toba and Pilaga Indians of the Gran Chaco* (American Folklore Society, Philadelphia, 1946, p.19), the Jaguar is the spirit of death and foe of the moon, (and p.109), the Jaguar is the original owner of Fire, and the Rabbit successfully steals it.

NOTES

1. Compare E. Pottier, 'L'Histoire d'une bete', *Rev. dé l'art anicine et moderne* XXVII, 1910, pp. 419–436.

2. For a short account of this doctrine see my 'Iconography of Dürer's "Knoten", and Leonardo's "Concatenation"', in the *Art Quarterly* VII, 1944. In Fig. 10 the three hares represent the Christian Trinity.

3. In Standish Hayes O'Grady, *Silva Gadelica* II. London, 1892, p. 321. In another version published in J. P. Campbell's *Popular Tales of the West Highlands*, Paisley and London 1899, I, pp. 303–4 the 'rope' is a *ladder set up against the Moon*; the magician cuts off the Hound's head, but restores it at the Earl's request, and this is a lesson to it, never to touch a Hare again. In both versions there are also a Boy and a Girl who are apparently doubtlets of the Hound and Hare.

In the Indian versions (*Jātaka*, IV, 324) the magician himself climbs the rope and is slain, but restored to life by his companions, who sprinkle him with the Water of Life.

4. Standish Hayes O'Grady, reference note 3, pp. 333–4.

5. Transformations of men are more often into (wer-) wolves, a sort of dog.

6. 'Atmayajña: Self-sacrifice'. *Harvard Journal of Asiatic Studies 6*. 1942. pp. 358–398. [Rpr. SP2, pp. 107–147.]

7. Caland, W., *Das Jaiminiya-Brahmana in Auswahl,* Amsterdam Johannes Mûller, 1919; pp. 13 and 14.

8. Fr. Edgerton, *The Panchatantra Reconstructed* 2, AOS. 3, 1924, pp. 365 f. and 296 f.

9. *Mathnawī*, III. 2738 f. and I. 997 f., with 1374, 1375 and Nicholson's notes.

10. E. P. Evans, *Animal Symbolism in Ecclesiastical Architecture*, New York 1896, p. 329: cf. note 2, above.

TWELVE

The Pilgrim's Way

THE five verses translated and commented on below occur in the *Aitareya Brāhmana*, VII. 15, and are found also in the *Sāṅkhâyana Srâuta Sūtra*. Rohita, our 'Rufus', has just returned to his village on hearing that his father Aikṣvāku has been stricken with dropsy by Varuṇa, because of the long delay in the fulfilment of the father's promise to sacrifice him (Rufus) to himself (Varuṇa, whom it is not difficult to equate with Mṛtyu, Death). The verses are addressed to Rufus in his capacity as a stay-at-home and householder; he is exhorted to travel in the 'forest', in search of a better fortune; in other words, to abandon the household life and become a homeless wanderer. The 'greater fortune' (*nânā* has here almost exactly its etymological force of 'no naught', and hence 'no small', but rather 'great') immediately intended for Rufus is to avoid death as a sacrifice to Varuṇa, to whom he had been dedicated at birth. Beneath the apparently episodal features of the story of Rufus and Śunaḥśepa, the substitute found in the sixth year of his wandering, there lies the universal motif of a going forth (*āgārad abhiniṣkrāntaḥ. . . . parivrajet*, Manu, VI. 41) in search of a way of escape from the death to which we are all appointed at birth, and which is by nature always a sacrifice to Varuṇa, whom it is not difficult to identify here and elsewhere with Mṛtyu, Death, the master of all that is under the Sun. The infection of death, as the story itself makes plain in connection with the release of the substitute, Śunaḥśepa, can only be escaped by a resort to Agni (so often described in the Vedas as the 'Pathfinder' *par excellence*) and by the performance of the offices which he enjoins, of which the most important in the present case is a celebration of Indra, the 'traveller's comrade' of our text.

The constant refrain, 'Just keep on going, just keep on going' (*cara-ēva*), the connection of the summons with Indra, and the 'solar' phraseology employed throughout, give us a key to the technicalities of the wording. We must bear in mind that it is precisely inasmuch as they are nomads and travellers, and not merely stay-at-home ploughmen (*kṛṣṭayaḥ*), that they are regularly spoken of in the Vedic texts as *carṣaṇayaḥ*. *Carṣaṇi*, as pointed out by Macdonell, *Vedic Grammar*, 122, is an agent noun from *car*, to 'go' or 'move', cf. Grassmann, *Wōrterbuch zum Rig-veda*, 'ursprunglich "wandernd" (von car)'. Monier-Williams' derivation from *kṛṣ* is not impossible, but semantically implausible, as can be very clearly seen in connection with RV. I. 46. 4 *pitā kuṭasya carṣaṇiḥ*, 'the moving, or active, or vigilant housefather', with reference either to Agni as housefather below or more likely in this context with reference to the Sun as housefather above. Grassmann renders our word in this context by 'empsige' (active), and Griffiths by 'vigilant'. *Nirukta*, v. 24, followed by Sāyaṇa, paraphrases *kuṭasya carṣaṇiḥ* by *kṛtasya karmaṇaś cāyitâdityaḥ*, rendered by Sarup 'who observes the deed, the action, i.e. the sun'.[1]

The Sun is, indeed, the 'overseer of *karma*', or in other words, Providence (*prajñāna*); but if vision and motion coincide *in divinis*, it nevertheless remains that the word *carṣaṇi* denotes a motion; that we understand that the motion also implies a vision, does not justify us in a free translation of the word that means motion by another word that means vision.

It is, of course, by his one foot, or feet, that the Sun, or Death, is present in the heart, and when these are withdrawn, the creature is 'cut off', or dies (SB. x. 5. 2. 13). It is, in other words, by a thread (*sūtrātman*), AV. x. 8. 38; SB. VIII. 7. 3. 10. etc.) that the Sun, which is the spiritual-essence (*ātman*) of all things (RV. I. 115, 1; JUB. III, 2–3, etc.) is connected with (*samyukta*, BG. XIII. 26, cf. *Svet. Up*. v. 10) born beings, as the Knower of the Field with the Field. It is in this way that the Spirit, birthless and unchanging (BG. II. 26, etc.) is thought of as Body-dweller (*dēhin, śarīrin*), and as ever-born and ever-dying (*nityaṁ-jātaṁ nityam . . . mṛtam*, BG. II. 26), thus that the Spirit 'proceedeth from within, as multifariously born' (*antaś carati bahudhā jāyamānaḥ, Muṇḍ Up*. II. 2.6).[2] It is this incessant and unwearying peregrination of the Spirit (the Divine procession) that Rufus is reminded in the fourth verse of our text; when the end of the road (*adhvanaḥ pāram, Kaṭha Up.* III. 9) has been reached, and Fortune found, when Rufus' eye and the Sun's eye, who is himself the 'Rufus' of AV. XIII. 1, are one and the same Eye (*sūryaṁ cakṣur gacchatu*, RV. X. 16.3: *dass selbe ouge, dâ inne mic got siht; meine auge und gottes auge dass ist ein auge und ein gesicht,*[3] Eckhart, Pfeiffer, XCVI) when the Wayfarer (*carṣaṇi*) has become an awakened Comprehensor (*vidvān; yo aśakad boddhum, Kaṭha Up.* VI. 4), 'then is he fit for embodiment within the emanated worlds' (*tataḥ sargēṣu lōkēṣu śarīratvāya kalpatē, Kaṭha Up.* VI. 4),[4] a Traveller indeed (*carṣaṇi* as in RV. I. 46.4), fused but not confused (*bhēdâbhēda*) with the being of the Peregrine Falcon (*śyēna*) and Eagle (*suparṇa*) whose Eye extends to the vision of all things simultaneously.[5]

It is a veritable 'pilgrim's progress' that Indra urges upon the stay-at-home 'Rufus'. And bearing in mind that earthly pilgrimages are mimetic visitations of analogous 'centres' ('All roads lead to Rome', or similarly, to Jerusalem, or to Benares or whatever site it may be that represents for us the 'navel of the earth'), it can well be imagined that our verses became a song of the road, and were sung as such by early Indian pilgrims, just as in Europe, on their way to Compostella, men sang their *Congaudeant Catholici*. In intention, at least, our verses have something in common with the modern 'Onward Christian Soldiers'. There cannot be any doubt that Indian pilgrims had their marching songs; we have heard, indeed, bands of pilgrims singing on their way to the summit of Adam's Peak on Ceylon, and Badrināth in the Himâlayas, at the present day. We seem to hear our verses chanted by the leader of a band, and the loud response of the chorus, *Carâiva, carâiva*, 'Keep on going, keep on going'. However this may have been, it is unquestionable that our verses are a stirring call to Everyman to take up his bed and walk, and to keep on going until the 'end of the road' (*adhvanaḥ pāram, Kaṭha Up.* III. 9) is reached. Our somewhat humorous thought, 'It's a great life if you don't weaken', is here applied to the pursuit of man's last end; by which end we mean all that is implied by an escape from the clutches of Death, the infection of whose power extends over all things under the Sun, but not beyond the golden gates, the solar portals of the world (*sâuraṁ dvāram, lōkadvāram, Maitri Up.* VI. 30 and *Chāndōgya Up.* VIII. 6.5, etc.).

It is plainly stated in the prose text by which the verses of AB. VII. 15 are divided from one another, that Rufus in fact accepted Indra's advice, and that he wandered in the 'forest' for a period of six years; he became in fact what is elsewhere called a *parivrāijaka*, or 'perambulating' poor man, and, as suggested by the word *śrameṇa*, a *śramaṇa* or 'toiler'; the whole context very clearly implies the life, not of a *vānaprastha*, or forest dwelling anchorite, occupying a hut, but that of a wandering *sannyāsin*, or 'poor man', of whom it can generally be assumed that he has received the last initiations and that his funeral rites have been performed, so that he has become what Rūmī (*Mathnawī*, VI. 723f) calls a 'dead man walking', one who has 'died before death', or as KU. VI. 4 expresses it, 'has been able to wake up before the dissolution of the body' (*aśakad boddhum prâk śarīrasya visraṅsaḥ*),[6] we need hardly add that in India it has been taken for granted that thus to have died to all *proprium*, all sense of 'I and mine', is virtually synonymous with a liberation from mortality and from all other 'ills'. We may add that the state of the homeless wanderers is analogous to that of the 'Red Bird that hath no nest' (RV. X. 55.6), and to that of the Son of Man having no 'where to lay his head', for as the *Pañcaviṁśa Brāhmaṇa*, XI. 15.1, explains, '"Nest" is cattle, nest is children, nest is "home"'; the assimilation is the more significant inasmuch as the name 'Rufus' is one of the names of the Sun, and that our Rufus is of solar lineage; that the solar Indra should have been his *guru* is perfectly in order. Taking all these things into consideration in connection with the designation of Indra as the traveller's 'Comrade', it is impossible not to be reminded of the institution of Compagnonage which flourished in Europe during the Middle Ages, and even very much later, and for which an immemorial antiquity can be claimed. We cannot pursue these indications farther here, but refer the reader to the special number of *Le Voile d'Isis* dealing with 'Le Compagnonage' which appeared in April 1934. We shall only cite in connection with the pilgrim's staff the remark that 'On a donc lâ un équivalent exact du caducèe hermètique at du brahma-danda ou bâton brahmanique' (*ibid*, p.151), adding that the 'Three-strider's (*Viṣṇu's*) staff' has been recognized as an aspect of the Axis of the Universe[7] (Skr. *skambha*, *akṣa*, Gk. *Stauros*). There is, then, a metaphysics of travelling, just as we shall presently observe that there is a metaphysics of games. It need hardly be pointed out, after this, that with the decline of pilgrimage, the *art* of travelling has also been lost.

We print below a text and translation accompanied by comments.

The text is that of the Bibliotheca Indica edition of the *Aitarēya Brāhmaṇa*, vol. IV, p. 72, 1906, except that in the case of the two words marked by an asterisk we have adopted the readings of the *Sāṅkhâyana Srâuta Sūtra*, and that in the case of the first word of the text we understand, rather than *nâna śrāntāya*, *nânâśrāntāya*, i.e. *nânā* and *aśrāntāya* connected by *sandhi*. We have, then:

Nānâśrāntāya śrīr-astîti rōhita śuśruma:
Pāpō nṛṣadvarō jana, indra ic-carataḥ sakhā:
Carāiva, carāiva.

Puṣpiṇyō caratō jaṅghau, bhūṣṇur-ātmā phalagrahiḥ:
Sērē'sya sarve pāpmānaḥ, śrameṇa prapathē hatāś:
Carāiva, carāiva.

Āstē bhaga āsīnasyōrddhvas-tiṣṭhati tiṣṭhataḥ:
Śētē nipadyamānasya, carati caratō bhagaś:
Carāiva, carāvia.

Kaliḥ śayānō bhavati, sañjihānas-tu dvāparaḥ:
Uttiṣṭhas-tretā bhavati, kṛtaṁ sampadyate caraṅś:
Carāiva, carāiva.

Caran-vai madhu vindati, carant-svādum udumbaram:
Sūryasya paśya śrēmāṇaṁ, yō na tandrayatē caraṅś:
Carāiva, carāiva.

'Manifold fortune is his who wearieth not',
Thus have we heard,[8] O Rufus:
T'is an evil race that sitteth down,[9]
Indra companions the traveller[10]
Keep on going, keep on going!

Forth-springing are the traveller's shanks,[11]
His person thriveth[12] and beareth fruit:
All of his ills supine,[13]
Slain by the toil of his progress—
Keep on going, keep on going!

His weal who sitteth up, up-sitteth too,[14]
But his who standeth, standeth up:
His weal who falleth down, lies down,

But his who goeth is itself agoing[15]
Keep on going, keep on going!

Kali his lot who lieth down,
Dvāpara his who would fain cast off,
Tretā his who standeth up:
Kṛta he reacheth who moveth—
Keep on going, keep on going!

T'is the traveller that findeth the honey,
The traveller the tasty fig:[16]
Consider the fortune of the Sun,
Who never tireth of travelling!
Keep on going, keep on going!

Two major aspects of our text remain to be discussed with special reference to the third and fourth verses. Each of these verses speaks of four conditions, though not in quite the same order. The four states are those of sitting down or recumbence, sitting up or being fain to cast off, standing up, and procedure. In the fourth verse observe the sequence *śayānaḥ, saṁjihānaḥ, uttiṣṭha,* and *sampadyatē;* and compare RV.x.53.8 where the long-sought Agni has appeared and having been called upon to 'guard the pathways by contemplation wrought' and to 'beget', i.e. as Griffiths, following Sāyaṇa's *janaya = utpādaya,* justly renders, 'bring forth' the Heavenly Race, addresses the *mumukṣavaḥ* as follows: 'Here flows the River of the Rock: lay hold, stand up (*ut tiṣṭhata*), cross over (*pratarata*), O my comrades (*sakhāyaḥ*), there let us leave behind the ineffectual (*aśēvāḥ*) and cross unto the friendly (*śivān*) coursers (*vājān*).[17] Here there are also four conditions, those of an original recumbence (ophidian sloth) implied by the injunction to stand up, a readiness to abandon those who are to be left behind, a standing up, and a setting out (on the 'ways by contemplation wrought') towards a farther shore that has already been reached by those who are referred to as 'friendly'.[18] In the same way in RV. x. 124.3–4, Agni (whom we know to have possessed a titanic, autochthonic and ophidian nature *ante principium*) abandons (*jahāmi*) the fallen Agni, Soma and Varuṇa, bids 'farewell' to the Titan Father, 'chooses Indra', and 'proceeds' (*êmi*) from the non-sacrificial to the sacrificial part. Similarly *sthāṣṇu cariṣṇu,* in connection with the divine procession, where the Spirit, having long dwelt in the darkness, and in idleness (*na ca svaṁ kurut karma*) would now 'stand up and move', Manu, I. 56. We find, in fact, throughout the Vedic tradition a regularly recurring and logical sequence of ideas represented by the use of the roots *śī* ('lie'), *hā* ('abandon') or an equivalent passive desiderative form of *muc* ('release'), *sthā* ('stand up') or equivalent *jan* 'be born' or 'come into existence',[19] and car ('proceed') or equivalent *ê*, *gam*, *prapat*, *ruḥ* or *tar*: *saṁjihānaḥ* in our text being, accordingly, equivalent to *mumukṣuḥ*. On the other hand, the distinction of lying from standing and of standing from going, as also that of renunciation from possession, breaks down when the end of the road has been reached; that end is not an *arrested* motion, but a consummation in which there exists no longer any necessity for a *loco*motion: 'Seated, he travels afar, and recumbent, goeth everywhere' (*āsīnō dūraṁ vrajati, śayānō yāti sarvataḥ, Kaṭha Up.* II. 21).

The pilgrimage is a procedure from potentiality to act, non-being to being, darkness to light, that is in question. Observe the change of construction in the fourth line of the first verse; he who has successively been (in) three inferior states of being, now inasmuch as he proceeds (*caran*) reaches or attains (*sampadyatē*) the Kṛta state. Not only does *sampad* imply 'success' or 'final achievement' (cf. *sampatti* in this sense), but it should be noted that *sam* (here as in *sam-bodhi, sam-bhoga, sam-bhū* and the like) adds the value of completion, perfection, or universality to the root to which it is prefixed. *Sam* also adds to a root the meaning 'with': *sampad* being thus not merely to 'reach' but literally to 'march with' or 'accompany'; *sampad* implies an entering into and a coincidence with that which is reached, as in *Chāndogya Up.* VI. 8.6, *vāg manasi . . . sampadyagē* and VIII. 3.4 *paraṁ jyotir upasampadya.*

Kṛta is then our traveller's goal. His procedure from potentiality to act can be expressed in familiar terms by saying that he is on his way to become a *kṛtsna-karma-kṛt* ('one who has performed the whole task', BG. IV. 18) and *kṛtakṛtyaḥ* ('one who has done what there was to be done', *Aitarēya Āraṇyaka,* II. 5, *Maitri Up.* II. i and VI. 30). We are by no means forgetting that Kali, Dvāpara, Tretā and Kṛta are throws in dicing, respectively one, two, three and four, from lowest to highest. We had this in mind in employing the words 'fortune' and 'lot', and in the fourth verse might have rendered 'Kali he throws . . .' But that the terms of a game are employed does not in the least preclude an anagogic (*paramârthika*) connotation: of which we have an admirable example in checkers, where to this day in Indian vernacular, the piece which succeeds in crossing the field and thus reaches the other side or further shore, is crowned king and called like the liberated Comprehensor, *kāmâcā-rin*, a 'Mover-at-will', being able, in fact, to occupy any square on the field. There is, accordingly, no need to treat a meaning as 'throws of dice' and a meaning as 'aeons' as incompatible alternatives.[20] In Sanskrit, just as in Latin scholasticism, the word has multiple meanings, all of equal validity; as we have just seen, *kāmacārin* may mean either or both a 'crowned piece' and/or a 'comprehensor'. It is for the translator, if he can, to discover equivalent terms in which a corresponding series of meanings, and not only one of these meanings, inheres.

Finally, *kṛtam* implies 'perfection' and corresponds to *kṛtâtman*, 'perfected spirit' as this term is used in *Chāndogya Up*. VIII. 13, 'I as *kṛtātman* am regenerated in the uncreated (*akṛtam*) Brahma-world'. More often we find the term *sukṛtātman* as 'perfected spirit', and just as Śaṅkara explains *sukṛta* qualifying the (Brahma-) world in *Kaṭha Up*. III. i by the paraphrase *svakṛta*, 'self-made', so, but without accepting his ethical connotation (since, as plainly stated in *Chāndogya Up*. VIII. 13 'neither *sukṛtam* nor *duṣkṛtam* can pass over the Bridge of the Spirit', cf. BG. V. 15 or as Eckhart puts it, 'There neither vice nor virtue ever entered in'), we hold that *kṛtam* = *sukṛtam*, 'perfection', and that a *sukṛtātman*, in the words of *Taittirīya Up*. II. 7, 'is called "per-fected" because it made itself' (*tad ātmānam akuruta, tasmād sukṛtam ucyatē*),[21] cf. '*svayambhū*' = *autogenes*. It is, then, 'only by keeping on' (*carâiva, carâiva*) that, as regarded from our present position, perfection can be achieved; but when this Perfection has been realised, it will not be found to have been effected by our toil, of which the only traces left will be the prints of our feet on the Way: our toiling was not essential to the *being* of this Perfection, our own Perfection, but only dispositive to our *realisation* of it. As Eckhart expresses it, 'When I enter there, no one will ask me whence I came or whither I went'. The weary pilgrim is now become what he always was had he only known it, a Blast of the Spirit (*marutaḥ*, MU. II. i), and as such no longer a toiler (*śramaṇa*) but in and of the Spirit that bloweth as it listeth—*vāyu, devānām ātmā*, (*yaś*) *carati yathá vaśam*, RV. X. 168.4. *Carāiva, carāiva*.

ADDENDUM

THE PILGRIM'S WAY, A BUDDHIST RECENSION

We have omitted a great deal of material pertinent to the subject of 'The Pilgrim's Way'. We should like, however, to call attention to the very interesting Buddhist adaptations of the story of Rohita which are to be found in *Saṁyutta Nikāya*, I. 61–2 and *Aṅguttara Nikāya*, II. 48–9. Here there is a dialogue between the Buddha and the former Rishi Rohitassa (Rohitâśva, 'Red Horse') who had intended 'to reach the end of the world by travelling' (*ahaṁ gamanena lokass 'antam pāpunissami ti*), but not having succeeded, is now a Deva-putto. With a characteristic bias, the Buddhist sequel makes it appear that Rohitassa had been naïve enough to suppose that the end of the world could be reached merely by a persistent 'travelling' in the most literal sense of the word, and had not understood that it was the following of a Way of Life that was required.[22] Granting this implausible assumption, the remainder of the Buddhist version is perfectly logical. What the Buddha teaches is summed up in the verses:

> Not to be reached by (merely) travelling is World's end ever:
> Yet there is no release from grief unless World's End be reached.
> So let a man become world-knower, wise, world-ender (*lokantagu*) let him have led the holy life (*vusita-brahmacariyo*);
> Knowing World's End, as one who is quenched (*samitāvi*), he longeth not for this world or another.'

The former Rohitassa realises now, 'that there is no making an end of grief without reaching World's End. Nay, Sire (he says) in this very fathom-long body, along with its percepts and thoughts, I proclaim that the world has its being, and so too its origin and its passing away, and therein likewise one takes one's way to the passing away of the world' (*lokanirodho-gāminīṁ ca paṭipadanti*).

NOTES

1. A derivation of *cāyitā* from *cāy* to 'see' or 'observe' is evidently assumed here, as it is also implied in Griffiths' 'vigilant'. We do not by any means propose to exclude this connotation, but do not feel that a connotation should be substituted for a denotation when translating. We note that *kṛta* and *karma* can hardly be synonymous; a tautology (*jāmitva*) is hardly to be expected in Yāska. The Sun is, no doubt, an observer of all that is done within the house of the universe. But this is inasmuch as he is also the mover within it; which motion is not a locomotion, but by means of his rays or lines of vision, which are also called his feet. It is not the vision, but the motion that is stated in *carṣaṇiḥ*. These considerations lead us to suppose that we have here to do with an overlooked *sandhi*, and to propose the analysis *ca-āyitā*, taking *āyitā* to be the nominative of an agent noun derived from *ê*, to go; we render accordingly 'the mover both of perfected act (*kṛta*) and of action (*karma*)', the Sun being thus the universal cause at once of liberation and embodiment, as in MU. VI. 30 *sarga-svargâpavarga-hētur-bhagavādityaḥ*. Yāska, if indeed he is thus making use of the causative *āyitā*, must have in mind that the mover *in* is also the mover *of*; that the *kartā* is also the *kārayitā*. In any case, the Sun is in all things the ultimate 'doer': 'Of what "I" did, *Thou* art the doer' (*tad akaravam . . . tasya kartā'si*, JUB. I. 5.2). And how is He the doer? 'By me as being the Eye, all things are done' (*mayā cakṣuṣā karmāṇi kriyantē*, JUB. IV. 12. 2).

2. Similarly AV. X. 8. 13 *prajāpatiś carati garbhē antar, adṛśya-mānō babudhā vi jāyatē*: RV. III. i. 20 and I. 72. 7 *janmañ janman nihito jātavēdaḥ . . . antarvadvān*, etc.

3. 'The same eye whereby in me God sees; my eye and God's eye that is one eye and one vision'; continuing, 'one knowledge and one love'. With 'eye whereby in me God sees', cf. AĀ. II. 4. 1–3 *ātmā vā idam eka . . . sa jato bhūtāny abbyaikṣat* and KU. IV. 6 *vaḥ . . .pūrvam ajāyata . . . yō bhūtēbhir vyapaśyata.*

4. The desperate efforts that have been made by scholars not excepting Śaṇkara himself (see Rawson, *Kaṭha Upaniṣad*, pp. 179–180), to explain away this passage makes rather pitiful reading. Nothing can do away with the doctrine of one essence and two natures, mortal and immortal (BU. II. 3. 1 etc.). The mortal Brahman is the spirant Ātman, the Sun, and Agni, 'multifariously born'. Whoever becomes the Brahman must evidently participate in both natures, in the divine açtivity ('eternal work') and in the divine idleness ('eternal rest'). The work is indeed contained in the idleness, as finite in infinite; but this does not mean that it can be taken away from it; even the finite potentialities are essential to the infinity of possibility.

The wishful thinking which leads the exegete to evade the notion of an incessant cosmic incarnation is founded on a mistake, in which the *universal* birth of the Spirit is confused with the *particular* birth of the individual So-and-so. It is particular birth, *per necessitatem coactionis*, from which the Freed (*mukta*) are released; the universal birth, *per necessitatem infallibilitatis*, is an activity inseparable from the divine beautitude in which the Freed participate. It is, moreover, precisely the universal extension of being to all things which is implied by such designations of the perfected as 'Mover-at-will' (*kāmacārin*); and as one of the hymns in the *Siddhântamuktāvalī* expresses it, 'How can that Beatific Spirit (*ānandatmā*) which, when it enters into the Darkness (of the infrasolar worlds) on its wings of enjoyment and satisfaction, enlivens every world, be made out to be other than man's Last End?' Let us make no mistake; the Spirit, very Self, is that which 'wanders about from body to body' (*prati śarīreṣu carati*, MU. II. 7). The same is expressed by Nicholas of Cusa when he says that filiation and deification imply a 'remotion of all otherness (*ablatio omnis alteritatis* = Skr. *advâita*) and all diversity, and a resolution of all things into one which is also a transfusion of the one into all' (*De Fil. Dei*, cited by Vansteenberghe, *Beiträge zur Geschichte des Mittelalters*, xiv, Heft 2–4, p. 13, note 2). If to be unified (*ekam bhū*, passim), if to be oned with Death is to have escaped contingent death (BU. I. 2.7), this is a unification with one who is 'One as he is in himself *and* many as he is in his children' (SB. x. 5. 2. 16); with one who is 'undivided in divided things' (BG. XIII. 16 and XVIII. 20) at the same time that he 'divides himself, filling these worlds' (MU. VI. 26). Impossible, then, to think of an identification with the Divine Essence that is not also a possession of both its natures, fontal and inflowing, mortal and immortal, formal and informal, born and unborn. An *Ablatio omnis alteritatis* must imply a participation in the whole life of the Spirit, of 'That One' who is 'equally spirated, despirated' (RV. x. 129. 2), eternally 'unborn' and 'universally born'.

5. It is precisely as an 'eye' and by means of his 'rays', which are also his 'feet', that the Sun is constantly thought of as 'travelling' and 'observant' by what is one act of being; in this way 'he proceedeth super-seeing' (*abhicakṣāṇa êti*, RV. II. 40. 5). Somewhat in the same way the English word 'range' can be used either with respect to vision or with respect to an actual locomotion, and we speak too of the 'eye travelling'.

An interesting parallel can be adduced. It is well known that 'The Sun is just sound; so, they say, "He goes resounding"' (*svara êti*, JUB. III. 33). In the same way Mitra 'speaks' (*bruvāṇaḥ*, RV. III. 59, 1, etc.). At the same time, the Sun is always an 'eye'. It can be well understood, accordingly, how it is that the root *cakṣ* can convey either of the two meanings, to see or to say; just as English 'observe' can be used in either of these two senses. For a further discussion see my 'Beauté, Lumière et Son' in *Études Traditionelles*, 42, 1937, [see chapter 4 of the present volume], where we might have spoken of an identity of Beauty, Light, Sound *and* Motion *in divinis*.

6. The words *aśakad bōddhum* in this passage are of peculiar interest in connection with Gautama's acquired epithet, Buddha, the 'Wake'. Of Solar lineage and Sakya or Sakiya family (Sn. 423, etc.), he is often also referred to by Indra's name of Sakka (Sakra), Sn. *passim*. In other words, born in the royal line of 'those who could' the Buddha was one who 'did' awaken before the dissolution of the body.

It may be further observed that just as our 'Rufus' is the son of the solar Aikṣvāku, so the Buddha is described as *Okkākarājassa* Sakyaputto, 'the Sakyan child of king Okkāka' (Sn. 991), i.e. of Ikṣavāku, as he is called in the *Mahāvastu*, who must be either the same as or the immediate ancestor of our Aikṣvāku. The name implies 'Onlooker', cf. AĀ. II. 4. 3 *abhyâikṣat* cited in our note 2; needless to say that the Vedic Sun is the 'eye' of Varuṇa, and that the Buddha is repeatedly called the 'eye in the world' (*cakkhuṁ loke*).

The Ikṣvāku implied by our Aikṣvāku is doubtless the *ikṣvāku . . . rēvān marāyī* of RV. x. 60. 4–5, where he flourishes in Indra's following, course, or operation (*vratē*): and the ancestor of Bṛhadratha in MU.

7. *Daśakumāracarita*, introductory invocation.

8. *Śuśruma*, in the mouth of a Brahman, and like the Biblical 'as it is written', implies a quotation from Scripture (*śruti*) rather than the citation of a proverb.

9. We might have rendered *niṣadvaraḥ* by 'stick-in-the-mud'. There is, in fact, as will later be seen, a definite suggestion of an ophidian sloth, imputed to the stay-at-home whose evils (*pāpmānaḥ*) still adhere to him.

10. Literally, 'is the Comrade of the traveller', *caratah sākhā* as in Rūmī, *Mathnawī*, VI. 2643, 'The Friend is the guide on the way'. Indra's character as leader, forerunner and guide is well established in RV. where, for example, he is *pūrvayāvan* in III. 34. 2. There, too, Indra is typically *sakhi* (comrade) amongst *sakhāyaḥ*, (comrades), *passim*; as Agni and the Sun are typically *mitra* (friend). In RV. x. 32. 6–8 is the guide and teacher who shows the way to Agni; he is the 'Knower-of-the-field, (*kṣētravit*, cf. *kṣētra-jñaḥ* in BG. XIII), and 'One-who-knoweth-not-the-field verily asks of the Knower-of-the-

Field; instructed by the Knower-of-the-field he goeth forth' (*prâiti*). The use of *prâiti* is poignant in this context, since it is precisely when the royal Spirit goes forth (*prêtyēna*, BU. IV. 3. 38) that the contingent being with which it had been connected (*samyukta*) is unmade. The veritable *prêta* of the Vedic tradition is no shade or goblin of the deceased, but the Holy Ghost that is given up when 'we' give up the 'ghost'. The true traveller is already 'in the Spirit' (*ātmani*) rather than 'in himself'; dead and awakened before the dissolution of body-and-soul, when the Spirit 'goes forth', it is himself that goes forth, leaving behind him for ever the 'down-sitter' (*niṣadvaraḥ*) or pseudo-self, of which the constituent factors are due to suffer a retribution in the sphere to which they belong. When the dissolution of the body ensues in due course, 'Then shall the dust return to the earth as it was; and the spirit shall return unto God who gave it' (Ecclesiastes, 12:7). As for the dust, whoever has followed the Forerunner and Comrade is no longer in or of it. The solar Indra and the traveller are the 'conjoint pair of eagle comrades' (*sakhāyā*) of RV. I. 164. 20.

It may be remarked that Indra plays his part of Comrade both of the Buddha and of Mahāvīra, throughout their 'lives' or 'journeying' (*caritra*).

11. Keith's 'Flower-like the heels of the wanderer' may be rather more picturesque; we prefer to retain the more literal 'shanks'. There is no direct comparison of the shanks with a flower as there is of the feet when we speak of 'lotus-feet' (*padma-ca raṇa*). what is common to the shanks and a flower in the present comparison (*sādṛśya*) is the vigour that is connotated by the root *puṣ* and according to which we say 'springeth up like a flower' or speak of a 'springing up again' or of 'springy turf'. The traveller's shanks are springy, and 'spring forth' like a flower in this sense.

12. *Bhūṣṇur-ātmā*: in Keith's version, 'his body groweth'. The great Vedic scholar's rendering of *ātman* by 'body' here can be understood if we take account of his position as explained in his edition and translation of the *Aitarēya Āraṇyaka*, introduction p. 42, where he speaks of the 'naïve manner in which knowledge is made the characteristic of the Ātman' in the Advaita system, and adds that 'Such knowledge as is not empirical is meaningless to us and cannot be described as knowledge'. We agree that that kind of knowledge, or rather, gnosis, in which there is no distinction of knower from known (BU. IV. 3.30). 'There is no cessation of the knower's knowing, it is not, however, any second thing, other than and separated from himself, that he might know'; Plotinus, *Enneads*, V. 8. 10–11. 'No vision unless in the sense of identification . . . It is the other, the Intellectual Principle that sees . . . itself'; similarly the Christian teaching that God's knowledge is a speculative knowledge, (not derived from any source external to himself) is not what the modern scholar means by 'knowledge'. But such a limited sort of knowledge as the modern scholar lays claim to (even if we presume the unreality of all that is meant by a gnosis, 'meaningless to us') is not what is intended by the Vedic texts when they speak of a knowing without duality. Unless we assume, at least 'for the sake of argument' the validity of a gnosis, we are not equipped to understand, and therefore not equipped to translate the Vedic texts, ruthlessly logical as they are, once their fundamental assumptions have been accepted. Unless we accept these assumptions, our translation will amount to no more than a simple parsing; in order to translate without parody, we must proceed at least *as if* the basic assumptions held good.

As to the rendering of Ātman by body; we do not deny that in reflexive use, 'those who can think of nothing more noble than bodies' are somewhat handicapped. If one believes that one's body is oneself, Ātman must often mean 'body'; this is in fact the profane interpretation which is described in CU. VIII. 8. 5 as a 'devilish doctrine' (*asura upaniṣad*). We also recall Śaṇkarācarya's scathing remarks in connection with BG. XIII. 2, 'How is it, then, that there are Doctors who, like worldly men, maintain that "I am so-and-so" and that "This is mine"? Listen: it is because they think the body is their-self'.

In the present context it might have been observed that the pilgrim is in search of *life*, and that 'no one becomes immortal with the body' (SB. x. 4. 3. 9). Nor could it be primarily a 'body' that would be thought of as thriving when 'sins disappear', as Keith himself renders the following *śēre . . .pāpmānaḥ;* on this basis one would have expected at least to find 'his soul groweth', although from the point of view of the Vedic tradition even this would have been unsatisfactory, since it is no more a soul than a body that is thought of as immortal there.

The rare word *bhūṣṇu* (=*bhaviṣṇu*) is significant. In Manu, IV. 135, Bühler renders by 'one who desires prosperity'. The verbal form is optative, or perhaps it would be better to say that it expresses a tendency. Derived from *bhu*, to 'become', a comparison may be made with *bhuyas* 'becoming in a greater degree', 'becoming more', and with *bhūyiṣṭha,* 'become in the greatest degree', 'super', or in other words, 'altogether in being'. *Bhūṣṇur-ātmā* then implies that the true traveller's spirit is flourishing, progressing from potentiality to act, tending towards a perfected being. The Spirit in question is that Spirit which is seen but imperfectly in the animal (-man), the *paśu,* and is more and more clearly manifested in a Man, or Person, *puruṣa*—'He who knows more and more clearly his spiritual-essence (*yo ātmānam āvistārām veda*) enjoys an evident more (*āvir bhūyas*) . . . The spiritual-essence is more and more clearly manifested in the Man' (*puruṣe tv ēvávistārām ătmā*). It is this sort of 'moring' that the traveller enjoys—he is becoming what he is (*wird was er ist*), while the stay-at-home remains empirically 'himself' (the only 'self' he knows).

It is, of course, the whole man, body, soul, and spirit, that thrives, cf. AB. III. 3 *sarvair aṅgaih sarvenâtmanā samrddhyate ya evaṁ veda*; and it is for this reason that, not intending to emphasise any one part of the pilgrim's constitution more than another, we have rendered *ātman* by 'person' rather than by 'spirit'. 'Person' (*purusa*) is a real equivalent, whether we consider a reference to 'this man' (*ātman* in reflexive sense) or as referring to the Person, Universal Man and very Self the only knowing and discriminating subject in all things whatsoever (BU. III. 3. 11) and to which one should most resort (Ait. Up. v = AĀ. II. 5).

13. *'Śēte'*, 'lie down'; just as Vṛtra, smitten by Indra's bolt, 'lies down' (*aśayat*) in RV. I. 32. 7, and *passim.* For what should be understood by 'evil' (*pāpman*) see BU. I. 3; evils are whatever is 'misshapenly' (*apratirūpam*) spoken, inhaled, seen, heard, or conceived.

14. The state of being implied by *āste* 'sitteth up' is to be distinguished from that implied by the 'sitting down' (root *niṣad*) of the first verse. 'Sitting up' we take to be the same as being 'fain to cast off' in the fourth verse, while 'sitting down' or 'lolling' can hardly be differentiated from the 'recumbence' of the fourth verse.

15. Procedure (*caraṇa*) can also be represented as a climbing; it is thus that one reaches the top of the tree, ascending these worlds step by step (*ākramaṇâir ākramāṇaḥ,* JUB. I. 3. 2); there the Sun, the Truth, awaits the climber, on guard at the doorway of the worlds; and to say that if the climber has wings, he flies off, but otherwise falls (JUB. III. 13. 9, PB. XIV. i. 12, cf. v. 3.5) is the same as to say that if he can rightly answer the question 'Who art thou', he is admitted (JUB. III. 14. 5), but if he cannot, is dragged away by the factors of time (JUB. III. 14. 2, cf. Cant. I. 8, *si ignoras te, egredere*).

16. The 'honey' (*madhu*) and the 'tasty fig' (*svādum udumbaram*) are evidently reminiscent of RV. I. 164. 22. 'Upon the Tree the eagles (incarnate spirits = immanent Spirit) eat of the honey . . . upon its top, they say, the fig is sweet' (*yasmin vṛkṣē madhv adaḥ suparṇā . . . tasyed āhup pippalaṁ svādv agrē*).

17. *Sremāṇa*: the fortune or brilliance (*śrī*) of the first verse, as an abstract quality or

attribute of the Sun. English 'fortune' conveys the content of '*śrī*' only in part. The best definition of *śrī* as a royal attribute, or majesty, will be found in SB. XI. 4. 3. 1 (see my 'Janaka and Yājñavalkya' in IHQ. XIII. 274).

It must not be overlooked that the Way has been trodden by the Sun, solar Indra, himself. Ophidian *ante principium* (PB. XXV. 15. 4, and see my 'Angel and Titan' in JAOS. 55), the Sun is dimmed, unfortunate, or inglorious (*aśrīra*) when still infected by 'this evil' (*pāpâmuyā*) of 'potentiality' (*kṛtyā*, RV. X. 85. 29–30; to be contrasted with *kṛtam* in its literal meaning of 'act', in our fourth verse): but 'even as Ahi doth, so doth he free himself from the night, from evil' (*pāpmanaḥ*, SB. II. 3. 1. 6), 'even as Ahi, so is he (Indra) freed from all evil' (*pāpmanaḥ*, JB. II. 34); and 'He who follows the same course shall shine with the glory of the Suns' (PB. XXV. 15. 4). In saying 'Keep on going', the Comrade, although in disguise as a Brahman, is saying 'Follow in my steps'; the Way is marked throughout by the divine *padāni, vestigia pedis.* ('Mark my footsteps, good my page').

18. For those who are to be understood as having crossed over, and as released from death, see Br. I. 3. 10–16: these are Voice, becoming Fire; Smell, becoming the Gale; Sight, becoming Sun; Hearing, becoming the Airs; and Intellect, becoming the Moon. Observe that the crossing or translation is also a transformation.

19. As remarked by Sāyaṇa in comment on RV. V. 19.1 *sthitam padârthaṁ jātam*: conversely it is in the womb that the yet unborn 'lie', as in RV. V. 78. 9 *śaśayānah kumāro adhi mātari, niraîtu jīvaḥ* 'the prince (Agni) that lieth in the Mother, may he come forth alive'.

20. For the association of ideas involved in our text, cf. AV. IV. 17.7 'Death by hunger, likewise defeat at dice . . . we wipe off all that'. When Devas and Asuras gamble, it is for stakes of life and death. Cf. Jeremy Taylor, cited in Oxford N.E.D., *s.v.*, throw, II. 5, 'They . . . cast a dice . . . of the greatest interest in the world, next to the last throw for eternity'.

Very close to the thought of our text is that of CU. IV. 1. 6, 'Even as the lower throws of the dice are consummated in the highest throw (*kṛtaṁ samyanti*), so to this man whatever good that beings do, all is consummated in him'.

21. *Kṛtam* in *Īśā Up.* 17, *kṛtaṁ smara* must be similarly understood; it is well known what great importance is attached to the dying thought, as having a directive force, and in view of the fact that the dying man is thought of as an aspirant for passage through the midst of the Sun (previous verse 15, and cf. JUB. I. 3–5) it is inconceivable that he should be asked to consider past acts, which cannot follow him there; on the other hand, it can well be imagined that he is asked to consider that (Ātman) which has been 'done', fulfilled, perfected and self-effected, to consider in other words that very *kṛtam* which in the fourth verse of our text is the traveller's goal.

22. It is very curious to observe the subtle adaptation of familiar Brahmanical expressions to the purposes of a specifically Buddhist edification. *Lokanirodho* means the same as *lokassantam*, but rather as the station of the putting an end to the world, so far as the Wayfarer is concerned, than as reaching its end in terms of the spatial symbolism of the Brahmanical texts, which make use of such expressions as 'end of the road' (*adhvanaḥ pāram* = *visṇoḥ paramaṁ padam*, KU. III. 9), or in terms of the corresponding temporal symbolism (*saṁvatsar asyo' dream.* JUB. IV. 15). In the Brahmanical texts the *nirodha* is at World's End, but is not so much an ending or destruction of the world as it is the Sundoor itself, by which the *arhat* departs, leaving the world behind him; which Sundoor is 'a forwarding for the wise, but a barrier to the foolish' (*ādityam . . . lokadvāram prapadatāṁ viduṣāṁ nirodho' viduṣām*, CU. VIII. 6.5).

THIRTEEN

Mind and Myth

SOME recent discussions in this journal [*The New English Weekly*] of instinct and intellect, together with various articles on myth and folklore, have prompted me to offer the following reflections.

Instincts are natural appetities, which move us to what seem to be, and may be, desirable ends; to behave instinctively is to behave passively, all reactions being in the strictest sense of the word passions. We must not confuse these appetitive reactions with acts of the will. The distinction is well known: 'Acts of the sensitive appetite . . . are called passions; whereas acts of the will are not so called' (St. Thomas, *Sum. Theol.* I. 20. 1 ad 1); 'the Spirit is *willing*, but the flesh is *weak*'. Moreover, as Aristotle points out (*De Anima*, III. 10) appetite may be right or wrong; desire as such always looks to the present, not considering consequences; only mind is always right.

In speaking of 'mind', however, it must be remembered that the traditional dicta always presuppose the distinction of 'two minds', the one 'apathetic' (i.e. independent of pleasure-pain motivation), the other 'pathetic' (i.e. subject to appetitive persuasion); it is only the First Mind (in Scholastic philosophy, *intellectus vel spiritus*) that, just because it is disinterested, can judge of the extent to which an appetite (instinct) should be indulged, if the subject's real good, and not merely immediate pleasure, is to be served.

So, then, Hermes (*Lib.* XII. 1. 2–4) points out that 'In the irrational animals, mind co-operates with the natural-instinct proper to each kind; but in men, Mind works against the natural-instincts . . . So that those souls of which Mind takes command are illuminated by its light, and it works against their presumptions . . . But those human souls which have not got Mind to guide them are in the same case as the souls of the irrational animals, in which mind co-operates (with the appetites), and gives free course to their desires; and such souls are swept along by the rush of appetite to the gratification of their desires . . . and are insatiable in their craving.' From the same point of view, for Plato, the man who is governed by his impulses is 'subject to himself', while he who governs them is 'his own master (*Laws*, 645, *Republic*, 431, etc.).

The instinctive appetites of wild animals and of men whose lives are lived naturally (i.e. in accordance with human nature) are usually healthy; one may say that natural selection has taken the place of Mind in setting a limit to the gratification of these appetites. But the appetites of civilised men are no longer reliable; the natural controls have been eliminated (by the 'conquest of Nature'); and the appetites, exacerbated by the arts of advertisement, amount to unlimited wants, to which only the disinterested Mind can set reasonable bounds. Mr. Romney Green is only able to defend the instincts (1) by forgetting that these are really appetites or wants and (2) because he is really thinking of those desires of which his Mind does, in fact, approve. Captain Ludovici, on the other hand, is entirely right in saying that our instincts must be regulated by a higher principle. If we are to trust our instincts, let us be sure that they are not just any instincts, but only those that are proper to Man, in the highest sense of the word.

I was much interested in Mr. Nichols' review of Waley's translation, 'Monkey'. He is very right in saying that it is characteristic of this kind of literature to 'give the deepest significance in the most economical everyday form': that is, in fact, one of the essential values of all adequate symbolism. Where, however, he is mistaken is in calling such a work 'a mine of *popular* fantasy'. That is just what it is not. The material of 'folklore' should not be distinguished from that of myth, the 'myth that is not my own, I had it from my mother', as Euripides said; which is not to say that my mother's mother made it. What we owe to the people themselves, and for which we cannot be too grateful in these dark ages of the mind, is not their lore, but its faithful transmission and preservation. The content of this lore, as some (though all too few) learned men have recognised, is *essentially* metaphysical, and only accidentally entertaining.

In the present case the 'river', the 'bridge' and the 'boat' are universal symbols; they are found as such in the literature of the last three millennia and are probably of much greater antiquity. The episode quoted appears to be an echo of the *Mahākapi Jātaka* ('Great Monkey Birth-story'), in which the Bodhisattva (not Boddhi-, as Mr. Nichols writes) is the king of the Monkeys, and makes of himself the bridge by which his people can cross over the flood of sensation to the farther shore of safety; and that is an echo of the older *Samhita* text in which Agni (who can be equated on the one hand with the Buddha and on the other with Christ) is besought to be 'our thread, our bridge and our way', and 'May we mount upon thy back') while in the *Mabinogion* we have the parallel 'He who would be your chief, let him be your bridge' (*A vo penn bit bont*, Story of Branwen), with reference to which Evola remarked that this was the 'mot d'ordre' of King Arthur's chivalry. St. Catherine of Siena had a vision of Christ in the form of a bridge; and Rūmī attributed to Christ the words 'For the true believers I become a bridge across the sea'. Already in the *Ṛg Veda* we find the expression 'Himself the bridge, he speeds across the waters', with reference to the Sun, i.e. Spirit. And so on for the other symbols; the Tripitaka is, of course, the well known designation of the *Nikāyas* of the Pali Buddhist Canon, and here stands for 'Scripture', taken out of its literal sense and given its higher meaning. The floating away of the dead body reminds us that a catharsis, in the Platonic sense, i.e. a separation of the soul from the body, or in Pauline terms, of the Spirit from the 'soul', has taken place.

Vox populi vox Dei; not because the word is theirs, but in that it *is* His, viz. the 'Word of God', that we recognised in Scripture but overlook in the fairy-tale that we had from our mother, and call a 'superstition' as it is indeed in the primary sense of the word and *qua* 'tradition', 'that which has been handed on'. Strzygowski wrote, 'He (i.e. the undersigned) is altogether right when he says, "The peasant may be unconscious and unaware, but that of which he is unconscious and unaware is in itself far superior to the empirical science and realistic art of the 'educated man', whose real ignorance is demonstrated by the fact that he studies and compares the data of folklore and 'mythology' without any more than the most ignorant peasant suspecting their real significance".' (*Journal of the Indian Society of Oriental Art*, v. 59).

The truth is that the modern mind, hardened by its constant consideration of 'the Bible as literature' (I prefer St. Augustine's estimate, expressed in the words 'O axe, hewing the rock'), could, if it would make the necessary intellectual effort, turn to our mythology and folklore and find there, for example in the heroic rescues of maidens from dragons or in (what is the same thing) the disenchantments of dragons by a kiss (since our own sensitive souls are the dragon, from which the Spirit is our saviour), the whole story of the plan of redemption and its operation.

FOURTEEN

Symbols

SYMBOLS* and signs, whether verbal, musical, dramatic or plastic, are means of communication. The references of symbols are to ideas and those of signs to things. One and the same term may be symbol or sign according to its context: the cross, for example, is a symbol when it represents the structure of the universe, but a sign when it stands for crossroads. Symbols and signs may be either natural (true, by innate propriety) or conventional (arbitrary and accidental) traditional or private. With the language of signs, employed indicatively in profane language and in realistic and abstracted art, we shall have no further concern in the present connection. By 'abstracted art' we mean such modern art as wilfully avoids representation, as distinguished from 'principial art', the naturally symbolic language of tradition.

The language of traditional art—scripture, epic, folklore, ritual, and all the related crafts—is symbolic; and being a language of natural symbols, neither of private invention, nor established by conciliar agreement or mere custom, is a universal language. The symbol is the material embodiment, in sound, shape, colour or gesture as the case may be, of the imitable form of an idea to be communicated, which imitable form is the formal cause of the work of art itself. It is for the sake of the idea, and not for is own sake, that the symbol exists: an actual form must be either symbolic—of its reference, or merely an unintelligible shape to be liked or disliked according to taste. The greater part of modern aesthetics assumes (as the words 'aesthetic' and 'empathy' imply) that art consists or

* A derivative of *sumballo* (Greek) especially in the senses 'to correlate', 'to treat things different as though they were similar', and (passive) 'to correspond', or 'tally'.

should consist entirely of such unintelligible shapes, and that the appreciation of art consists or should consist of appropriate emotional reactions. It is further assumed that whatever is of permanent value in traditional works of art is of the same kind, and altogether independent of their iconography and meaning. We have, indeed, a right to say that we *choose* to consider only the aesthetic surfaces of the ancient, oriental, or popular arts; but if we do this, we must not at the same time deceive ourselves so as to suppose that the history of art, meaning by 'history' an explanation in terms of the four causes, can be known or written from any such limited point of view. In order to understand composition, for example, i.e. the sequence of a dance or the arrangement of masses in a cathedral or icon, we must understand the *logical* relation of the parts: just as in order to understand a sentence, it is not enough to admire the mellifluent sounds, but necessary to be acquainted with the meanings of separate words and the logic of their combinations. The mere 'lover of art' is not much better than a magpie, which also decorates its nest with whatever most pleases its fancy, and is contented with a purely 'aesthetic' experience. So far from this, it must be recognised that although in modern works of art there may be nothing, or nothing more than the artist's private person, behind the aesthetic surfaces, the theory in accordance with which works of traditional art were produced and enjoyed takes it for granted that the appeal to beauty is not merely to the senses, but through the senses to the intellect: here 'Beauty has to do with cognition'; and what is to be known and understood is an 'immaterial idea (Hermes), a 'picture that is not in the colours' (*Laṇkāvatāra Sūtra*), 'the doctrine that conceals itself behind the veil of the strange verses' (Dante), 'the archetype of the image, and not the image itself' (St. Basil). 'It is by their ideas that we judge of what things ought to be like' (St. Augustine).

It is evident that symbols and concepts—works of art are things *conceived*, as St. Thomas says, *per verbum in intellectu*—can serve no purpose for those who have not yet, in the Platonic sense, 'forgotten'. Neither do Zeus nor the stars, as Plotinus says, remember or even learn; 'memory is for those that have forgotten', that is to say, for us, whose 'life is a sleep and a forgetting'. The need of symbols, and of symbolic rites, arises only when man is expelled from the Garden of Eden; as means, by which a man can be reminded at later stages of his descent form the intellectual and contemplative to the physical and practical levels of reference. We assuredly have 'forgotten' far more than those who first had need of symbols, and far more than they need to infer the immortal by its mortal analogies; and nothing could be greater proof of this than our own claims to be superior to all ritual operations, and to be able to approach the truth directly. It was as signposts of the Way, or as a trace of the Hidden Light, pursued by hunters of a supersensual quarry, that the motifs of traditional art, which have become *our* 'ornaments', were originally employed. In these abstract forms, the farther one traces them backward, or finds them still extant in popular 'superstition', agricultural rites, and the motifs of folk-art, the more one recognises in them a polar balance of perceptible shape and imperceptible information; but, as Andrae says (*Die ionische Säule*, Schlusswort), they have been more and more voided of content on their way down to us, more and more denatured with the progress of 'civilisation', so as to become what we call 'art forms', as if it had been an aesthetic need, like that of our magpie, that had brought them into being. When meaning and purpose have been forgotten, or are remembered only by initiates, the symbol retains only those decorative values that *we* associate with 'art'. More than this, we deny that the art form can ever have had any other than a decorative quality; and before long we begin to take it for granted that the art form must have originated in an 'observation of nature', to criticise it accordingly ('That was before they knew anything about anatomy', or 'understood perspective') in terms of progress, and to supply its deficiencies, as did the Hellenistic Greeks with the lotus palmette when they made an elegant acanthus of it, or the Renaissance when it imposed an ideal of 'truth to nature' upon an older art of formal typology. We interpret myth and epic from the same point of view, seeing in the miracles and the *Deus ex machina* only a more or less awkward attempt on the part of the poet to enhance the presentation of the facts; we ask for 'history', and endeavour to extract an historical nucleus by the apparently simple and really naïve process of eliminating all marvels, never realising that the myth is a whole, of which the wonders are as much an integral part as are the supposed facts; overlooking that all these marvels have a strict significance altogether independent of their possibility or impossibility as historical events.

FIFTEEN

The Interpretation of Symbols

THE scholar of symbols is often accused of 'reading meanings' into the verbal or visual emblems of which he proposes an exegesis. On the other hand, the aesthetician and art historian, himself preoccupied with stylistic peculiarities rather than with iconographic necessities, generally avoids the problem altogether; in some cases perhaps, because an iconographic analysis would exceed his capacities. We conceive, however, that the most significant element in a given work of art is precisely that aspect of it which may, and often does, persist unchanged throughout millennia and in widely separated areas; and the least significant, those accidental variations of style by which we are enabled to date a given work or even in some cases to attribute it to an individual artist. No explanation of a work of art can be called complete which does not account for its composition or constitution, which we may call its 'constant' as distinguished from its 'variable'. In other words, no 'art history' can be considered complete which merely regards the decorative usage and values as a motif, and ignores the *raison d'être* of its component parts, and the logic of their relationship in the composition. It is begging the question to attribute the precise and minute particulars of a traditional iconography merely to the operation of an 'aesthetic instinct'; we have still to explain why the formal cause has been imagined as it was, and for this we cannot supply the answer until we have understood the final cause in response to which the formal image arose in a given mentality.

Naturally, we are not discussing the reading of subjective or 'fancied' meanings in iconographic formulae, but only a reading of the meaning of such formulae. It is not in doubt that those who made use of the symbols (as distinguished from ourselves who merely look at them, and generally speaking consider only their aesthetic surfaces) as means of communication expected from their audiences something more than an appreciation of rhetorical ornaments, and something more than a recognition of meanings literally expressed. As regards the ornaments, we may say with Clement, who points out that the style of Scripture is parabolic, and has been so from antiquity, that 'prophecy does not employ figurative forms in the expressions for the sake of beauty of diction' (*Misc.* VI. 15);[1] and point out that the iconolater's attitude is to regard the colours and the art, not as worthy of honour for their own sake, but as pointers to the archetype which is the final cause of the work (Hermeneia of Athos, 445). On the other hand, it is the iconoclast who assumes that the symbol is literally worshipped as such; as it really is worshipped by the aesthetician, who goes so far as to say that the whole significance and value of the symbol are contained in its aesthetic surfaces, and completely ignores the 'picture that is not in the colours' (*Laṇkāvatāra Sūtra*, II. 117). As regards the 'more than literal meanings' we need only point out that it has been universally assumed that 'Many meanings underlie the same Holy Writ'; the distinction of literal from ultimate meanings, or of signs from symbols, presupposing that 'whereas in every other science things are signified by words, this science has the property that the things signified by the words have themselves also a signification' (St. Thomas, *Sum Theol.* III, App. 1.2.5 ad 3 and 1.10.10c).[2] We find in fact that those who themselves speak 'parabolically', for which manner of speaking there are more adequate reasons than can be dealt with on the present occasion, invariably take it for granted that there will be some who are and others who are not qualified to understand what has been said: for example, *Matt.* 13: 13–15; 'I speak to them in parables; because they seeing, see not; and hearing, they hear not, neither do they understand . . . For this people's . . . ears are dull of hearing, and their eyes they have closed; lest at any time they should see' etc. (cf *Mark,* 8:15–21). In the same way Dante, who assures us that the whole of the *Commedia* was written with a practical purpose, and applies to his own work the Scholastic principle of fourfold interpretation, asks us to marvel, not at his art, but 'at the the teaching that conceals itself beneath the veil of the strange verses'.

The Indian rhetorician, too, assumes that the essential value of a poetic dictum lies not so much in what is said as in what is suggested or implied.[3] To put it plainly, 'A literal significance is grasped even by brutes; horses and elephants pull at the word of command. But the wise man (*paṇḍitaḥ* = doctor) understands even what is unsaid; the enlightened, the full content of what has been communicated only by a hint.'[4] We have said enough, perhaps, to convince the reader that there are meanings immanent and causative in verbal and visual symbols, which must be read *in* them, and not, as we have said above, read *into* them, before we can pretend to have understood their reason, Tertullian's *rationem artis*.[5]

The graduate, whose eyes have been closed and heart hardened by a course of university instruction in the Fine Arts or Literature is actually debarred from the complete understanding of a work of art. If a given form has for him a merely decorative and aesthetic value, it is far easier and far more comfortable for him to assume that it never had any other than a sensational value, than it would be for him to undertake the *self-denying* task of entering into and consenting to the mentality in which the form was first conceived. It is nevertheless just this task that the professional honour of the art historian requires of him; at any rate, it is this task that he undertakes nominally, however great a part of it he may neglect in fact.

The question of how far an ancient author or artist has understood his material also arises. In a given literary or plastic work the iconography may be at fault, by defect of knowledge in the artist; or a text may have been distorted by the carelessness or ignorance of a scribe. It is evident that we cannot pass a valid judgment in such cases from the standpoint of our own accidental knowledge or ignorance of the *matiere*. How often one sees an emendation suggested by the philologist, which may be unimpeachable grammatically, but shows a total lack of understanding of what could have been meant originally! How often the technically skilled restorer can make a picture look well, not knowing that he has introduced insoluble contradictions!

In many cases, however, the ancient author or artist has not in fact misunderstood his material, and nothing but our own historical interpretation is at fault. We suppose, for example, that in the great epics, the miraculous elements have been 'introduced' by an 'imaginative' poet to enhance his effects, and nothing is more usual than to attempt to arrive at a kernel of 'fact' by eliminating all incomprehensible symbolic matter from an epic or gospel. What are really technicalities in the work of such authors as Homer, Dante, or Valmiki, for example, we speak of as literary ornaments, to be accredited to the poet's imagination, and to be praised or condemned in the measure of their appeal.[6] On the contrary: the work of the prophetic poet, the texts for example of the *Ṛg Veda* or of Genesis, or the logio of a Messiah, are only 'beautiful' in the same sense that the mathematician speaks of an equation as 'elegant'; by which we mean to imply the very opposite of a disparagement of their 'beauty'. From the point of view of an older and more learned aesthetic, beauty is not a mere effect, but, properly belongs to the nature of a formal cause; the beautiful is not the final cause of the work to be done, but 'adds to the good an ordering to the cognitive faculty by which the good is known as such';[7] the 'appeal' of beauty is not *to* the senses, but *through* the senses, *to* the intellect.[8]

Let us realise that 'symbolism' is not a personal affair, but as Emil Mâle expressed it in connection with Christian art, a calculus. The semantics of visible symbols is at least as much an exact science as the semantics of verbal symbols, or 'words'. Distinguishing 'symbolism' accordingly, from the making of behaviouristic signs, we may say that however unintelligently a symbol may have been used on a given occasion, it can never, so long as it remains recognisable, be called unintelligible: intelligibility is essential to the idea of a symbol, while intelligence in the observer is accidental. Admitting the possibility and the actual frequency of a degeneration from a significant to a merely decorative and ornamental use of symbols, we must point out that merely to state the problem in these terms is to confirm the dictum of a well-known Assyriologist, that 'When we sound the archetype, the ultimate origin of the form, then we find that it is anchored in the highest, not the lowest'.[9]

What all this implies is of particular significance to the student, not merely of such heiratic arts as those of India or the Middle Ages, but of folk and savage art, and of fairy tales and popular rites; since it is precisely in all these arts that the parabolic or symbolic style has best survived in our otherwise self-expressive environment. Archeologists are indeed beginning to realise this. Strzygowski, for example, discussing the conservation of ancient motifs in modern Chinese peasant embroideries, endorses the dictum that 'the thought of many so-called primitive peoples is far more spiritualised than that of many so-called civilised peoples', adding that 'in any case, it is clear that in matters of religion we shall have to drop the distinction between primitive and civilised peoples'.[10] The art historian is being left behind in his own field by the archeologist, who is nowadays in a fair way to offer a far more complete explanation of the work of art than the aesthetician who judges all things by his own standards. The archeologist and anthropologist are impressed, in spite of themselves, by the antiquity and ubiquity of formal cultures by no means inferior to our own, except in the extent of their material resources.

It is mainly our infatuation with the idea of 'progress' and the conception of ourselves as 'civilised' and of former ages and other cultures as being 'barbarous'[11] that has made it so difficult for the historian of art—despite his recognition of the fact that all 'art cycles' are in fact descents from the levels attained by the 'primitives', if not indeed descents from the sublime to the ridiculous—to accept the proposition that an 'art form' is already a defunct and derelict form, and strictly speaking a 'superstition', i.e. a 'stand over' from a more intellectual humanity than our own; in other words, exceedingly difficult for him to accept the proposition that what is for us a 'decorative motif' and a sort of upholstery is really the vestage of a more abstract mentality than our own, a mentality that used less means to mean more, and that made use of symbols primarily for their intellectual values, and not as we do, sentimentally.[12] We say here 'sentimentally', rather than 'aesthetically', reflecting that both words are the same in their literal significance, and both equivalent to 'materialistic'; *aesthesis* being 'feeling', sense the means of feeling, and 'matter' what is felt. To speak of an aesthetic experience as 'disinterested' really involves an antinomy; it is only a noetic or cognitive experience that can be disinterested. For the complete appreciation or experiencing of a work of traditional art (we do not deny that there are modern works of art that only appeal to the feelings) we need at least as much to *eindenken* as to *einfühlen*, to 'think-in' and 'think-with' at least as much as to 'feel-in' and 'feel-with'.

The aesthetician will object that we are ignoring both the question of artistic quality, and that of the distinction of a noble from a decadent style. By no means. We merely take it for granted that every serious student is equipped by temperament and training to distinguish good from bad workmanship. And if there are noble and decadent periods of art, despite the fact that workmanship may be as skilful or even more skilful in the decadent than in the noble period, we say that the decadence is by no means the fault of the artist as such (the 'maker by art'), but of the man, who in the decadent period has so much more to say, and means so much less. More to say, the less to mean—this is a matter, not of formal, but of final causes, implying defect, not in the artist, but in the patron.[13]

We say, then, that the 'scientific' art historian, whose standards of explanation are altogether too facile and too merely sensitive and psychological, need feel no qualms about the 'reading of meanings into' given formulae. When meanings, which are also *raisons d'être*, have been forgotten, it is indispensible that those who can remember them, and can demonstrate by reference to chapter and verse the validity of their 'memory', should re-read meanings into forms from which the meaning has been ignorantly 'read out', whether recently or long ago. For in no other way can the art historian be said to have fulfilled his task of fully explaining and accounting for the form, which he has not invented himself, and only knows of as an inherited 'superstition'. It is not as such that the reading of meanings into works of art can be criticised, but only as regards the precision with which the work is done; the scholar being always, of course, subject to the possibility of self-correction or of correction by his peers, in matters of detail, though we may add that in case the iconographer is really in possession of his art, the possibilities of fundamental error are rather small. For the rest, with such 'aesthetic' mentalities as ours, we are in little danger of proposing over-intellectual interpretations of ancient works of art.

NOTES

1. Cf. the Hasidic Anthology, p. 509; 'let us now hear you talk of your doctrine; you speak so beautifully'. 'May I be struck dumb ere I speak beautifully.' As Plato demanded, '*About what* is the sophist so eloquent?' a question that might be put to many modern artists.

2. We need hardly say that nothing in principle, but only in the material, distinguishes the use of verbal from visual images, and that in the foregoing citation, 'representations' may be substituted for 'words'.

3. *Pancatantra*, I. 44.

4. Edgerton, Fr., 'Indirect suggestion in poetry; a Hindu theory of literary aesthetics'. *Proceedings of the American Philological Society* LXXVI. 1936. pp. 687 f.

5. Tertullian, *Docti rationem artis intelligunt, indocti voluptatem.*

6. As remarked by Victor-Emile Michelet, *La Secret de la Chevalerie*, 1930, p. 78 'L'enseignment vulgaire considère que le poème épique, en vertu de sa tradition et de la technique du genre, renforce le recit des expoits guerriers par des inventions d'un merveilleux plus ou moins conventionnel destiné à servir d'agrément et d'element decoratif.'

7. St. Thomas, *Summa Theol.* I. 5.4 ad 1, and Comm. on Dionysius, *De Div. Nom.* V.

8. And thus, as recognised by Herbert Spinden (*Brooklyn Museum Quarterly*, Oct. 1935), 'Our first reaction is one of wonder, but our second should be an effort to understand. Nor should we accept a pleasurable effect upon our unintelligent nerve ends as an index of understanding.'

9. Andrae, W., *Die ionische Säule*, 1933, p. 65. The reader is strongly recommended to the whole of Andrae's 'Schlusswort'. Cf. Zoltan de Takacs, *Francis Hopp Memorial Exhibition*, 1933 (Budapest, 1933), p. 47; 'The older and more generally understood a symbol is, the more perfect and self-expressive it is' and p. 34; 'the value of art forms in (the) prehistoric ages was, therefore, determined, not simply by the delight of the eyes, but by the purity of traditional notions conjured by the representation itself.'

10. Strzygowski, J., *Spuren indogermanischen Glaubens in der bildenden Kunst*, 1936, p. 334.

11. Gleizes, A., *Vie et Mort de l'occident chrétien, Sablons* (1936), p. 60 'Deux mots, *barbarie et civilisation*, sont à la base de tout developement historique. Ils donnent à la notion de progrès la continuité qu'on lue désire sur tous les terrains particuliers en évaillant l'idée d'infériorité et de supériorité. Ils nous débarrassent de tout souci d'avenir, la barbarie etant derrière nous et la civilisation s'améliorant chaque jour.' [translated by Aristide Messinesi as *Life and Death of the Christian West*, London, 1947.] I cite these remarks not so much in confirmation, as to call attention to the works of M. Gleizes, himself a painter, but who says of himself "Mon art je l'ai voulu métier . . . Ainsi, je pense ne pas ètre humainement inutile'. M. Gleizes' most considerable work is *La Forme et l'Histoire: vers une Conscience Plastique*, Paris, 1932.

12. Despite the recognition of a typical 'descent', the notion of a meliorative 'progress' is so attractive and so comfortably supports an optimistic view of the future that one still and in face of all the evidence to the contrary fancies that primitive man and savage races 'drew like that' because they 'could not' represent natural effects as we represent them; and in this way it becomes possible to treat all 'early' forms of art as striving towards and preparing the way for a more 'mature' development; to envisage the supercession of form by figure as a favourable 'evolution'. In fact, however, the primitive 'drew like that' because he imagined like that, and like all artists, wished to draw as he imagined; he did not in our sense 'observe', because he had not in view the statement of singular facts; he 'imitated' nature, not in her effects, but in her manner of operation. Our 'advance' has been from the sublime to the ridiculous. To complain that primitive symbols do not *look like* their referents is as naïve as it would be to complain of a mathematical equation, that it does not resemble the locus it represents.

13. It is extraneous to the business of the art historian or curator, *as such*, to distinguish noble from decadent styles; the business of these persons as such is to know what is good of its kind, exhibit, and explain it. At the same time, it is not enough to be merely an art historian or merely a curator; it is also the business of man as patron, to distinguish a hierarchy of values in what has been made, just as it is his business to decide what it is worth while to make now.

SIXTEEN

The Symbolism of Archery

'Homage to you, bearers of arrows, and to you bowmen, homage!
Homage to you, fletchers, and to you, makers of bows!'
TS. IV. 5.3.2 and 4.2

THE symbolic content of an art is originally bound up with its practical function, but is not necessarily lost when under changed conditions the art is no longer practiced of necessity but as a game or sport; and even when such a sport has been completely secularized and has become for the profane a mere recreation or amusement it is still possible for whoever possesses the requisite knowledge of traditional symbolism to complete this physical participation in the sport, or enjoyment of it as a spectacle, by an understanding of its forgotten significance, and so restore, for himself at least, the 'polar balance of physical and metaphysical' that is characteristic of all traditional cultures.[1]

The position of archery in Turkey, long after the introduction of firearms had robbed the bow and arrow of their military value, provides us an excellent example of the ritual values that may still inhere in what to a modern observer might appear to be a 'mere sport'. Here archery had become already in the fifteenth century a 'sport' under royal patronage, the sultans themselves competing with others in the 'field' (*meidān*). In the sixteenth century, at the circumcision festivals of the sons of Muhammad II, competing archers shot their arrows through iron plates and metal mirrors, or shot at valuable prizes set up on high posts: the symbolisms involved are evidently those of 'penetration', and that of the attainment of solar goods not within the archer's direct reach; we may assume that, as in India, the 'doctrine' implied an identification of the archer himself with the arrow that reached its mark.

Maḥmūd II in the first quarter of the nineteenth century was one of the greatest patrons of the archers' guilds, and it was for him and 'in order to revive the Tradition (*iḥjā' al sunna*)—that is to say, in renewed 'imitation of the Way of Muhammad', the standard of human conduct—that Muṣṭafā Kānī compiled his great treatise on archery, the *Telkhīṣ Resāil er-Rümāt*,[2] in which the contents of a long series of older works on the subject is resumed and a detailed account is given of the whole art of manufacturing and using the bow and arrow.

Kānī began by establishing the canonical justification and legitimate transmission of the archer's art. He cited forty Hadith, or traditional sayings of Muhammad, the first of these referring to the Qur'ān (VIII. 60): 'Prepare against them whatsoever thou canst of force', where he takes 'force' to mean 'archers'; another Hadith attributes to Muhammad the saying that 'there are three whom Allah leads into Paradise by means of one and the same arrow, viz. its maker, the archer, and he who retrieves and returns it', the commentator understanding that the reference is to the use of the bow and arrow in the Holy War; other Hadith glorify the space between the two targets as a 'Paradise'.[3] Kānī went on to 'derive' the bow and arrow from those that were given by the angel Gabriel to Adam, who had prayed to God for assistance against the birds that devoured his crops; in coming to his assistance, Gabriel said to Adam: 'This bow is the power of God; this string is his majesty; these arrows the wrath and punishment of God inflicted upon his enemies'. From Adam the tradition was handed on through the 'chain' of Prophets (it was to Abraham that the compound bow[4] was revealed) up to Muhammad, whose follower Sa'd b. Abī Waḳḳāṣ, 'The Paladin of Islam' (*fāris al-islām*) was the first to shoot against the enemies of Allah under the new dispensation and is accordingly the 'Pīr' or patron saint of the Turkish archers' guild, in which the initiatory transmission has never (unless, perhaps, quite recently) been interrupted.[5]

At the head of the archers' guild is the 'sheikh of the field' (*sheikh-ül-meidān*). The guild itself is a definitely secret society, into which there is admission only by qualification and initiation. Qualification is chiefly a matter of training under a master (*usta*), whose acceptance of a pupil, or rather disciple, is accompanied by a rite in which prayers are said on behalf of the souls of the Pīr Sa'd b. Abī Waḳḳāṣ, the archer imams of all generations and all believing archers. The master hands the pupil a bow, with the words: 'In accordance with the behest of Allah and the Way (*sunna*) of his chosen messenger . . .' The disciple receives the bow, kisses its grip, and strings it. This prescribed procedure, preparatory to any practical instruction, is analogous to the rites by which a disciple is accepted as such by any dervish order. The actual training is long and arduous; the pupil's purpose is to excel, and to this end he must literally devote himself.

When the disciple has passed through the whole course of instruction and is proficient, there follows the formal acceptance of the candidate by the sheikh. The candidate must show that he can hit the mark and that he can shoot to a distance of not less than nine hundred strides: he brings forward witnesses to his mastery. When the sheikh is satisfied the disciple kneels before him and takes up a bow that is lying near him, strings it, and fits an arrow to a string, and having done this three times he replaces it, all with extreme formality and in accordance with fixed rules. The sheikh then instructs the master of ceremonies to take the disciple to his master, from whom he will receive the 'grip' (*ḳabẓa*). He kneels before the master and kisses his hand: the master takes him by the right hand in token of a mutual covenant patterned on that of the Qur'ān, (XLVIII. 10–18), and whispers the 'secret' in his ear. The candidate is now a member of the archers' guild and a link in the 'chain' that reaches back to Adam. Henceforth he will never use the bow unless he is in a condition of ritual purity; before and after using the bow he will always kiss its grip.[6] He may now take part freely in the formal contests, and in case he becomes a great master of long distance shooting he may establish a record which will be marked with a stone.

The reception of the 'grip' is the outward sign of the disciple's initiation. He has, of course, long been accustomed to the bow, but what is meant by the 'grip' is more than a mere handling of the bow; the grip itself implies the 'secret'. The actual grip, in the case of the compound bow used by the Turks and most Orientals, is the middle part of the bow, which connects its two other parts, upper and lower. It is by this middle piece that the bow is made one. It is only when one tries to understand this that the metaphyscial significance of the bow, which Gabriel had described as the 'power' of God, appears: the grip is the union of Allah with Muhammad. But to say this is to formulate the 'secret' only in its barest form: a fuller explanation, based on the teachings of Ibn 'Arabī is communicated to the pupil. Here it is only indicated that what links the Deity above to the Prophet below is the *Ḳuṭb* as Axis Mundi, and that this is a form of the spirit (*al-Rūh*).

The Indian literature contains an almost embarrassing wealth of matter in which the symbolic values of archery are conspicuous. RV. VI. 75.4 as understood by Sāyaṇa says that when the bow tips consort (that is, when the bow is bent), they bear then the child (the arrow) as a mother bears a son, and when with common understanding they start apart (releasing the arrow), then they smite the foe; and it is evident that the arrow is assimilated to Agni, the child of Sky and Earth, whose birth coincides with the separation of his parents.[7] In BD. I. 113, where all the instruments of the sacrifice are regarded as properties of Agni, the two ends of the bow are again correlated with Sky and Earth and other sexually contrasted pairs, such as the pestle and mortar; and we are reminded not only of the Islamic interpretation cited above, but also of Heracleitus (Fr. LVI): 'The harmony of the ordered-world is one of contrary tensions, like that of the harp or bow'.[8] The arrow being the offspring of the bow, the identification of the bow ends with the celestial and terrestrial worlds is clearly indicated in AV. I. 2 and 3, where the 'father' of the arrow is referred to as Parjanya, Mitra, Varuna, etc., and its 'mother is the Earth (*pṛthivī*)'; this is even literally true in the sense that the reed of which the arrow is made is produced by the earth fertilized by the rains from above and affords a good illustration of the exegetical principle that the allegorical meaning is contained in the literal. In these two hymns the bowstring and the arrow are employed with spells to cure diarrhoea and strangury; the bowstring because it constricts, the arrow because it is let fly: 'As the arrow flew off, let loose from the bow, so be thy urine released' (*yatheṣukā parāpatad avasṛṣṭādhi dhanvanaḥ, evā te mūtram mucyatām*); here the relation of the flight of the arrow is to a physical release, but it will presently be seen how this flight, as of birds, is an image equally of the delivery of the spirit from the body.

In AV. I. 1 the archer is the Lord of the Voice (*Vācaspati*) with the divine mind; recalling RV. VI. 75.3, where 'she is fain to speak' and, drawn to the ear, 'whispers like a woman', it is clear that the bowstring corresponds to the voice (*vāc*) as organ of expression, and the arrow to audible concept expressed. So in AV. V. 18.8 the

Brāhmans, the human representatives of the Lord of the Voice, are said to have sharp arrows that are not sped in vain, the tongue being their bowstring and their terrible words their arrows; while in BU. III. 8.2, penetrating questions are described as 'foe-piercing arrows'. This conception underlies the use of *iṣ* (to 'shoot'), compare *iṣu, iṣukā* ('arrow') and our own vernacular 'shoot' meaning 'speak out'; in AB. II. 5, 'impelled by the Mind, the Voice speaks' (*manasā vā iṣitā vāg vadati*); the voice indeed acts, but it is the mind that activates (JUB. I. 33.4).

Thus an 'arrow' may be either literally a winged shaft or metaphorically a 'winged word': Skr. *patatrin*, 'winged', denoting either 'bird' or 'arrow' covers both values; for the swift and unhindered flight of thought is often compared to that of birds and the symbolism of birds and wings is closely connected with that of arrows. The language of archery can, indeed, be applied to all problems of thought and conduct. Thus sādh, whence *sādhu* as 'holy man' and as an exclamation of approval, is to 'go straight to the mark'; *sādhu* may qualify either the archer (RV. I. 70.6) or the arrow (RV. II. 24.8), and 'it is not for the King to do anything or everything, but only what is straight' (*sādhu*, ŚB. V. 4.4.5); that is to say, he may no more speak at random than shoot at random. *Ṛju-ga*, 'that which goes straight', is an 'arrow'; and 'as the fletcher straightens (*ujuṁ karoti*) the shaft, so the wise man rectifies his will' (Dh. 33, cf. 80, 145 and M. II. 105); in the *Mahājanaka Jātaka*, VI. 66) a fletcher at work straightening (*ujuṁ karoti*) an arrow is looking along it with one eye closed, and from this the moral is drawn of single vision.

Since the bow is the royal weapon *par excellence* and such great stress is laid upon the King's rectitude it will not be irrelevant to point out that the Sanskrit and Pali words *ṛju* and *uju*, cited above and meaning 'straight', pertain to a common root that underlies 'right', 'rectify', 'regal' (Lat. *regere* and *rex* and Skr. *rājā*). From the traditional point of view, a king is not an 'absolute' ruler, but the administrator of a transcendental law, to which human laws are conformed.[9] More than once Śankara makes the case of the fletcher profoundly absorbed in his task an exemplum of contemplative concentration (on BU. III. 9.28.7 and on Bādarāyaṇa, *Śarīraka Mīmāṅsa Sūtra*, VII. 11, p.800 Bib. Ind. ed.); and as St. Bonaventura remarked: *'Ecce, quomodo illumination artis mechanicae via est ad illuminationem sacrae Scripturae, et nihil est in ea, quod non praedicet veram sapientiam' (De red. artium ad theologiam,* 14).

Aparādh, the opposite of *sādh*, is to 'miss the mark', hence 'go astray', 'deviate', 'fail', 'sin': the two values can hardly be distinguished in TS. VI. 5.5.2, where Indra, having loosed an arrow at Vṛtra, thinks 'I have missed the mark' (*aparādham*); compare II. 5.5.6, where one who misses his mark (*avavidhyati*) grows the more evil (*pāpiyān*), while he who does not fail of it is as he should be. The phrase is common, too, in Plato, where as in India and Persia it pertains to the metaphor of stalking or tracking (ἰχνεύω, *mṛg*), the origin of which must be referred to a hunting culture, of which the idiom survives in our own expression to 'hit (or miss) the mark', *frapper le but*. From *vyadh* (to 'pierce') derive *vedha* and *vedhin* ('archer') and probably *vedhas* ('wise' in the sense of 'penetrating'). This last word some derive from *vid* (to 'know' or 'find'), but there are forms common to *vyadh* or *vid*, notably the imperative *viddhi*, which can mean either or both 'know' and 'penetrate'; the ambiguity is conspicuous in JUB. IV. 18.6. *Mund. Up.* II. 2.2 (discussed below) and BG. VII. 6. A Brahman's verbal arrows 'pierce' his detractors AV. V. 18.15). Comparison of an expert monk to an 'unfailing shot' (*akkhaṇa-vedhin*)[10] is very common in the Pali Buddhist literature, often in combination with other terms such as *durepātin* ('far-shooting'), *Sadda-vedhin* ('shooting at a sound') and *vālavedhin* ('hair-splitting') (A. I. 284, II. 170, IV. 423, 494; M. I. 82, etc). *Mil.* 418 describes the four 'limbs' of an archer that a true monk should possess:

> Just, O king, as the archer, when discharging his arrows, plants both his feet firmly on the ground, keeps his knees straight, hangs his quiver against the narrow part of his waist, keeps his whole body steady, sets up his bow with both hands,[11] clenches his fists, leaving no opening between the fingers, stretches out his neck, shuts his mouth and eye, takes aim (*nimittam ujuṁ karoti*), and smiles at the thought 'I shall pierce';[12] just so, O king, should the Yogin (monk) . . . thinking, 'With the shaft of gnosis I shall pierce through every defect . . .' And again, O king, just as an archer has an arrow-straightener for straightening out bent and crooked and uneven arrows . . . And again, O king, just as an archer practices[13] at a target . . . early and late . . .

Just as an archer practices early and late,
And by never neglecting his practice earns his wages,
So too the Sons of the Buddha exercise the body,
And never neglecting that exercise, become adept (*arhat*).

The bow is the royal weapon *par excellence*; skill in archery is for the king, what the splendor of divinity is for the priest (ŚB. XIII. 1.1.1–2). It is in their capacity as *Kṣatriyas* that Rāma and the Bodhisattva can perform their feats of archery. Like the king's own arms, the two 'arms' of the bow are assimilated to *Mitrā-varuṇau, mixta persona* of sacerdotium and regnum; in the coronation rite the priest hands over the bow to the king, calling it 'indra's dragon-slayer', for the king is the earthly representative of Indra, both as warrior and as sacrificer, and has dragons of his own to be overcome; he gives him also three arrows, with reference to the terrestrial, aerial, and celestial worlds (ŚB. V. 3.5.27f, V. 4.3.7).

The bow as symbol of power corresponds to the conception of the power of God, bestowed by Gabriel on Adam, for his protection, as cited above from Turkish sources. It is from this point of view, that of dominion, that we can best understand the widely disseminated rites of the shooting of arrows to the Four Quarters; cf. RV. VI. 75.2: 'With the bow let us conquer the regions'. In the *Kurudhamma Jātaka*, (II. 372) we learn that kings at a triennial festival 'used to deck themselves out in great magnificence, and dress up like Gods . . . standing in the presence of the *Yakkha Cittarāja*, they would shoot to the four points of the compass arrows painted with flowers'. In Egypt the shooting of arrows toward the four quarters was a part of the Pharaonic enthronement rite.[14] In China, at the birth of a royal heir, the master of the archers 'with a bow of mulberry wood and six arrows of the wild Rubus shoots toward Heaven, Earth, and the Four Quarters' (*Li Chi*, X. 2.17);[15] the same was done in Japan.[16]

The archetype of the rite that thus implies dominion is evidently solar; that the king releases four separate arrows reflects a supernatural archery in which the Four Quarters are penetrated and virtually grasped by the discharge of a single shaft. This feat, known as the 'Penetration of the Sphere' (*cakka-viddham*, were *cakka* implies the 'round of the world') is described in the *Sarabhanga Jātaka*, (V. 125f), where it is attributed to the Bodhisatta Jotipāla, the 'Keeper of the Light' and an 'unfailing shot' (*akkhaṇa-vedhin*).

Jotipāla is the king's Brahman minister's son, and although the bow, as we have seen, is typically the weapon of the Kṣatriya, it is quite in order that it should be wielded by a Brahman, human representative of the brahma (*sacerdotium*) *in divinis*, 'Who is both the sacerdotium and the regnum' ŚB. x. 4.1.9), and like any avatāra, 'both priest and king'. Jotipāla is required by the king to compete with the royal archers, some of whom are likewise 'unfailing shots', able to split a hair or a falling arrow. Jotipāla appeared in disguise, hiding his bow, coat of mail, and turban under an outer garment; he had a pavilion erected, and standing within it, removed his outer garment, assumed the regalia, and strung his bow; and so, fully armed, and holding an arrow 'tipped with adamant' (*vajiragga*—the significance of this has already been pointed out), 'he threw open the screen (*sāniṃ vivaritvā*) and came forth (*nikkhamitvā*) like a prince of serpents (*nāga-kumāro*) bursting from the earth. He drew a circle[17] in the middle of the four-cornered royal courtyard (which here represents the world), and shooting thence, defended himself against innumerable arrows shot at him by archers stationed in the four corners;[18] he then offered to wound all these archers with a single arrow, which challenge they dared not accept. Then having set up four banana trunks in the four corners of the courtyard, the Bodhisattva 'fastening a thin scarlet thread (*ratta-suttakam*) to the feathered end of the arrow, aimed at and struck one of the trees; the arrow penetrated it, and then the second, third, and fourth in succession and finally the first again, which had already been pierced, and so returned to his hand, while the trees stood encircled by the thread.'[19]

This is, clearly, an exposition of the doctrine of the 'thread spirit' (*sūtrātman*), in accordance with which the sun, as point of attachment, connects these worlds to himself by means of the Four Quarters, with the thread of the spirit, like gems upon a thread.[20] The arrow is the equivalent of the 'needle', and one might say that in the case described above the quarters are 'sewn' together and to their common centre; the feathered end, or nock of the arrow to which the thread is attached corresponding to the eye of the needle.[21] In ordinary practice an arrow leaves no visible trace of its passage. It may be observed, however, that an arrow with a slender thread attached to it can be shot across an otherwise impassable gulf; by means of this thread a heavier line can be pulled across, and so on until the gulf is spanned by a rope; in this way the symbolism of archery can be combined with that of the 'bridge'. The principle is the same in the case of modern life-saving apparatus, in which a line is shot, in this case from a gun, from the shore to a sinking ship, and by means of this line a heavier 'life-line' can be drawn across.

The Chinese, moreover, actually employed an arrow with an attached line in fowling, as can be clearly seen on an inlaid bronze of the Chou dynasty now in the Walters Art Gallery, Baltimore. The Eskimo, too, made use of arrows with demountable heads and an attached cord in hunting sea otter.[22] In the same way in the case of a cast net with attached line, and in the case of the lasso; and likewise in fishing, where the rod corresponds to the bow and the eyed fishhook to the arrow of a needle. In all these cases the hunter, analogous to the deity, attaches the prey to himself by means of a thread, which he draws in. In this sense Shams-i-Tabrīz: 'He gave me the end of a thread—a thread full of mischief and guile—"Pull", he said, "that I may pull; and break it not in the pulling"'.[23]

A famous passage in the *Mahābhārata*, (I.123. 46f. in the new Poona edition) describes the testing of Droṇa's pupils in archery. An artificial eagle (*bhāsa*) has been prepared by the craftsmen, and set up at the top of a tree to be a mark. Three pupils are asked: 'What do you see?' and each answers: 'I see yourself, the tree and the eagle'. Droṇa exclaims: 'Away with you; these three will not be able to hit the mark'; and turning to Arjuna, 'the mark is for you to hit'. Arjuna stands stretching his bow (*vitatya kārmukam*), and Droṇa continues; 'Do you also see the tree, myself and the bird?' Arjuna replies: 'I see only the bird'. 'And how do you see the bird?' 'I see its head, but not its body'. Droṇa, delighted, says: 'Let fly' (*muñcasva*). Arjuna shoots, cuts off the head and brings it down. Droṇa then gives him the irresistible weapon, 'Brahma's head', which may not be used against any human foe; and there can be little doubt that this implies the communication of an initiatory *mantram*, and the 'secret' of archery.[24] The evident 'moral' is one of single-minded concentration.

In public competition[25] Arjuna performs a number of magical feats using appropriate weapons to create and destroy all sorts of appearances, and then from a moving chariot shoots five arrows into the mouth of a moving iron boar, and twenty-one into the opening of a cow's horn suspended and swinging in the air.[26] In the great competition for the hand of Draupadī[27] her father has made a very stout bow which no one but Arjuna will be able to bend, and has made also 'an artificial device suspended in the air and together with it a golden target' (*yantraṁ vaihāyasam . . . kṛtimaiṁ, yantreṇa sahitam . . . laksyaṁ kāñcanam*), announcing that 'whoever strings this bow and with it and these arrows pass it and pierce the target (*atītya lakṣyaṁ yo veddhā*) shall have my daughter'. When the competing princes are assembled, Draupadī's brother addresses the assembly:

> Hear me, all ye children of the Earth: This is the bow, this the mark and these the arrows; hit the mark with these five arrows, making them pass through the opening in the device (*yantrachidreṇābhyatikramya lakṣyaṁ samarpayadhvaṁ khagamair daśārdhaiḥ*).[28]
>
> Whoever, being of a good family, strong and handsome, performs this difficult feat shall have my sister to wife this day, I tell no lie.

This only Arjuna is able to do; his arrows penetrate the target itself, with such force as to stick in the ground beyond it.

The language itself of all these texts expresses their symbolic significance. The feat itself is essentially Indra's, of whom Arjuna is a descent, while Draupadī, the prize, is explicitly Śrī (Fortuna, Tyche, Basileia). With hardly any change of wording the narrative could be referred to the winning of a more eminent victory than can be won by concrete weapons alone. This will appear more clearly in the citation from the *Muṇḍaka Upaniṣad*, below. In the meantime it may be observed that *muñcasva* ('let fly') is from *muc* (to 'release'), the root in *mokṣa* and *mukti* ('spiritual liberation', man's last 'aim'). *Kārmuka* ('bow') is literally 'made of *kṛmuka* wood', a tree that ŚB. VI. 6.2.11 derives from 'the point of Agni's flame that took root on earth'; thus the bow, like the point of the arrow[29] participates in the nature of fire. The primary meaning of yantra is 'barrier'; the suspended perforated yantra through which the arrows are to be shot can hardly be thought of but as a sun symbol, that is, a representation of the Sun door, through which the way leads on to Brahma: 'Thereby men reach the highest place.'[30] That the mark, whatever its form may have been, is 'golden' reflects the regular meanings of 'gold', viz., light and immortality; and that it is to be reached through a perforated disk, such as I take the 'device' to have been, corresponds to such expressions as 'beyond the sky' (*utteraṁ divaḥ*[31]) or 'beyond the sun' (*pareṇa ādityam*[32]), of which the reference is to the 'farther half of heaven' (*divi parārdha*[33]), Plato's υιπερουράνιος τόπος, of which no true report has ever been made[34] and is nameless,[35] like those who reach it. Kha-ga, 'arrow', is also 'bird', and literally, 'farer through empty space'; but kha is also 'void',[36] and as such a symbol of Brahma—'Brahma is the Void, the Ancient Void of the pneuma . . . whereby I know what should be known' (*kham brahma, kham purāṇaṃ vāyuram . . . vedainena veditavyam*[37]).

It is, in fact, in the notion of the penetration of a distant and even unseen target that the symbolism of archery culminates in the *Muṇḍaka Upaniṣad* (II. 2.1–4). In the first two verses Brahma is described as the unity of contraries, *summum bonum*, truth immortal: 'That is what should be penetrated, penetrate it, my dear' (*tad veddhavyaṁ, somya viddhi*). The third and fourth verses continue:

> Taking as bow the mighty weapon (Oṁ) of the Upaniṣad,
> Lay thereunto an arrow sharpened by devotions (*upāsana-niśitam*)[38]
> Draw with a mind of the same nature as That (*tadbhāva-gatena cetasā*):
> The mark (*lakṣyaṁ*) is That Imperishable; penetrate it (*viddhi*)[39] my dear!
> Oṁ is the bow, the Spirit (*ātman*, Self)[40] the arrow, Brahma the mark:
> It is penetrable[41] by the sober man; do thou become of one substance therewith (*tanmayo bhavet*), like the arrow.

Here the familiar equation, Ātman = Brahman, is made. The penetration is of like by like; the spiritual self represented by the arrow is by no means the empirical ego, but the immanent Deity, self-same self in all beings: 'Him one should extract from one's own body, like the arrow from the reed' (KU. VI. 17); or, in terms of MU. VI. 28, should 'release' and 'let fly' from the body like an arrow from the bow.

In MU. the phrasing differs slightly but the meanings remain essentially the same: there are obstacles to be pierced before the target can be reached. In MU. VI. 24: 'The body is the bow, the arrow

Oṃ, the mind its point, darkness the mark (*lakṣyaṁ*)[42]; and piercing (*bhitvā*)[43] the darkness, one reaches that which is not wrapped in darkness, Brahma beyond the darkness, of the hue of the Sun (i.e. "golden"), that which shines in yonder Sun, in Fire and Lightning.'[44] In vi. 28 one passes by, or overcomes (*atikramya*) the objects of the senses (*sensibilia*, τὰ αισθήτα), and with the bow of steadfastness strung with the way of the wandering monk and with the arrow of freedom-from-self-opinion (*anabhimānamayena caiveṣuṇā)* knocks down (*nihatya*) the janitor of Brahma's door[45]—whose bow is greed, bowstring anger, and arrow desire—and reaches Brahma.

The penetration of obstacles is a common feat; it has been noted above in Turkish practice, and in *Jātaka*, v. 131 Jotipāla pierces a hundred planks bound together as one (*ekābaddham phalakasataṁ vinijjhitvā*). In *Visuddhi Magga*, 674 an archer performs the difficult feat of piercing a hundred planks (*phalakasataṁ-nibbijjhanam*) at a distance of some fifty yards; the archer is blindfolded and mounted on a moving wheel (*cakka-yante aṭṭhāsi*); when it comes round so that he faces the target, the cue (*saññā*)[46] is given by the sound of a blow struck on the target with a stick; and guided by the sound, he lets fly and pierces all the planks. The archer represents the 'Gnosis of the Way' (*maggañāña*), while the given cue is that of 'Adoptive Gnosis' (*gotrabhū-ñāna*) and can be regarded as a 'reminder' of the end to be reached; the bundle of planks signifies the 'trunks or aggregates of greed, ill-will and delusion' (*lobhadosa-moha-kkhandhā*); the 'intention' or 'aim' (*ārammaṇa*) is Nibbana (*Nirvāṇa*).[47]

Remarkable parallels to the foregoing texts can be cited from other sources. Thus Shams-i-Tabrīz: 'Every instant there is, so to speak, an arrow in the bow of the body: if it escapes from the bow, it strikes its mark'.[48] In what means the same he exclaims: 'Fly, fly, O bird, to thy native home, for thou hast escaped from the cage, and thy pinions are outspread . . . Fly forth from this enclosure, since thou art a bird of the spiritual world';[49] and indeed: 'it is as a bird that the sacrificer reaches heaven.'[50] His great disciple Rūmī said: 'Only the straight arrow is put on the bow, but this bow (of the self) has its arrows bent back and crooked. Be straight, like an arrow, and escape from the bow, for without doubt every straight arrow will fly from the bow (to its mark).[51]

In the same way Dante:[52] 'And thither now (i.e. to the Eternal Worth as goal),[53] as to the appointed site, the power of that bowstring beareth us which directeth to a happy mark whatso it doth discharge'.[54] With 'Oṁ is the arrow' may be compared the *Cloud of Unknowing*, (Chap. 38): 'Why pierceth it heaven, this little short prayer of one syllable?' to which the same unknown author replies in the *Epistle of Discretion*: 'Such a blind shot with the sharp dart of longing love may never fail of the prick, which is God'.[55]

In conclusion, I shall allude to the practice of archery as a 'sport' in Japan at the present day, making use of a valuable book compiled by Mr. William Acker, the American pupil of Mr. Toshisuke Nasu, whose own master, Ichikawa Kojurō Kiyomitsu, 'had actually seen the bow used in war, and who died in the bow-house while drawing his bow at eighty years of age'. The book[56] is a translation of Toshisuke Nasu's instructions, with an added commentary. The extracts show how little this 'sport' has the character of mere recreation that the notion of sport implies in secular cultures:

> The stance is the basis of all else in archery. When you take your place at the butts to shoot, you must banish all thought of other people from your mind, and feel then that the business of archery concerns you alone . . . When you thus turn your face to the mark you do not merely look at it, but also concentrate upon it . . .you must not do so with the eyes alone, mechanically, as it were—you must learn to do all this from the belly.

Again:

> By *dōzukuri* is meant the placing of the body squarely on the support afforded by the legs. One should think of oneself as being like Vairocana Buddha (i.e. the sun), calm and without fear, and feel as though one were standing, like him, in the centre of the universe.[57]

In the preparation for shooting, the greatest stress is laid on muscular relaxation, and on a state of calm to be attained by regular breathing; just as in contemplative exercises, where likewise the preparation is for a 'release'. In taking aim (*mikomo*, from *miru*, to see, and *komu*, to press) the archer does not simply look at the target, but 'presses into' or 'forces into' it his vision, as it were anticipating the end to be reached by the arrow itself. The archer's breathing must be regulated, in order to 'concentrate one's strength in the pit of the abdomen—then one may be said to have come to a real understanding of archery'.[58] In this emphasis on deep breathing the 'Zen' (Skr. *dhyāna*) factor is apparent, and on the stress that is laid on the 'spirit' (*kī*, Chinese *chi*, Skr. *ātmạn, prāṇa*) in the same connection, the Taoist factor. Mr. Acker remarked that all Japanese arts and exercises are referred to as 'ways' (*mīchī*, Chinese *tao*), that is, spiritual disciplines:

> . . . one may even say that this is especially so in archery and fencing for there are archers who will tell you that whether or not you succeed in hitting the mark does not matter in the slightest—that the real question is what you get out of archery spiritually.[59]
>
> The consummation of shooting is in the release . . . the Stance, Preparation, Posture, Raising the Bow, Drawing, and Holding, all these are but preparatory activities. Everything depends upon an unintentional involuntary release, effected by gathering into one the whole shooting posture . . . the state in which the release takes place of itself, when the archer's breathing seems to have the mystic power of the syllable Oṁ . . . At that moment the posture of the archer is in perfect order—as though he were unconscious of the arrow's having departed . . . such a shot is said to leave a lingering resonance behind—the arrow moving as quietly as a breath, and indeed almost seeming to be a living thing . . . Up to the last moment one must falter neither in body nor in mind . . . (Thus) Japanese archery is more than a 'sport' in the Western sense; it belongs to Bushido, the Way of the Warrior. Further, the Seven Ways are based upon spontaneous principles, and not upon mere reasoning—
>
> Having drawn sufficiently,
> No longer 'pull', but 'drive' it
> 'Still without holding.'
> The bow should never know
> When the arrow is to go.

The actual release of the arrow, like that of the contemplative, whose passage from *dhyāna* to *samādhi*, *contemplatio* to *raptus*, takes place suddenly indeed, but almost unawares, is spontaneous, and as it were uncaused. If all the preparations have been made correctly, the arrow, like a homing bird, will find its own goal; just as the man who, when he departs from this world 'all in act' (*kṛtakṛtya, kataṁ karanī-yam*), having done what there was to be done, need not wonder what will become of him nor where he is going, but will inevitably find the bull's eye, and passing through that sun door, enter into the empyrean beyond the 'murity' of the sky.

Thus one sees how in a traditional society every necessary activity can be also the Way, and that in such a society there is nothing profane; a condition the reverse of that to be seen in secular societies, where there is nothing sacred. We see that even a 'sport' may also be a yoga, and how the active and contemplative lives, outer and inner man can be unified in a single act of being in which both selves cooperate.

NOTES

1. This article, in its original form, was to have appeared in the special number of *Études traditionelles*, to be devoted to 'Sport', in the year 1940. Of this journal nothing has been heard since the occupation of Paris.

2. First printed at Constantinople in 1847 A.D. A detailed account of this work and of Turkish archery has been published by Joachim Hein ('Bogenhandwerk und Bogensport bei den Osmanen', *Der Islam*, XIV, 1925, 289–360, and XV, 1926, pp. 1–78); my account is based on Hein's work.

3. In either direction the 'Path' leading directly from the archer's place to the (solar) target is obviously an 'equivalent', in horizontal projection, of the Axis Mundi: and in walking on this Path the archer is therefore always in a 'central' and 'paradisiacal' position with respect to the rest of the 'Field' as a whole. It will be further observed that in the alternate use of the two targets there is a shooting in two opposite directions, one from and one toward the archer's original stand; the shooting from a stand beside the second target involves a return of the arrow to its first place, and it is clear that the two motions are those of 'ascent' and 'descent' and that the 'Path' is a sort of Jacob's Ladder.

4. 'Compound bows first appear in Mesopotamia in the dynasty of Accad (*ca.* twenty-fourth century B.C.)', W. F. Albright and G. E. Mendenthall, 'The Creation of the Compound Bow in Canaanite Mythology', *Journal of Near Eastern Studies*, I (1942), 227–29, citing H. Bonnet, *Die Waffen der Vöker des alten Orients* (Leipzig, 1926), pp. 135–45.

5. A. N. Poliak, 'The Influence of Chingiz-Khān's Yāsa Upon the General Organization of the Mamlūk State', *Bull, School Oriental Studies*, X (1942), p. 872, note. 5, refers to Arabian lancers who formed an hereditary corporation and concealed 'the secrets of their professional education' from the lay public, pointing out that the art of these

rammāḥs 'was a conservative one, claiming descent from Sasanian and early Islamic warriors'; these data are derived from a work cited as *Kitāb fi 'Ilm al-Furūsīya*, MS, Aleppo (*Aḥmadīya*).

6. Cf. 'Anu shouted aloud and spake in the assembly, kissing the bow', in *Babylonian Legends of Creation* (London, 1931), p. 67, sixth tablet, ls. 64, 65.

7. Agni Anīkavat, being its point (*anīka*), is the essential part of the divine arrow that does not swerve and with which the gods struck the dragon in the beginning; and so virtually the whole of the arrow, since 'where the point goes, there the arrow goes' (ŚB. II.3.3.10, II. 5.3.2, II. 5.4.3.8; AB. I. 25, etc.). It comes to the same thing that he is also the point of the bolt (*vajra*) with which the dragon was smitten (ŚB. III. 4.4.14); for it is from the point of this bolt as their etymon that arrows are 'derived' (TS. VI. 1.3.5; ŚB. I. 2.4.1); and *vajra* meaning also 'adamant'; we often find that a solar hero's arrows are described as 'tipped with adamant'. From the concept of love (*kāma*) as a fire, and Agni having 'five missiles', comes the iconography of Kāmadeva, the god of love, as an archer.

8. Cf. Plato, *Symposium*, 187A, and *Republic*, 439B. That for any efficacy there must be a co-operation of contrasted forces is a basic principle of Indian and all traditional philosophy. ['Without Contraries is no Progression', Blake.]

9. See my *Spiritual Authority and Temporal Power in the Indian Theory of Government*, (New Haven, 1942). note 14a, and *passim*. Law, or justice (*dharma*) is the principle of kingship (BU. I. 4.14, etc.); and this 'justice' differs only from the truth (*satyam*) in that it is applied (Śaṅkara on BU. I. 4.15). Government, in other words, is an art. based on an immutable science; and as in the case of other arts, so here, *ars sine scientia nihil*.

10. The Pali Text Society's Pali dictionary explanations of *akkahaṇa* are admittedly unsatisfactory. The real equivalent is Skr. *ākhaṇa* ('target'), as in JUB. I. 60.7.8 and CU. I. 2.7.8. Cf. *ākha* in TS. VI. 4.11.3, Keith's note, and Pāṇini III. 3.125, *vartt.* 1.

With *sadda-vedhin* (*śabda-*) cf. *Mbh.* (Poona, 1933), I. 123. 12–18 where Ekalavya, the Naiṣādha, who has acquired his skill (*laghutva*) in archery (*iṣvastra*) by making a clay image of Droṇa and practicing before it as his master, shoots seven arrows into the mouth of a dog whom he hears barking, but does not see.

11. *Dve hatte sandhiṭṭhānam āropeti* (misunderstood by Rhys Davids) can only mean 'setting up the bow', i.e. putting its two parts together, *sandhi-ṭṭhānam* being the junction and 'grip'; cf. *Jātaka* III. 274 and IV. 258 *dhanum adejjhaṁ katvāna*, lit. 'making the bow to be not-twofold', *Mhv.* VII. 19 *dhanuṁ sandhāya*, and *Mil.* 352 *cāpāropana*, 'breaking down and setting up the bow' (as one 'breaks down' a gun). *Āropeti* is to 'make fit together', and can also be used of stringing the bow, as in *Jātaka*, V. 129 *dhanuṁhi . . . jiyam āropetvā*; while *sandahati* (*saṁdhā*) to 'join' can also be used of setting the arrow to the string, as in *Jātaka*, IV. 258 *usuṁ sandhāya*.

A glossary of archer's terms, Skr. and Pali, would require a separate article, and I have mentioned only some that have a bearing on the significance of archery.

12. Cf. *Jātaka*, IV. 258: 'Thinking, "I shall pierce him, and when he is weakened, seize him".' *Nimittam ujuṁ karoti* could also be rendered 'makes a right resolve'.

13. *Upāsati* (Skr. *upās*) is ordinarily to 'sit near', 'sit under', 'wait upon', 'honour', 'worship'; *Mil.* 352 speaks of a hall, *upāsana-sālā* (= *santhāgāra*, S. V. 453), in which a skilled archer teaches his disciples (*antevāsike*, resident pupils, cf. A. IV. 423). In other words, the practice of archery is literally a 'devotion'. In *Jātaka*, V. 127f. Jotipāla is sent to a Master in Takkasilā to learn the whole art (*sippam*). A fee of 'a thousand' is paid. When the boy has become an expert, the master gives him a sword, and 'a bow of ram's-horn and a quiver, both of them deftly joined together' (*sandhiyutta-*), and his corselet and turban (thus establishing the pupil as a master in due succession).

'Early and late' may mean by day and night. In *Mbh.* (Poona) I. 123.7 Arjuna resolves to practice by *abhyāsa*, of which the primary sense is a 'shooting at' (cf. 'intend', 'intention', self-*direction*) and the derived meaning 'exercise', 'practice', or 'study' of any kind.

14. A. Moret, *Du caractère religieux de la royauté pharaonique* (Paris, 1902), pp.105–6 (p.106, note. 3: 'Il semble que cette cérémonie ait pour but de definir le pouvoir qu 'a Pharaon-Horus de lancer, comme le soleil, ses rayons dans les quatre parties du monde'). In the relief from Karnak (E. Lepsius, *Denkmäler* [Leipzig, 1850–59], III, Pl. 36b) Thothmes III is represented thus shooting, guided by Horus and Seth; in the late relief of the twenty-fifth dynasty (E. Prisse d'Avennes, *Monuments égyptiens* [Paris, 1847], Pl. XXXIII; H. Schäfer, *Ägy-tischer und heutiger Kunst und Weltgebaüde der alten Ägypter* [Berlin, 1928], Abb. 54, and *idem*, 'König Amenophis II als Meister-Schütz', *Or. Literat. Zeitschr.*, [1929], col. 240–43) the queen is shooting at circular loaves, which are evidently symbols of the Four Quarters; the inscription states that she receives the bows of the North and South and that she shoots toward the Four Quarters; this is in the *sed* rite which, later in a reign, repeats the rites of enthronement and deification, apparently renewing the king's royal power. This rite is accompanied by, or may perhaps replace another in which four birds are released to fly to the Four Quarters; bird and arrow are equivalent symbols.

In ŚB. I. 2.4.15f. and TB. III. 2.9.5f., where the priest brandishes the wooden sword four times, however, this is done to repel the Asuras from the Three Worlds and 'whatever Fourth World there may or may not be beyond these three'. But in the Hungarian coronation rite the sword is brandished, as the arrows are shot, toward the Four Quarters of this world.

ŚB. V. 1.5.13f. and V. 3.5.29, 30 describe the ritual use of seventeen arrows and that of three arrows. The seventeen arrows correspond to the 'seventeenfold Prajāpati', the seventeenth marking the place for the goal post about which the chariots are to turn in the ritual race (we know from other sources that this post represents the sun); and it is explicit that the shooting symbolizes and implies 'the rule of one over many'. The three arrows, one that penetrates, one that wounds, and one that misses, correspond to the Three Worlds.

15. This was regarded by B. Karlgren ('Some Fecundity Symbols in Ancient China', *Bull. Mus. Far Eastern Antiquities*, II, Stockholm, 1930, p. 51) as a fecundity ritual performed for the sake of male children, represented by the arrows: C. G. Seligman ('Bow and Arrow Symbolism', *Eurasia Septentrionalis Antiqua*, IX [1934], 351) criticizing Karlgren, rightly pointed out that the primary significance of the rite is that of 'a supreme assertion of power'. Neither author, however, seems to realise that the erotic significance of shooting (still quite familiar) and that of shooting as a symbol of dominion are by no means mutually exclusive meanings. Thus, the sun's rays, which he shoots forth (cf. Phoebus Apollo) are at the same time dominant and progenitive (cf. TS. VII. 1.1.1, ŚB. VIII. 7.1.16–17, and A. K. Coomaraswamy, 'The Sun-Kiss', *Journ. Amer. Oriental Soc.*, LX [1940], p. 50, note 13, 14). In the same way Skr. *sṛj*, to 'let fly', can apply either to the release of an arrow or to the act of procreation, and it is in fact thus that Prajāpati 'projects' (*sṛjati*) his offspring, thought of as 'rays'.

16. *Heike Monogatari* (thirteenth century); see A. L. Sadler, 'The Heike Monogatari', *Trans. Asiatic Soc. Japan*, XLVI (1918), Pt. 2, 120.

17. The printed text has *maṇḍapa*, 'pavilion', but the v.l. *maṇḍala* is to be preferred. That the archer stands within a circle and shoots thence to the four corners of a square field has a meaning related to that of a dome on a square structure, heaven and earth being typically 'circular' and square; it is true that the earth can also be regarded as a circle, and the domed structure may be circular also in plan, still the earth is square in the sense that there are four 'Quarters'. The archer's position relative to the four targets

is quintessential, and virtually 'elevated'; the 'field' corresponds to all that is 'under the Sun', the ruler of all he surveys.

18. The Bodhisatta's invulnerability corresponds to that of the solar Breath (*prāṇa*) of JUB. I. 60.7–8 and CU. I. 2.7–8.

19. This mention of a second penetration of the first target should be noted; without this the circle would have been left 'open'. One could not ask for better proof of the metaphysical content of what many would think of as mere story-telling. The serious student will soon learn that all true folk and fairy tale motifs have such a content; and that it would be idle to pretend that the most primitive peoples lacked adequate idioms for the expression of the most abstract ideas, whether in verbal or visual arts. It is *our* language that would be impoverished if their idioms were forgotten.

20. ŚB. VI. 7.1.17, VIII. 7.3.10 (the Sun is the fastening to which the Quarters are linked by a pneumatic thread); BU. III. 6.2; BG. VII. 7; *Iliad*, VIII. 18f; Plato, *Theatetus*, 153C, D; *Laws* 644E, 'One Golden Cord'; Dante, *Paradiso*, I, 116 *questi la terra in se stringe*; W. Blake, 'I give you the end of a golden string'; etc.

'At a place in Gilgit there is said to be a golden chain hanging down to earth from the sky. Any persons suspected of wrong-doing or falsehood were taken to the place and forced to hold the chain [as in Plato *Laws*, 644E] while they swore that they were innocent or that their statements were true. This suggests the Homeric reference (*Iliad*, VIII. 18 *et seq.*), and the Catena Auerea Homeri, which was handed down through the Neo-Platonists to the alchemists of the Middle Ages' (W. Crooke, *Folklore*, XXV [1914]. 397).

21. 'Tis the thread that is connected with the needle: the eye of the needle is not suitable for the camel', i.e. soul-and-body (Rūmī, ed. by R. L. Nicholson, *Mathnawī*, I. 3065: cf. I. 849, cords of causation; II. 1276, rope and well).

22. O. T. Mason, 'North American Bows, Arrows and Quivers', *Smithson. Rept. 1893* (Washington, 1894), pp. 631–79. I am indebted to Dr. Carleton S. Coon of the University Museum, Pennsylvania, for this reference.

23. In R. A. Nicholson, *Dīwān of Shams-i-Tabrīz* (Cambridge, 1898), Ode 28. 'Keep thy end of the thread, that he may keep his end' (Hafiz, I. 386.2); 'Fish-like in a sea behold me swimming, Till he with his hook my rescue maketh' (W. Leaf, *Versions from Hafiz* [London, 1898]. XII. 2). Any full discussion of the Islamic symbols of the spirit would require a separate article. Far Eastern parallels could also be cited, e.g. the story of 'The Spider's Thread' in *Tales Grotesque and Curious*, by R. Akutagawa, trans. by G. Shaw (Tokyo, n.d.), the thread is broken by the climbers' egotism.

24. In *Mbh*. I. 121.21, 22 we are told that Droṇa himself had received from (*Paraśu-*) Rāma his 'weapons, together with the secrets of their use' (*astrāṇi . . . saprayogarahasyāni*) and the 'Book of the Bow' (*dhanurvedam*).

A *Dhanurveda*, dealing with the whole art of war and arms 'auch über geheime Waffen, Zaubersprüche, Königsweihe und Omina' is attributed to the *Ṛṣi Viśvāmitra*; and there are other Dhanurvedas extant in manuscript (M. Winternitz, *Geschichte der indischen Literatur*, Leipzig, 1920, III, 532).

M. Williams, *Sanskrit Dictionary*, cites the word *kārmukopaniṣaṭ* ('secret of the art of shooting') from the *Bālarāmāyaṇa*.

25. *Mbh*. I. 125.

26. In the Mahāvrata rite (a winter solstice festival) three arrows are shot by a king or prince, or the best archer available, at a circular skin target suspended between two posts; the archer stands in a moving chariot that is driven round the altar; the arrows are not to pass through, but to remain sticking in the target. That is done to 'break down' (*avabhid*) the sacrificer's evil *pāpman*), as the target is 'broken down' by the arrows TS. VII. 5.10). A skin is often the symbol of darkness (for RV. see H. G.

Grassmann, *Wörterbuch, zum Rig-Veda* [Leipzig, 1873], s. v. tvac, sense 9), and darkness, death, and sin or evil (*pāpman*) are one and the same thing (*Brāhmaṇas, passim*). So it is to free the sun from darkness, and by analogy the sacrificer from his own darkness, that the rite is performed.

27. *Mbh.* I. 176–79.

28. In S.V. 453 the Buddha finds some Licchavi youths exercising in a gymnasium (*santhāgāre upāsanaṁ karonte*) shooting 'from afar through a very small "keyhole"' (*durato va sukhumena tāḷa-chiggaḷena*) and splitting an arrow, flight after flight without missing (*asanam atipatente poṅkhānupoṅkham avirādhitam. Tāḷa-chiggaḷa* (= *tāḷa-chidda*) is here evidently not an actual keyhole but the equivalent of the yantra-chidra of *Mbh.*, an aperture that may very well have been called in archer's slang a 'keyhole', just as we speak of any strait gate as a 'needle's eye'; in this sense one might have rendered *yantra-chidra* in *Mbh.* by 'keyhole'. The term is, furthermore, most appropriate inasmuch as the sun door, passing which one is altogether liberated (*atimucyate*), is a 'hole in the sky' (*divaś chidra*, JUB. I. 3.5; *childra ivādityo dṛśyate*, AĀ. III. 2.4), while the arrow equated with the Atman or with Oṁ (*Muṇḍ, Up.* II. 2.4, VI. 24) could well have been thought of as the pass 'key'. In the same connection it may be observed that in traditional art actual keyholes are commonly ornamented with the device of the sun bird (often the bicephalous Garuḍa or Haṁsa), through which the key must be passed before there can be access to whatever is within. To this sun bird corresponds the 'suspended device' of *Mbh.*

In S. (*loc. cit.*) the Buddha proceeds to ask the archers whether their performance, 'to shoot like that, or to pierce one strand of a hair, a hundred times divided, with another strand is the more difficult?' The answer is obvious. He continues: 'That is just what they do, who penetrate the real meaning of the words. This is grief' (*atha ko . . . paṭivijjhanti ye* IDAṀ DUKKHAṀ *ti yathābhūtam paṭivijjhanti*).

With *atipātente* above, cf. M. I. 8.2 *tiriyaṁ tālacchāvam atipāteyya* 'pierces an umbrageous palm'; but in JV. 130, 1.1, *pātesi* is 'knocks down'. The more usual word for 'piercing' is *vijjhati*, as in the expression *Vāla-vedhi*, 'splitting a hair'. It may be remarked here that in JV. 130 *koṭṭhakam parikhipanto viya* is misunderstood by the translator (H. T. Francis); the Bodhisatta knocks down (*pātesi*) his opponents' 120,000 arrows and 'throws round *himself* a sort of house' of which the walls are the fallen arrows, neatly stacked; it is from within this 'arrow-enceinte' (*sara-gabbha*) that he afterwards rises into the air 'without damaging the "house"'.

29. See footnote 7.

30. MU. VI. 30. The 'path' is that one of the sun's 'rays' that pierces through his disk, *ūrdhvam ekaḥsthitas teṣām yo bhitvā sūrya-maṇḍalam brahmalokam atikramya* in MU. like *yantrachidreṇābhyatikramya* in *Mbh.* cited above; cf. Hermes Trismegistus, *Lib.* XVI. 16 ἀκτὶς ἐπιλάμπει διὰ τοῦ ἡλιοῦ.

For a more detailed account of the sun door and its form and significance see my 'Svayamātṛṇṇā: Janua Coeli', *Zalmoxis*, II (1939), 3–51. [Rpr. SP 1, pp. 465–520.]

31. AV. X. 7.3.

32. JUB. 1.6.4.

33. RV. I. 164.12; ŚB. XI. 2.3.3, etc.

34. *Phaedrus*, 247C.

35. *Nyāsa Up.* 2.

36. Cf. my '*Kha* and Other Words Denoting Zero . . .', *Bull. School of Oriental Studies*, VII (1934), pp.487–97. [Rpr. SP2, pp.220–230.]

37. BU. V. 1.

38. In RV. VI. 75.15 arrows are 'sharpened by incantations' (brahmasaṁśita), just as in ŚB. I. 2.4 the wooden ritual sword is sharpened by and held to participate in the

nature of the cutting Gale. *Upāsana* has been remarked above (Note 13) as 'exercise'; in the present context the 'exercise' is contemplative, as in BU. I. 4.7 *ātmety evopāsīta*, 'Worship Him as Spirit', or 'thy Self'.

39. *Viddhi*, as noted above, is the common imperative of *vyadh* or *vidh* to pierce or penetrate, and *vid* to know or find. Cf. BG. VII. 7 *prakṛtiṁ viddhi me parām*, 'penetrate (or know) my higher nature', i.e., the 'that-nature' of the Muṇḍaka verse. In the same way JUB. IV. 18.6 (*Kena Up.*) *'tad eva brahma tvaṁ viddhi ne'dam yad idam upāsate'*, 'Know (or penetrate) only Brahma, not what men worship here'. The ambivalence recurs in Pali; thus, in Udāna 9, *attanā verdi* is rendered by Woodward as 'of his own self hath pierced (unto the truth)' ['in', or 'with the spirit' would be equally legitimate], the commentary reading: *sayam eva aññāti, paṭividdha* 'knows or penetrates'. In S.I.4 *paṭividhitā*(v.l.-*vidhitā*) is interpreted as *ñānema paṭividdha*, 'those who have by gnosis penetrated', and this can hardly be called with Mrs. Rhys Davids an 'exegetical pun', for we do not call the double entendre in our word 'penetrating' a 'pun'. The fact is that the 'pursuit' of truth is an art of hunting; one tracks it down (*mṛg*, ἰχνευω), aims at it, hits the mark, and *penetrates* it. Cf. *Jātaka*, 340, 341, *pacceka-bodhi-ñānam paṭivijjhi*, 'he penetrated the gnosis of a *Pacceka Buddha*', and *Vis.* 288 *lakkhana-paṭisaṁvedhena, li*, 'by penetration of the mark' but here 'by penetration of the characteristics' (of a state of contemplation). In KB. XI. 5 *manasā preva vidhyet* is 'with his mind, as it were, let him pierce'; cf. MU. VI. 24, where the mind is the arrow point.

An analogous symbolism is employed in *Visuddhi Magga*. I. 284, where *sūci-pāsavedhanam* is a 'needle's eye borer' used by the needle maker; the needle stands for recollection (*sati* = *smṛti*) and the borer for the prescience (*pañña*) = *prajñā*) connected with it.

On *penetrabilia* and *penetralia* cf. Isodorus, *Diff.* I.435 (Migne, vol. 83, col. 54) *penetralia autem sunt domorum secreta, et dicta ab eo quod est penitus* (*penitus* is 'within', and not to be confused with 'penitent'): Mellifluus (*ca.* 540 A.D.) *ad regni superni penetrabilia non pervenit quisquam nisi egerit paenitentiam*; cited by R. J. Getty, '*Penetralia* and *penetrabilia* in Post-Classical Latin'. *Amer. Journ. Phil.*, LVIII (1936), pp.233–44. Cf. also Rūmī, *Mathnawī*, ed. R. A. Nicholson, I.3503, 'As the point of the spear passes through the shield'.

40. Cf. Udāna 9 attanā vedi cited in the preceding note. The condition of entry is that one should realise '"That" is the truth, "That" the Spirit (or Self. the real self of all beings), "That" art thou' (CU. VI.9.4; cf. JUB. III. 143 and my 'The "E" at Delphi', *Review of Religion*, V (1941), pp.18–19. [Rpr. SP1, pp.43–5.]

41. Cf. BG. VI. 54 *sakyo hy ahaṁ viddhah*, 'I can, indeed, be penetrated (or known)'.

42. Not here, of course, the ultimate mark, but the obstacle.

43. As in MU. VI. 30 *sauraṁ dvāram bhitvā*, 'piercing the Sundoor'. All this symbolism is paralleled in that of the roof; the expert monk, rising in the air, breaks through the roof plate of the dome (kaṇṇika-maṇḍalam bhinditvā, *DhA.* III.66, etc.); cf. my 'Symbolism of the Dome', *Indian Hist. Quart.* XIV (1938) Pt. iii. [Rpr. SP1, pp. 415–458.

44. Three forms of Agni. Brahma is 'that in the lightning which flashes forth' (*Kena Up.* 29).

45. *Abhimāna*, arrogance, is the ego delusion, the notion 'I am' and 'I do'. To overcome the janitor is to open the way in, and is an equivalent of the 'keyhole' symbolism. In JUB. I.5 the sun (disk) is the janitor and he bars the way to those who expect to enter in by means of their good works; but cannot hinder one who invokes the truth, which is that his deeds are not 'his own', but those of the sun himself, one who disclaims the notion 'I do', or as in JUB. III. 14.5 denies that he is another than the sun himself; cf. Rūmī, *Mathnawī*, I. 3056–65, the world door is a way in for the wise, and a barrier to the foolish (CU. VIII. 6.5; cf. RV. IX. 113.8).

46. Saññā (*saṁjñā*) is also 'awareness'; A. II. 167 defines four levels of consciousness, of which the first and lowest is renunciation (*hāna*, repudiation, repentance), the second the taking up of a stand (*ṭhiti*), the third the transcending of dialectic (*vitakka*), while the highest involves indifference (*nibbida*) and revulsion (*virāga*) and is the nature of penetration (*nibbedha* = *nirvedha*). The stand (*thiti*) corresponds to the skilled stance of the archer; like the archer with his skill, the monk is a 'man of skilled stance' (*thāna-kusalo*) by his conduct (*sīla*), a 'far-shooter' in that in all phenomenal things he recognizes 'that is not mine, I am not that, that is not my Self', one 'who hits the mark' in that he understands the meaning of 'grief' (*dukkham*) as it really is, and the 'cleaver of a great mass' in that he pierces the trunk of ignorance *avijjā-khandham* (A. II. 171; cf. II. 202). M. I. 82 compares the perfected disciple to an instructed, practiced, devoted archer (*dhanūggaho sikkhito katahattho katūpāsano*), who can easily, even with a light shaft, pierce an umbrageous palm (*tiriyaṁ tālacchāyam atipāteyya*). The Bodhisattva's great feats of archery (by which, like Arjuna and Rāma, he wins a bride) are described in *Jātaka*, I. 58 (where it is to be understood that he performed all those feats that were performed by Jotipāla in the *Sarabhaṅga Jātaka*) and the *Lalita Vistara* (Ch. XII), where he pierces five iron drums, seven palm-trees, and 'an iron figure of a boar, provided with a (perforated) device' (*yantra-yukta*, cf. *yantra-sahitam* cited and explained above from *Mbh.*) with a single arrow which passes through all these and buries itself in the earth beyond them, and when the assembly marvels, the Gods explain (S. Lefmann, *Lalita Vistara*, Halle, 1902, p.156, verse omitted in P. E. Foucaux's translation, Paris, 1884, from another edition of the text) that 'former Buddhas have likewise, with the arrows of "emptiness" and "impersonality" (*śūnya-nairātma-bāṇaiḥ*) smitten the enemy, depravity, and pierced the net of (heretical) "views", with intent to attain to the supreme Enlightenment'; cf. MU. VI. 28. The Buddha is, indeed, 'of superlative penetration' (*ativijjha*) by his prescience (*paññā*, S. I. 193, V. 226).

47. It was unnecessary for the purposes of the text to explain the symbolism of the turning wheel, which must have been quite apparent to an Indian audience. This is evidently the 'wheel of becoming' (*bhava-cakka*), 'the turning wheel of the vortex of becoming' (*āvṛtta-cakram iva saṁsāra-cakram*, MU. VI. 29), and, like 'chariot' and 'horse', the physical vehicle on which the spirit rides; the blindfolded archer is the incarnate and unseeing elemental self (*bhūtātman*, i.e. *śarira ātman*, bodily self), caught in the net, overcome by *karma*, filled with many things and 'carted about' (*rathita*) MU. III. I-IV. 4; the bodily self (*kāyo* = *attā*, cf. *Dīgha-Nikāhya*, I. 77 *añño kāyo*), unseeing, overspread by the net, filled up and 'carried about on karma-car' (*karma-yantita*), *Th.* I. 567 f.

The stance upon a moving wheel corresponds to Arjuna's, who shoots from a moving car, as mentioned above. For the equivalent of a turning wheel and a car may be cited TS. I. 7.8 and ŚB. V. 1.5.1f. where the high priest (*brahmā*) 'mounts a car-wheel' (*rathacakran . . . rohati*, TB. I. 3.6.1) and there enacts a chariot race. This carwheel is mounted on the point of a post and made to revolve, and is thus just what *Vis.* refers to as a *cakkayanta*: and because a car is essentially the 'bolt' (*vajra*), as are also arrows (see TS. V. 4.11.2, VI. 1.3.4.5; ŚB. I. 2.4.1–6), the operation implies a 'victory over all the Quarters' (*Sāyaṇa* on TS. I. 7.8), as in the case of shooting toward the Quarters, mentioned above. For the equation, car = flesh or bodily self, KU. III. 3–9, *Jātaka*, VI. 252 will suffice; cf. Plato, *Phaedrus*, 247. In the same way the body can be compared in the same context to a chariot and to a potter's wheel (*cakra*), MU. II. 6 (mark the contrast of *cakra-vṛtta*, 'spun on the wheel' and *Cakravartin*, the 'spinner of the wheel'), All these things, like the body itself, are 'engines' (*yantra*): well for him who, from such a merry-go-round, can hit the unseen mark!

On the general symbolism of wings cf. RV. VI. 9.5 'Mind is the swiftest of flying things'; JUB. III. 13. 10 where the sound of Oṁ serves the sacrificer as wings with which to reach the world of heaven; PB. XIX. 11.8, XXV. 3.4; Plato, *Phaedrus*, 246–56; Dante, *Paradiso*, XXV. 49–51.

48. *Dīwān*, T.1624 a, cited by R. A. Nicholson, *Dīwān of Shams-i-Tabrīz* (Cambridge, 1938), p. 336. Cf. 'the mark of truth, that they may aim aright' (*Homilies of Narsai*, XXII), and 'should he miss, the worse for him, but if he hits becomes like as (the mark)', TS. II. 4.5.6.

49. *Ibid*, Odes XXIX, XLIV.

50. PB. V. 3.5; cf. TS. V. 4.11.1.

51. *Mathnawī*, I. 1384, 1385, Nicholson's translation.

52. The following is cited, in *Voile d'Isis*, 1935. p. 203, from an Ilahī of Yunīs Emre (fl. thirteenth-fourteenth century): *'Ta vie est comme une flèche sur un arch tendu à fond, puisque l'arc est tendu, pourquoi rester sans mouvement? Suppose donc que tu as lancé cette flèche.'*

53. *Paradiso*, I. 107.

54. *Ibid.* I.124–7.

55. 'Blind shot' is not, of course, a shot at random, but at an unseen mark.

56. Nasu and Aka (Acker), *Toyō kyūdo Kikan* (Tokyo, 1937). Now obtainable only from the author, Freer Gallery, Washington. I have not seen Martin Filla, *Grundlagen und Wesen der altjapanesischen Sportkünste* (Würzburg-Aumühle).

57. All this implies an indentification of one's (real) Self with the mark, as in the *Muṇḍaka Up.* cited above (*tadbhāva-gatena cetasā . . . tanmayo bhavet*). 'If you do not make yourself equal to God, you cannot know God; for like is known by like' (Hermes Trismegistus, XI. ii. 20b).

58. Cf. CU. I. 3.4,5 where, as in chanting, 'so in other virile acts such as the production of fire by friction, running a race, or bending a stiff bow, one does these things without breathing in and out', i.e. without panting, getting out of breath or excitement.

59. That is to say that hitting the mark in fact should be a result of one's state of mind; an evidence, rather than the cause of his spiritual condition. 'Thy concern is only with the action (that it be "correct"), never with its results: neither let the results of action be thy motive, nor refrain from acting' BG. II. 47).

SEVENTEEN

Khwāja Khaḍir and the Fountain of Life, in the Tradition of Persian and Mughal Art

IN India, the Prophet, Saint, or Deity known as Khwāja Khizr (Khaḍir), Pīr Badar, or Rāja Kidār, is the object of a still surviving popular cult, common to Muslims and Hindus. His principal shrine is on the Indus near Bakhar, where he is worshipped by devotees of both persuasions; the cult is however hardly less widely diffused in Bihar and Bengal. In the Hindu cult, the Khwāja is worshipped with lights and by feeding Brahmans at a well, and alike in Hindu and Muslim practice, by setting afloat in a pond or river a little boat which bears a lighted lamp. Iconographically Khwāja Khizr is represented as an aged man, having the aspect of a *faqīr*, clothed entirely in green,[1] and moving in the waters with a 'fish' as his vehicle.

The nature of Khwāja Khizr can be inferred from his iconography as outlined above, and also from the Indian legends. In the ballad of Niwal Daī, which is localized at Safīdam[2] in the Pañjāb, Niwal Daī is the daughter of Vāsuki, the chief of the Serpents. The Aryan Pāṇḍava Rājā Parikṣit has encountered Vāsuki, and forced him to promise his daughter to him in marriage, though from Vāsuki's point of view this is a disgraceful misalliance. Vāsuki is then stricken with leprosy, owing to a curse pronounced by the Priest Sījī[3] whose cows have been bitten by the Serpents. Niwal Daī undertakes to obtain for his healing the Water of Life (*amṛta*), from the closed well which she alone can open, but which is in the domains of Rājā Parikṣit.[4] When she reaches the well, which is covered over by heavy stones, she moves these by her magic power, but the waters sink down out of reach; this is because Khwāja Khizr, their master, will not release them until Niwal Daī, whom none but her own parents Vāsuki and his queen Padmā have ever yet seen, permits herself to be seen; when Niwal Daī showed herself, then Khwāja Khizr 'sent the waters up bubbling'. Rājā Parikṣit, aroused by the sound, gallops to the well, and though Niwal Daī hides in her serpent form, forces her to put on her human aspect, and after a long argument at the well, convinces her that she is bound by the previous betrothal, and in due course marries her.[5]

The scene at the well may also have been the original theme of the composition represented in a number of seventeenth and eighteenth century Mughal paintings, where a prince on horseback is shown at a well, from which a lady has drawn up water.[6] The motif of a dynasty originating in the marriage of a human King with a Nāginī is widely diffused in India, and in the last analysis can always be referred back to the rape of Vāc, the Apsaras or Virgin of the Waters whose origin is with the powers of darkness and whom the Father-Creator has not 'seen' before the transformation of darkness into light, *in principio*; in this connection it is noteworthy that in the ballad, Niwal Daī has never seen the Sun or Moon, and has been kept hidden in a whirlpool (*bhauṅrī*) until she comes forth to uncover the Well at the World's End, in which are the Waters of Life.[7] That she assumes a human form is her 'manifestation'. It will be realised, of course, that just as in the European parallels, where a mermaid, or the daughter of a magician, marries a human hero, so in the later Indian folk tales and romances the redactor may not have always fully 'understood his material'.

Khwāja Khizr appears again in another Indian folk tale of a very archaic type, the Story of Prince Maḥbūb.[8] The king of Persia has a son by a concubine, who, in the absence of any other child, becomes the heir apparent. Subsequently the true queen becomes pregnant. The first prince fears that he will be displaced, invades the kingdom, slays his father, and usurps the throne. In the meantime the true queen escapes, and is cared for by a farmer; a son is born, who is called Maḥbūb, and the 'Darling of the World'. Later he goes alone to court, and becomes the victor in athletic contests, particularly as an archer. The people recognise his likeness to the late king. On his return home his mother tells him of his birth, and both set out on their travels in order to avoid the usurper's suspicion. Mother and son reach a desert land, and there in a mosque beside a mountain they meet a *faqīr* who gives them bread and water that are inexhaustible, and two pieces of wood, one of which can serve as a torch, the other possessing this virtue, that within a radius of fourteen cubits from the place where it is held, the deepest sea will become fordable, and no more than a cubit in depth. As mother and son are then wading through the sea knee-deep, they meet with a ruby-bearing current. They cross the sea and reach India, where they sell one of the rubies at a great price. It comes into the hands of the king of that country. He finds out its source, and seeks the hero, who has in the meantime built a new and great palace by the seaside. Maḥbūb undertakes to procure more of the same kind. He sets out alone, lights the torch (this shows that he is about to enter a world of darkness), and aided by the rod traverses the sea till he reaches the ruby current. He follows it up until he finds its source in a whirlpool. He jumps in and falls down the black watery chimney until he touches solid ground and finds the waters flowing out from an iron gateway of a conduit. Passing through this he finds himself in a wonderful garden, in which is a palace. In this palace he finds a room in which is a freshly severed head, from which drops of blood are falling into a basin, and are carried out as rubies with the current into the conduit and so to the whirlpool and up into the sea. Twelve *parīs*[9] then appear, take down the head, bring forth the trunk, lay the parts together, and taking up burning candles execute a dance round the couch, so swift that Maḥbūb can see only a circle of light. Then stooping over the bed, they wail 'How long, O Lord, how long? . . . When will the sun of hope arise on the darkness of our despair? Arise, O King, arise, how long will you remain in this deathlike trance?'[10]

Then from the floor of the palace there rises up the form of the *faqīr* previously mentioned, and now clad in garments of light. The *parīs* bow down to him, and ask 'Khwāja Khizr, has the hour come?' The *faqīr*, who is indeed none but the immortal Khwāja Khizr, explains to Maḥbūb that the corpse is his father's, who had been murdered by the usurper Kassāb; Maḥbūb's ancestors have all been *magi*[11]; all have been buried in the under-water palace, but Maḥbūb's father has remained unburied, for none had performed his funeral rites; Maḥbūb, as son, should now do this. Maḥbūb accordingly makes prayer to Allāh on behalf of his father's soul.

Immediately the head is joined to the body, and the dead king rises up alive.[12] Khizr vanishes, and Maḥbūb returns to India with his father, who is thus reunited with the widowed queen. When the king of India comes for the rubies, Maḥbūb pricks his own finger, and the drops of blood falling into a cup of water become the required gems, for as Maḥbūb now knows, every drop of blood that flows in the veins of the kings of Persia is more precious than rubies. Maḥbūb marries the princess of India. An expedition to Persia dethrones the usurper Kassāb, and his head is taken and hung in the underground palace, but every drop of blood becomes a toad.

The true nature of Khwāja Khizr is already clearly indicated in the two stories summarised above, as well as in the iconography. Khizr is at home in both worlds, the dark and the light, but above all master of the flowing River of Life in the Land of Darkness: he is at once the guardian and genius of vegetation and of the Water of Life, and corresponds to Soma and Gandharva in Vedic mythology, and in many respects to Varuṇa himself, though it is evident that he cannot, either from the Islamic or from the later Hindu point of view be openly identified with the supreme deity. We shall find these general conclusions amply confirmed by further examinations of the sources of the Islamic legends of al-Khaḍir.

In the Qur'ān (Sūra XVIII, 59–81) occurs the legend of Mūsā's search for the *Ma'jma 'al-Baḥrain*,[13] which is probably to be understood as a 'place' in the far west at the meeting of two oceans; Mūsā is guided by a 'servant of God', whom the commentators identify with al-Khaḍir, whose abode is said to be upon an island or on a green carpet in the midst of the sea. This story can be traced back to three older sources, the Gilgamesh epic, the Alexander Romances, and the Jewish legend of Elijah and Rabbi Joshua ben Levi.[14] In the Gilgamesh epic the hero sets out in search of his immortal 'ancestor' Utnapishtim who dwells at the mouth of the rivers (*ina pi narati*), like Varuṇa whose abode is 'at the rivers' source', *sindhūnām upodaye*, *Ṛg Veda*, VIII, 41, 2; his object being to be informed with respect to the 'plant-life', prototype of the Avestan *haoma*, Vedic *soma*,[15] whereby man can be saved from death. In the Alexander Romances Alexander sets out in search of the Fountain of Life, which is accidentally found, and significantly 'in the land of darkness', but cannot be found again. A recension of this legend occurs in the *Shāh Nāma*, where Alexander sets out in search of the Fountain of Life, which lies in the Land of Darkness beyond the place of the setting of the Sun in the western waters; Alexander is guided by Khizr, but when they come to a parting of the ways, each follows a different path, and Khizr alone accomplishes the quest. Those of Alexander's followers who bring back with them stones from the Land of Darkness find on their return that these are precious stones.[16] The story is retold at greater length in Nizāmī's *Iskandar Nāma*, LXVIII-LXIX; here Alexander learns from an ancient man (probably Khizr himself in human form) that 'of every land, the Dark Land is best, in which is a Water, a life-giver' and that the source of this River of Life is in the North, beneath the Pole Star.[17] On the way to the Dark land, in every arid land the rain falls and grass springs up, 'Thou wouldst have said: "The trace of Khizr was on that road; that verily, Khizr himself was with the king".'[18] They reach the northern limit of the world, the sun ceases to rise, and the Land of Darkness lies before them. Alexander makes the prophet Khizr his guide, and Khizr 'moving with greenness'[19] leads the way, and presently discovers the fountain, from which he drinks, becoming immortal. He keeps his eye on the spring, while waiting for Alexander to catch up with him; but it disappears from sight, and Khizr himself vanishes, realising that Alexander will not succeed in his quest. Niẓāmī goes on to relate another version according to the 'account of the elders of Rūm'; here the quest is undertaken by Ilyās[20] and Khizr, who sit down by a fountain to eat their repast, consisting of dried fish; the fish falling into the waters, comes to life, and thus the seekers are made aware that they have found the Fountain of Life, from which both drink. Nizāmī then proceeds to the Kur'ānic version, and interprets the Fountain as one of Grace, the true Water of Life being the Knowledge of God. A similar interpretation of the ancient material occurs in the New Testament, (John, 4). Niẓāmī attributes Iskandar's failure to his eagerness, whereas in the case of Khizr 'the Water of Life arrived unsought', with reference to the fact that it is revealed indirectly by its effect on the fish, when Khizr has no suspicion that he has already reached it.

The finding of the Fountain by Ilyās and Khizr occurs in Persian art as the subject of miniatures illustrating the *Iskandar Nāma*.[21] One of these, from a late sixteenth century manuscript belonging to Mr A. Sakisian, is reproduced in colour as frontispiece to his *La*

Miniature persane, 1929, and in monochrome by L. Binyon, *Persian Painting*, 1933, Pl. LXIa; here the two prophets are seated by the Well in a verdant landscape, two fish are seen lying on a platter and a third, evidently alive, is in Khizr's hand; it is clear that he is pointing out to Ilyās the significance of the miracle. Ilyās is robed in blue, Khizr wears a green robe with a brown cloak. In another, and unpublished version of the seventeenth century, belonging to the Freer Gallery the arrangement is similar, but only one fish is seen on the platter. A third example, in the Museum of Fine Arts, Boston, and of late fifteenth century date, is reproduced in *Ars Asiatica*, XIII. Pl. VII, no. 15; Ilyās and al-Khaḍir are seen in the foreground beside the stream, in darkness; Alexander and his followers above, as in the Freer Gallery example, where the arrangement of the darks and lights is reversed. The Freer Gallery example seems to be the more correct in this respect, inasmuch as the whole quest takes place within the Land of Darkness, but the immediate vicinity of the Fountain of Life is understood to be lighted up by the sheen of its flowing waters. The Finders of the Well are both nimbate.

In the Syrian *Lay of Alexander*, and in the Qur'ānic version, the fish swims away, and in the latter is said to reach the sea. A connection with the story of Manu and the 'fish' may be predicated in the Manu myth (*Śatapatha Brāmaṇa*, I. 8. 1); the 'fish' (*jhaṣa*) is from the beginning alive, but very small, and precariously situated, for it comes into Manu's hands when he is washing, and asks him to rear it. Manu provides it with water, and after it has grown great, releases it in the sea; and when the Flood comes, it guides the Ark through the Waters by means of a rope attached to its horn. A noteworthy variant of the Manu legend, with a closer parallel to the Alexander and Qur'ānic versions with respect to the dessication of the 'fish' occurs in *Jaiminīya Brāhmaṇa*, III. 193, and *Pañcaviṁśa Brāhmaṇa*, XIV. 5. 15; here Śarkara, the '*śiśumāra*', refuses to praise Indra, Parjanya therefore strands him on dry land and dries him up with the north wind (the cause of the desiccation of the fish is thus indicated). Śarkara then finds a song of praise for Indra, Parjanya restores him to the ocean (as does Khizr, though unintentionally, in the Qur'ānic version), and by the same laud Śarkara attains heaven, becoming a constellation. There can be no doubt that the constellation Capricornus, Skr. *makara, makaraśi*, is intended. *Makara, Jhaṣa*, and *śiśumāra* are thus synonymous;[22] and this Indian Leviathan clearly corresponds to the *kar*-fish, 'greatest of the creatures of Ahuramazda', who swims in Vourukasha, guarding the Haoma tree of life in the primordial sea (*Bundahiś*, XVIII; *Yasna*, XLII. 4, etc.); and to the Sumerian goat-fish, the symbol and sometimes the vehicle of Ea, god of the waters (Langdon, *Semitic Mythology*, pp.105–6). That in the late Indian iconography Khizr's vehicle is an unmistakable fish, and not the crocodilian *makara*, need not surprise us, for other instances of the alternative use of *makara* and 'fish' could be cited from Indian iconographic sources; in some early representations, for example, the river-godess Gangā is shown supported by a *makara*, but in the later paintings by a fish.

In the Pseudo-Callisthenes (C) version of the Alexander legend, Alexander is accompanied by his cook, Andreas. After a long journey in the Land of Darkness, they come to a place gushing with waters, and sit down to eat; Andreas wets the dried fish, and seeing that it comes to life, drinks of the water, but does not inform Alexander. Subsequently Andreas seduces Alexander's daughter Kale, and gives her a drink of the Water of Life (of which he had brought away a portion); she having thus become an immortal goddess is called Nereis, and the cook is flung into the sea, becoming a god; both are thus denizens of the other world. There can be no doubt that Andreas here is the Idrīs of Qur'ān, Sūra XIX, 57ff. and Sūra XXI, 85, whom Islamic tradition identifies with Enoch, Ilyās, and al-Khaḍir. From the account of Idrīs in Ibn al-Qiftī's *Tārikh al-Ḥukamā'a* (c. 1200) it appears that he plays the part of a solar hero, and is immortal.

Al-Khaḍir also presents some point of resemblance with Saint George, and it is in this connection and as patron of travellers that we meet with a figure which is probably that of al-Khaḍir in carved relief over the gateway of a caravanserai on the road between Sinjār and Mosul, of the XIIIth century; the figure is nimbate, and is thrusting a lance into the mouth of a scaly dragon.[23]

The figure of a man seated on a fish occurs apparently as a Hindu work built into the bastion of the fort at Raichur, in the Deccan; it is stated to have a 'crown of river-serpent hoods', and has therefore been called a 'nāga king', but these hoods are not clearly recognisable in the published reproduction.[24] Mediaeval Indian art affords numerous examples of Varuṇa seated on a *makara*.[24]

A brief reference may be made to European parallels similarly derivative in the last analysis from Sumerian sources. Khaḍir corresponds to the Greek sea-god Glaukos (Friedländer, *loc. cit.* pp. 108ff., 242, 253, etc., Barnett, *loc. cit.* p.715). Khaḍir belongs to the Wandering Jew type. Parallels between Glaukos and Vedic Gandharva are noteworthy; the Avestan designation of Gandarva as *zairipāsna* 'green-heeled' tends to a connection of Gandharva with Khaḍir. Gandharva, as suggested by Dr. Barnett may correspond to Kandarpa, i.e. Kāmadeva, and in this connection it may be observed that the erotic motif common to Glaukos and Gandharva-Kāmadeva appears in connection with Khizr in the Niwal Daī ballad, where Khizr will not release the waters unless he has sight of Niwal Daī; as might be looked for if we think of him as the Gandharva, and of her as the *apsaras* or Maiden (*yoṣā*) of the Waters, or equally if we correlate Khizr with Varuṇa, cf. *Ṛg Veda*, VII. 33. 10–11 where Mitra-Varuṇa are seduced by the sight of Urvaśī, as is emphasized in the *Sarvânukramaṇī*, I. 166 *urvaśim apsarasaṁ dṛṣṭvā . . . reto apatat*, and Sāyaṇa, *retaś caskanda* evidently following *Nirukta*, V. 13. The same situation is implied in *Ṛg Veda*, VII. 87. 6 with respect to Varuṇa alone who descends as a white drop (*drapsa*) and is called a 'traverser of space' (*rajasaḥ vimānaḥ*) and 'ruler of the deep' (*gambhīra-śaṅsaḥ*), epithets that might well be applied to Khizr. It remains to be observed that in Christian iconography the figure of the river-god Jordan,[25] commonly found in representations of the Baptism of Jesus, bears a certain likeness to the conception of Glaukos and Khizr. In some cases the Baptism was thought of as taking place at the junction of two rivers, Jor and Danus. Sometimes there is found a masculine river-god, and a feminine figure representing the sea; both riding on dolphins, like the numerous types of Indian dwarf Yakṣas riding on *makaras*. All these types in the last analysis may be referred back to prototypes of which our earliest knowledge is Sumerian, in the concept of Ea, son and image of Enki, whose essential name Enki means 'Lord of the Watery Deep'. Ea was the ruler of the streams that rose in the Underworld, and flowed thence to fertilize the land; precious stones are likewise his. In iconography, Ea has the goat-fish, and holds in his hands the flowing-vase, the source of the 'bread and water of immortal life'. Ea has seven sons, of whom Marduk inherits his wisdom and slew the dragon Tiamat. Another son was Dumuziabzu, the 'Faithful Son of the Fresh Waters', the Shepherd, the Semitic form of whose name is

Tammuz, well known as the 'Dying God' of vegetation; comparable in many respects with Soma, and as 'Lord of the Realm of the Dead' with Yama. The further Sumerian parallels are too many and too close to admit of adequate discussion here.[26] It suffices to have demonstrated the wide diffusion and ancient origin of the figure of Khwāja Khizr as it occurs in Persian and Indian iconography. In connection with Mughal art may be cited the remark of H. Goetz, who in discussing the sources of Mughal art speaks of a 'teils absolute Identität teils engste Verwandschaft mit solchen der grossen altorientalischen Kulturen, und zwar zu gut Teilen schon der klassischen sumerischen Zeit'.[27] That the figure of Khizr comes into independent prominence precisely in Mughal art of the eighteenth century—all the Indian examples that I have seen are in the 'Lucknow style'—when considered in connection with the adoption of the fish as royal emblem by the rulers of Oudh, seems to show that some revival of the cult took place at this time and in this area.

NOTES

1. In accordance with the meaning of al-Khaḍir, the 'Green Man'.

2. Safīdam, probably a corruption of *sarpa-damana*, 'Quelling of the Serpent'. For the legend of Niwal Daī see Temple, *Legends of the Panjab*, I, pp.414, 418–19.

3. Usually Saṅjā (perhaps for Skr. *Saṁjña*). This priest (Brahman) who serves Vāsuki, but acts against him, suggests Viśvarūpa who in *Taittirīya Saṁhitā*, II. 5. 1 is called the Purohita of the Angels, and Uśanas Kāvya who in *Pañcaviṁśa Brāhmaṇa*, VII. 5. 20 is the Purohita of the Titans, but is won over to the side of the Angels.

4. A location of the Well in the domains of the human Parikṣit is hardly 'correct', (it is really on the borders of both worlds, in a forest equally accessible to Vāsuki and Parikṣit), but it will be observed that the waters are not merely protected by the heavy stone covering, but also subject to Khizr's will, they are not 'flowing'. Vedic equivalents for the 'heavy stone' which hinders access to the waters are abundant, e.g. IV. 28. 5 *aphitāni aśnā*, VI. 17. 5 *adrim acyutam*, IV. 16. 8 *apaḥ adrim*, IV. 1. 15 *dṛdhram ubdham adrim*, IV. 18.6 *paridhim adrim*, and when the stony obstacle is broken, then "the waters flow from the pregnant rock", *sṛṇvantnv apaḥ . . . babṛhānasya adreḥ*, V. 41. 12; cf. *Śatapatha Brāhmaṇa* IX. 1. 2. 4 in connection with the baptism of the fire-altar, which begins 'from the rock', because it is from the rock that the waters come forth, *aśmano hy apaḥprabhavanti*. Vāsuki in the ballad corresponds to Ahi, smitten by Indra, but 'still waxing in sunless gloom', *Ṛg Veda*, V, 32. 6.

5. In the theme condensed above it is easy to recognise the Vedic creation-myth of the conflict between Angels and Titans (Devas and Asuras), Indra and Ahi-Vṛtra; the abduction of Niwal Daī is the rape of Vāc, (*Ṛg Veda*, I. 130, where Indra *vacām muṣāyati*); Khwāja Khizr, the master of the waters, the Vedic rivers of life, is Varuṇa.

6. E. G. Blochet, *Peintures hindoues de la Bibliothèque Nationale*, Paris, 1926. Pls. v and xxiii.

7. The world under water, the home of the serpent race (*ahi, nāga*), Varuna's 'watery origin' (*yonim apyam, Ṛg Veda*, ii, 38, 8), 'in the western gloom' (*apācine tamasi, ib.* vi, 6, 4), is not lighted by the Sun, it is 'beyond the Falcon' (*Jaiminīya Brāhmaṇa*, iii, 268), but the shining of the Waters is everlasting (*ahar-ahar yāti aktur apām, Ṛg Veda*, ii. 30. 1).

8. Shaikh Chilli, *Folk tales of Hindustan*, Allahābād, 1913, pp. 130 ff., with a modern picture of Khwāja Khizr as an old man blessing Maḥbūb, Pl. xxxiii. The story of Prince Maḥbūb is essentially the relation of an achievement of the Grail Quest by a solar hero, the son of a widowed mother, and brought up in seclusion and innocence of his true character, as in the Perceval cycle. Maḥbūb corresponds to Vedic Agni and Sūrya; Ḳassāb to Indra.

9. Apsarases; Grail maidens.

10. The 'wailing women' and 'deathlike trance' of the Fisher King are essential features of the Grail myth.

11. Equivalent to Skr. *māhin*, 'magician', a designation especially applicable to the Titans and, secondarily to the premier Angels, particularly Agni, the 'ancestors' represent the solar heroes of former cycles.

12. The Grail Quest is achieved.

13. Baḥrain, an island in the Persian Gulf, has been identified by many scholars with the Sumerian Dilmun, where dwelt the gardener Tagtut after the flood: see Delitzsch, *Wo lag das Paradies*, p.178, and Langdon, *Sumerian Epic*, pp. 8ff.

14. For Islamic legend, other parallels, and further references see *Encyclopedia of Islam*, s. v. Idrīs, al-Khaḍir and Khwādja Khiḍr; Warner, *Shah Nama of Firdausi*, vi, pp. 74–8 and 159–162; Hopkins, 'The Fountain of Youth', JAOS. xxvi; Barnett, 'Yama, Gandharva, and Glaucus', *Bull. School Oriental Studies*, iv; Grierson, *Bihar Peasant Life*, pp. 40–3; Garcin de Tassy, *Mémoire sur des Particularités de la Religion Musalmane dans l'Inde*, pp. 85–9; Wünsche, *Die Sagen vom Lebensbaum und Liebenswasser*, Leipzig, 1905; Friedländer, *Die Chadhirlegende und der Alexander-Roman*, Leipzig, 1913.

15. Cf. Barnet, *loc. cit.*, pp. 708–10.

16. Cf. *Ṛg Veda*, vii. 6. 4 and 7, where Agni is said to bring forth the Maidens (rivers of life) eastward from the 'western darkness' (*apācine tamasi*) and to bring back 'treasures of earth' (*budhnyā vasūni*) 'when the Sun rises' (*uditā sūryasya*).

17. Al-Khaḍir's realm, known as Yūḥ (also a name of the Sun), where he rules over saints and angels, is situated in the far North; it is an Earthly Paradise, a part of the human world which remained unaffected by the Fall of Adam and the curse (see Nicholson, *Studies in Islamic Mysticism*, pp. 82, 124).

18. According to 'Umārah, Khizr is 'Green' because the earth becomes green at the touch of his feet.

19. *Khazra*, either 'verdure' or 'sky'.

20. The prophet Elias, with whom Khizr is often identified.

21. Cf. *Iskandar Nāma*, lxix. 57, 'verdure grows more luxuriantly by the fountain'. *Ibid.* 22, the spring is described as a 'fountain of light', and this corresponds to *Vendidād*, Fargad xxi, where light and water proceed from a common source; cf. also Vedic Soma as both light and life, a plant and a fluid (*amṛta*, the Water of Life, cf. Barnett, *loc. cit.*, p. 705, note 1).

22. In *Bhagavad Gītā*, x. 31, Kṛṣṇa is *jhaṣānām makaraḥ*, the *makara* is therefore regarded as the foremost amongst the *jhaṣas*, or monsters of the deep. The word *makara* occurs first in *Vājasaneyi Saṁhitā*, xxiv. 35; *śiṁśumāra* in *Ṛg Veda*, i. 116. 18. For a full discussion of the *makara* in Indian iconography (especially as vehicle of Varuṇa and banner of Kāmadeva) see my *Yakṣas*, 1931,ii, p. 47ff. and further references there cited.

The 'fish' vehicle, of course, implies the rider's independence of local motion in the unbounded ocean of universal possibility; just as wings denote angelic independence of local motion in the actual worlds.

23. Sarre und Herzfeld, *Archäologische Reise im Euphrat-und Tigris-Gebiet*, Vol. I, pp. 13, and 37–8, Berlin, 1911.

24. *Annual Report, Archaeological Department, Nizam's Dominions*, 1929–30 (1933), p. 17 and Pl. 11, b.

24. See my *Yakṣas*, II.

25. For example, in the Baptistry at Ravenna (Berchem and Clouzot, figs. lii and 220); Jordan here holds a vase from which the waters are flowing.

26. For the Sumerian deities see S. H. Langdon, *Semitic Mythology*, Ch. 2; for the flowing vase etc., Van Buren, *The Flowing Vase and the God with Streams*, Berlin, 1933, and as regards India, my *Yakṣas*, II. For the iconographic link between the Asiatic full vase and Christian Grail vessel see Gosse, *Recherches sur quelques représentations du Vase Eucharistique*, Geneva, 1894.

27. *Bilderatlas zur Kulturgeschichte Indiens in der Grossmoghul-Zeit*, 1930, p. 71. 'An in part absolute identity and an in part very close Kinship with the sources of the great cultures of the ancient East and even to a considerable extent with the sources of the classical Sumerian period.'

EIGHTEEN

Eckstein

IN a remarkable book, *Consider the lilies, how they grow* (Matt. 6:28) published by the Pennsylvania German Folklore Society, 1937, Mr Stoudt, whose interpretation of Pennsylvania German art is based entirely on 'the historical manifestations of mystical religion' (with special emphasis on Jacob Boehme, Dante, St Bernard, and the Bible), was for a long time puzzled by the diamond motif; until finding a passage in the writings of Alexander Mach where (in accordance with the Biblical texts cited below) 'Christ was spoken of as the *Eckstein* . . . he realised that the (German) word for diamond was the same as for cornerstone' (p. 76). The device occurs on stove-plates, and in this connection Mr Stoudt appropriately cites the instruction by Clement of Alexandria to the early Christians to place the accepted symbols of Christ on their domestic utensils.

So far, so good. We can, however, go further, and enquire in what senses Christ is thus referred to both as 'diamond' and as 'cornerstone,' or more literaly 'angle (-stone)'.[1] In Ps. 118:22 = Matt. 21:42 = Luke, 22:17, we have 'The stone which the builders rejected, the same is become the head of the corner' (κεφαλὴν γωνιάς, caput anguli); in Eph. 2:20, 'Himself the chief corner-stone' (ὄντος ἀκρογωνιαίου ἀυτου χρισου Iησοῦ. ipso summo angulari lapide Christo Jesu) the text continuing: 'in whom each separate building fitly framed together (συναρμοδογομένη, constructa = Skr. *saṁskṛta*) groweth into a holy temple (εἱς ναὸν αγιον) in the Lord, in whom ye also are builded together (coedificamini) for a habitation of God in the Spirit (ἑν Πνεύματι = Skr. *ātmani*).' The evident intention of the text is to depict the Christ as the *unique* principle upon which the whole edifice of the Church depends. The principle of anything is neither one among other parts of it, nor a totality of parts, but that in which all parts are reduced to a unity without composition. The figure is parallel to that of membership in the Mystical Body of Christ. But a 'corner stone' in the accepted sense of a stone at the corner of a building, however important, and even if an uppermost quoin be intended, is only one of four equal supports; we cannot logically speak of *the* corner-stone; and any one corner stone rather reflects than is the dominating principle of a building. We begin to suspect that the meaning of 'corner-stone' may have been misunderstood: that that in which men are 'all builded together' cannot be thought of as a corner-stone in the sense of *a* stone at the corner or angle of the building.

To know what is meant by the evidently equivalent expressions 'head of the angle' and 'chief angular (-stone)' we must ask first what is meant by the 'angle' or 'angular (-stone'). To speak of a 'corner' begs the question because, for us, a corner is always one of many, typically four; 'angle', which may imply either the corner or the peak of a building or pediment, is intentionally non-committal. Γ'ωνία may refer either to position, as being at an angle, or to shape, as in 'polygon', or when it means the 'cutwater of a bridge'. Γωνια is that which is prominent or stands out, and is used metaphorically in this sense in the Septuagint I, Sam. 14:38); 'all the chief of the people', Vulgate *angulos populorum*; the Hebrew word rendered by *angulos* is *pinnāp*, plural of *pinnoth* (סִנְּדּה). English 'quoin' or 'coign', the etymological equivalent of γωνία, may be either a corner stone at any level, or may be coping, according to the context.[2]

The words meaning 'angle' or 'angular' are combined with others meaning 'head' and 'extremity'. Κεφαλή 'head', and architecturally 'capital', can only apply to whatever forms the summit of anything. Ἄκρος implies extremity,[3] in whatever direction, as in 'acrolithic', a statue of which the extremities, head, hands, and feet, are of stone, but often with special reference to the top or highest part, as in 'acropolos'. Ἀκροτήριον is the pedestal for a figure or other finial at the top or corners of a pediment or on a coping (or sometimes refers to pedestal and figure together). Such a pedestal or finial, in the case of a stone structure, might very properly have been called an ἀκρογωνιαῖος λιθος.

What was the shape of the building implied or taken for granted by our texts? It would be convenient to think of a domed or tent-roofed building, but a rectangular building with a peaked roof is more plausible, in view of the probable derivation of the form of Solomon's temple from that of the Tabernacle, also the traditional form of the Ark. The gable end view of such a building states its essentials in vertical projection. If now we equate ἀκρογωνιαῖος λίθος with ἀκροτήριον it will surely be to the uppermost angle-stone and not to either of the lateral angle-stones that the Christ would have been compared. He is assuredly the peak of the roof. Our view is accordingly that the real meaning of the text could be best conveyed in modern English by 'is become the keystone of the arch,' or 'roofplate of the vault'. We see him, in other words, in that position at the summit of a dome which is regularly occupied in Christian architecture by the figure of the Pantakrator, or a corresponding monogram or a solar symbol, or even by an architectural 'eye' surmounted by a 'lantern'.[4] He is the keystone, coping stone, or roof-plate of the cosmic structure which is also his 'Mystical Body', monument and dwelling place, and of which the individual man is a microcosmic analogy.

We can now advantageously call attention to some rather impressive Oriental parallels. In *Jātaka*, I. 1. 200–1 and DhA. I. 269 a 'rest-hall' (*vissamana-śālā*)[5] is being built. The building cannot be completed without a roof-plate, which cannot be made of green wood, but only of seasoned. The woman Sudhammā, 'Perfect Virtue', has prepared in advance a seasoned roof-plate. The builders, who wish to keep the merit of the work for themselves, are forced to use this *kaṇṇika* against their will: the celestial palace, for such it is in the last analysis, cannot otherwise be completed. The roof-plate of hard wood which the builders would have rejected becomes the keystone of the roof. Because Sudhammā has supplied the crowning element of the structure, her name is given to the rest-hall itself.[6] The name sudhammā is manifestly that of a principle, and is identical in meaning with the *kusalā dhammā* ('efficient powers of consciousness,' i.e. 'perfect virtues', but not exclusively in an ethical sense) of *Mil.* 38 as cited in the next paragraph.

As we have shown elsewhere, the roof-plate is the key piece of the roof, as the roof itself is the most essential feature of the building, which is above all a shelter.[7] The roof-plate or, in some cases, the roof-ridge, becomes accordingly the subject of numerous parables, for example *Mil.* 38, 'Just as the rafters of a peak-roofed building move towards, rest upon and meet together in (*samosaraṇā*) the peak, and this peak is acknowledged to be the summit (*agga* = *agra*) of all, just so each and all of the efficient powers of consciousness (*kusalā dhammā*)[8] have at-one-ment (*samādhi*, etymologically and semantically 'synthesis') for their head (*pamukha*), rest upon and slope towards at-one-ment', or in terms of a further comparison, as the four wings of an army are related to the king, environing him and depending upon him as their head.

Our roof-plate seen from below hangs in the vault of the roof not obviously supported from below, but it is nevertheless virtually the capital of a central pillar; just as a king-post although supported by a cross beam is virtually the upper part of a column extending downwards to and supported by the floor. The central pillar thus implied may be compared to the centre-pole of a tent or the handle of an umbrella; the equation of roof with umbrella is explicit. Such a central pillar corresponds also to the trunk of the Tree of Life and to the vertical of the Cross, Gk, *stauros*, Skr. *skambha*; and it is the central principle of the whole construction, which departs from it below and returns to it above, as can be readily seen if we consider a building in its simplest aspect, which is that of a tepee or pyramid. The actual employment of such a central pillar is implied in an earlier form of the parable quoted above, viz. in AĀ. III. 2.1, where 'Just as all the other beams (*vaṁśa*, literally 'bamboo') are unified in (*samāhitāh*) in the hall-beam (*śālā-vaṁśa*), so in this Breath (*prāṇa*) the powers (*indriyāṇi*) of eye, ear and mind, the body and whole self (*sarva ātmā*) are unified'. Here, as usual, the 'Breath' in the singular refers to the Brahman and Ātman, the Spirit.[9]

The building itself is the cosmos in a likeness, and therefore a likeness of the 'body' of the cosmic (*lokāvatī*, MU. VI. 6) Man, the 'mystical body' of Christ 'of which ye are members':[10] the roof-plate in which the rafters, which are also 'beams' (in both senses of the word) meet (as the angles of a pyramid, or ribs of an umbrella, or radii of a circle meet in a point), is the Sun of Men (*sūryo nṛn*, RV. I. 146. 4), the 'one lotus of the sky' (BU. VI. 3.6). The pillar expressed or implied, about which the whole building is constructed and of which its four corners or quarters (represented by other pillars or by vertically superimposed series of quoins) is the centre or 'heart'[11] of the building on any floor, circle (*cakra, loka*) or level of reference (however many the storeys may be): and cosmically, the Sun-pillar[12] extending from the centre of the sky to the navel of the earth, and pillar of Fire extended conversely from the navel of the earth to the centre of the sky, the 'pillar of life at the parting and meeting of the ways' (RV. v. 5.6, v. 139.3, etc.), Branstock or fiery trunk of the Tree of Life and Burning Bush, the Shaft of Light or Bolt that at once divides and connects together heaven and earth, and with which the Dragon was smitten in the beginning, the vertical of the Cross of light—*stauros* and *skambha*. In this omniform pillar extending from floor to roof of the cosmos all things inhere in one form, the single form that is the form of very different things: 'There inheres this all, there whatever stirs, whatever breathes . . . that concurrently (*sambhūya*, 'assembled', 'combined', etc.) is one simply' (*ekam eva*, AV. v. 8. 7–11) corresponds to Eph. 2:20 'in whom ye also are builded together', and apocryphal *Acts of John*, 98–99: 'a cross of light set up, in which was one form and likeness, and in it another multitude of diverse forms . . . This cross, then, is that which fixed all things apart and joined all things unto itself . . . and then also, being one, streamed forth into all things.'[13] *Vajra* as 'bolt' coinciding with *Skambha* as Axis Mundi, similar doctrine can be recognised in Heraclitus, xxxvii, 'the thunderbolt (κεραυνός) governs (οἰακίζει) all things', or—as might have been said, οἰκίζει, 'builds all things'.[13]

The 'head' of this pillar is the solar and man-regarding (*nṛ-cakṣus*) Face of God, the omniform and omniscient Sun, who is also the Spirit whose kiss endows all things with being (SB. VIII. 3.2. 12–13), and connects all things to himself in one con-spiration. His Orb is moreover not only the roof-plate of the cosmos, but the door of the worlds, through which one is altogether liberated, breaking out of the cosmos—'No man cometh to the Father save by me . . . I am the way . . . I am the door' (John, 14:6 and 10:9). Architecturally, the 'head of the angle' is our roof-plate, coping stone, and acroter, the capital of an axial pillar, which is really one of pneumatic light, and if not structurally realized is nevertheless ideally present. Macrocosmically, this 'head of the angle' is the Sun in the zenith; and whoever returns to this Sun, the Truth, as like to like, by an *ablatio omnis alteritatis*,[14] becomes a Mover-at-will and for him it is 'evermore day'.

In various countries the hardest and brightest stone or metal known has been the symbol of indestructibility, invulnerability, stability, light, and immortality. The North American Indian preserves to this day what was probably already a Paleolithic use of 'flint' in this sense,[15] the Egyptian pyramidion was made of granite 'polished like a mirror'; the adamant (diamond) of the classical world was probably of Indian origin; the Chinese had their jade, but also derived from India with Buddhism the symbolic values of *vajra*, which they rendered by the character *chin* (Giles 2032) of which the primary value is metal, especially gold, and also weapon.

Skr. *vajra* is not only the lightning, thunder-bolt, shaft, or lance with which Indra smote the Dragon in the beginning, and Axis Mundi and Sacrificial Pillar, *skambha* and σταυρός (Skr. *sthāvaraḥ*, 'firm'), but also 'diamond', and in the latter sense with special reference to the qualities of hardness, indestructibility, and intellectual brilliance. We have, for example, such expressions as *vajrāsana*, 'diamond throne'[16] (on which the Buddha and all former Munis have been seated at the Navel of the Earth), and *vajra-kāya*, 'diamond body', an immortal body of light. Skr. *aśri*, angle, corner, and *aṁśa*, part, corner, edge, point, etc., are related to ακρος, *acer*, *acies*.[17] The *vajra* as weapon or sacrificial post is constantly spoken of as 'angular', for example 'four-edged' (*catur-aśri*) in RV. IV. 22.2; in AB. II. 1 and KB. X. 1 the sacrificial post (*yūpa* = στυρός) and the bolt (*vajra*) are identified, and the one is to be made 'eight-angled' (*aṣṭaśri*) like the other.[18] It is evident that *vajra* as 'adamant' or diamond is a naturally eight-angled stone. In the same way, Pali *attaṅsa*, 'eight-edged,' is both 'diamond', and 'pillar', typically of a heavenly palace (for references see PTS, *Pali Dictionary*, *s.v.*). Chinese *chin* (Jap. *kongō*, Skr. *vajra*) in combination with other characters gives us such expressions as 'golden crow' (Sun), and 'diamond pivot, or axis' (Moon). The character for 'axis', *shu* (Giles 10092) implies also 'centre', and whatever is fundamental: *T'ien shu* is the pole or axis on which the sky turns; *shu yü* (Giles 13626) is controlling power, guiding mind, ἡγεμών. Without going further into the analysis of these expressions it will be sufficiently evident that the complex of ideas in which the notions of adamantine quality and of the polar or solar axis of the universe are inseparably connected is part and parcel of a universal and widely distributed tradition, in the light of which our Biblical phrases discussed above should be envisaged.

We shall conclude with a reference to the notion of a corner-stone or angular stone which is also an extremity in terms of Egyptian architecture. No architectural unit that can be thought of would do better than a pyramidion (the crowning member of a pyramid) fit the phrase 'head of the angle', or simply 'angle' as used in OT. to mean chief or leader. The pyramidia of Weserka-ra (tenth dynasty) and of Amenemhat III (twelfth dynasty) are described in *Ann. du Service des Antiquités*, XXX, 105ff, and III, 206ff. The characteristic of these pyramidia is their solar symbolism. Of the first, 'une grande pointe de pyramide en granit noir', we are told that 'Auhaut de chacune des ses faces, le disque solaire étend ses ailes protectrices', the four solar symbols being those of the 'divinités des quatre points cardinaux, Ra, Ptah, Anubis et les astres nocturnes'. The second 'est taillé avec une régularité singulière et il a été poli à miroir . . . La face est occupée par un beau disque ailé flanqué des deux Uraeus; entre les deux ailes est gravé un groupe formé . . . des deux yeux, des trois lutsh et du disque non ailé' (in which the centre of the circle is marked): 'Chaque face, répondant à une des *maisons* du monde, est consacrée à la divinité qui protège cette *maison*'. The normal arrangement of a central point, surrounded by four guardians of the quarters will be recognized immediately. The legends engraved on the four sides of the pyramidion are dialogues between the deceased or his priest and the guardian deities of the respective 'houses': on the East, for example 'Sout ouvert la face du roi Nimāri (name of the king as child of Ra, the Sun) pour qu'il donne au roi Amenemhaît de se lever en dieu maître de l'Éternité et indestructible'. Ainsi parle le prêtre, et le dieu Harmakhis, guardien de la *maison* est répond, "Harmakhis a dit: J'ai donné l'horizon excellent au roi du Sud et du Nord qui prend l'heritage dex deux terres"—ici il s'addresse directement au roi,—"pour que tu t'unisse à lui; ainsi m'a-t-il plu. Et l'horizon prend la parole à son tour. "L'horizon a dit que tu te reposes sur lui; ainsi m'a-t-il plu".' And similarly on the other sides.

To this it must be added that the hieroglyph for 'pyramidion', *bnbn.t* (also the 'point of an obelisk'), in the combination *bnbn.tj* becomes an epithet of the Sun-god, 'He of the pyramidion'.[19]

The deceased king is thus at the same time accepted by the four faces or four-fold aspect[20] of the Sun, and identified with the Sun, while the two kingdoms, north and south, are analogically Heaven or Earth, of which he receives the inheritance; the pyramid itself representing not merely the tomb, but at the same time the cosmic embodiment or dwelling place of the resurrected king, now becomes a member of the 'mystical body' of the Sun. The apex of the pyramid, which is also the Sun, is architecturally the unique principle in which, as one may say, all the rest is builded together and exists more eminently. If *bnbn.t* is also the 'point of an obelisk', which corresponds to the 'Sunpillar' of other traditions, even this pillar may be said to be represented by the tenon which projects from the lower surface of the pyramidion and holds it fast when set in place. And if now Christ is the 'angle' or 'head of the angle', it is clear that this could have been stated in Egyptian architectural phraseology by saying instead of 'is become the head of the corner', 'is become the *bnbn.t*'. It is not absolutely impossible that the Hebrew expression itself was ultimately of Egyptian origin, and ought to be thus restored.

NOTES

1. Cf. Wynkyn de Worde, *Pilgr. Perf.* 183, 'The diamonde moost precyous to mankynde, thy swete sone Jesus.'

2. Just as in the typically Orissan architecture, where the *āmalaka* form is repeated as a corner-stone at various levels of the tall spire, and also forms the coping-stone; the corner-stones being really quarter-*āmalakas*, and only the crowning stone exhibiting the whole form. The crowning *āmalaka* is here indeed the 'head of the angle', both inasmuch as the four angles of the spire converge upwards towards it, and inasmuch as their form subsists in it more eminently, at the same time more fully and on a higher level of reference. For an example see my *History of Indian and Indonesian Art*, [N.Y. 1965] fig. 216.

3. Skr. *agra* is generally 'top', but can also mean 'extremity' in any direction; it is also metaphorically 'prior', 'foremost', etc.

4. See my 'Symbolism of the Dome', [Rpr. SPI, pp.415–458.] Special mention is made of the fact that the roof-plate is 'perforated': there can be no question that it is the architectural equivalent of the Sundoor through which one is altogether liberated; the 'perforation' is the 'eye' of the heavenly dome, or in other words the Sun; 'I am the door, by me if any man enter in, he shall be saved,' etc. (John, 14:9)

5. Cf. *vissamana-ṭṭhāna* in S.I. 201, Comm., and *vissameti* (causative), in J. III. 36 where the host 'gives rest' to weary travellers. 'Come unto me, all ye that labour and are heavy laden, and I will give you rest . . . How often would I have gathered thy children together' (Matt 11:28 and 23:37). The root is *vi-śram*, to 'cease from toil'. The anagogic significance is obvious; for its is precisely the Wayfarer (*parivrājaka, carṣaṇi*) that 'labours' (*śramati*), and hence the usual designation of the monk, ascetic, almsman, etc., as a 'Labourer' (*śramaṇa*). The Rest House at the end of the road, at

worlds' end, where the burden is laid down, is then *viśramaṇa* in the sense that whoever enters there is no longer a 'Labourer', no longer under a rule, but altogether 'liberated' (from himself). And just as in the Vedic rite the sacrificer in 'building up' Agni is at the same time building up for himself a 'body of light', so whoever like Sudhammā 'builds up' a rest-house is at the same time building up the heavenly mansion, and laying up treasure in heaven:

> A house was building, and your bitter sighs
> Came hither as toil-helping melodies,
> And in the mortar of our gem-built wall
> Your tears were mingled mid the rise and fall
> Of golden trowels tinkling in the hands
> Of builders gathered wide from all the lands.
> —Is the house finished? Nay, come help to build . . .
>
> (William Morris)

6. Sudhammā is actually the wife of Magha (the solar Indra), in the same sense that the Church is the bride of Christ, and the Sudhammā Devasabhā (of which there is a representation in relief at Bharhut, see Cunningham, *Stupa of Bharhut*, pl. xvi) is the palace of Indra and analogue of the rest-hall for which 'Perfect Virtue' provides the roof-plate.

7. A material shelter being needed only by those who are 'under the sun'. Liberation, a breaking out of the cosmos by the Sundoor, is often described as a breaking through the roof or roof-plate, and the Buddha as being thus liberated is often referred to as *vivaṭa-chado*, 'he whose roof has been opened up'; of which, moreover, the abandonment of the household life and adoption of the open-air life of a 'Wanderer' is already a prefiguration.

8. These powers of consciousness, or virtues or acts of the practical intellect (collectively *dhammā*, here nearly equivalent to *indriyāṇi*, *prāṇāḥ*, and, *devāḥ*) are 'contact (of subject with object), sensibility, recognition, will, awareness, counsel, habit' (*phassā, vedanā, saññā, cetanā, viññāna, vitakka, vicāra*). When these have been unified (*ekatobharā*), operation no longer involves a temporal sequence of acts, but becomes a single act of being (*Mil.* 63).

9. For detailed discussion of all the architectural symbols discussed in the preceding paragraphs see my 'Symbolism of the Dome' (*loc. cit.*), 'Uṣṇiṣa and Chatra' (*Poona Orientalist*, III, 1938, 'Inverted Tree' [Rpr. SP2, pp. 376–404.] and 'Svayamātṛṇṇā: Janua Coeli' [Rpr. SP2, pp. 465–520.] René Guénon, 'Le symbolisme du dôme and 'Le dôme et la roue,' *Etudes traditionelles*, XLIII, 1938, and P. Mus, *Barabaḍur*, parts IV and V.

10. Cf. *Mund.* II. 1.4. 'Fire is his head; His eyes, the moon and sun; the airts His ears; His voice the revealed Vedas; the gale His breath; His heart the all; from His feet the earth; He is indeed the Spirit immanent in every being' (*sarrabhûrātàtmā*).

11. The axial pillar of a Japanese pagoda (stūpa), around which there winds a spiral stair, is actually called the 'heart pillar' (*shinbashira*) and thus distinguished from the four 'guardian pillars' (*shitĕn-bashira*) of the 'corners'.

12. AB. V. 28. 1, *ādityaḥ yū paḥ, pṛthivi vediḥ*. AB. II. 1, *vajro vai yû pa*.

13. For the *skambha*, Axis Mundi, as Brahman, and single form of all things, see the whole of AV. X. 7 and 8. The doctrine is of fundamental import in the whole of the Vedic ontology.

14. For Nicolas of Cusa, the condition of *filiatio* and *theosis* is thus defined. Cf. 'If any man come unto me and hate not . . . yea, and his own soul also, he cannot be my disciple' (Luke, 14:26); 'The word of God . . . piercing even to the dividing asunder of

soul from spirit' (Heb. 4:12, cf. Dionysius, *De div. nom.* IX. 3). 'Whoso cleaveth to God becometh one spirit with him' (I Cor. 6:27).

15. The Navajo conception of 'flint armour' is the equivalent of Milton's 'in a rock of Diamond arm'd' (*Paradise Lost*, VI. 364), and Buddhist *vajra-kāya*.

16. 'As a rock of Diamond, stedfast evermore' (Spenser, *Fairy Queen*, I. 6. 4). For values of *vajra* see also my *Elements of Buddhist Iconography*, 1935, pp. 14–15.

17. Of the two Indian (Pali) words *kūṭa* and *kaṇṇika* which denote the peak or roofplate of a house to which the rafters converge, the former is from a root *kuṭ* to bend (from an angle), whence also *kūṭi* (cf. Eng. 'cot' and 'hut'), a small house with an edged or domed roof, or even a large shrine with a spire; and the latter a diminutive of *kaṇṇa* (Skr. *karna*), of which the primary meaning is 'corner', and related both to *aśri*, etc. and to *śṛṅga*, 'horn', and architecturally 'spire'. Thus the *kaṇṇika* (the 'roofplate') rejected by the builders in the Sudhamma story (p. 171 above) would be quite literally 'corner stone' but for the fact that it is made not of stone but of hard wood; the symbolism is, of course, unaffected by this material accident.

18. Indian pillars in architectural use are typically (although not always) both four-and eight-angled at the same time, i.e. square in section above and below, and sometimes also in the middle, but for the rest chamfered so as to be eight-angled in section.

19. Cf. also in Greece, 'this earlier aspect of the Sun-God as a pyramidial pillar' Arthur Evans, 'Mycenean Tree and Pillar-cult'. *Journal of Hellenic Studies*, 1901, p. 173.

20. On the ultimate significance of the four faces of God see P. Mus, 'Has Brahmā four faces?' in *Journal of the Indian Society of Oriental Art*, V, 1937.

NINETEEN

Quod factum est in ipso vita erat

Ὃ γέγονεν ἐν αὐτῷ ζωὴ ἦν.

THESE words,[1] taken from John, 1: 3, 4 are cited in the form in which they are given in nearly all of the earlier codices, and in which they are quoted by the Scholastics, e.g. Meister Eckhart in *Expositio S, Evangelii sec. Johannem* (ed. J. Christ and J. Koch, Stuttgart-Berlin, 1936, p.56), and by Origen in *Comm. in Ev. Joannio,* II.16.[2] I render, 'What has been made (or, 'has become', or 'was begotten') was life in Him', or in Sanskrit *Yad bhūtam* (or *jātam*) *tad svātmani jīva āsīt.*

Both Meister Eckhart and St Bonaventura, the latter in *I Sent.*, d. 36, a.2, q.1 ad 4 citing St Augustine's *res factae . . . in artifice creato dicuntur vivere*, recognise the analogy of the human and divine artificers; in both cases the pattern of what is to be made pre-exists in the maker's living mind, and is alive in it, and remains alive in it even when the *factibile* has become a *factum* or after it has been destroyed. Our intention is to indicate the immediate and universal background against which these ideas subsist.

This background is essentially that of the traditional doctrine of the 'two minds', or two aspects of the mind, the one in act and the other in action. Combining Aristotle's *Metaphysics*, XII.7.8, 1072b 20f. and XII. 9.5, 1074 a 34f. With *De anima*, III.5, 430 a f., we find that of these two the first, or Mind[3] 'in act' (ἐνεργείᾳ)—'in itself, (καθ' αδτήν) in its own act of being—is 'apart' (χωριστός) 'from sensibles' (τῶν αἰσθητῶν), 'contemplative' (θεωρητικός), 'impassible' (ἀπαθής), without remembrance[4] and unmixed; 'it does not think', or rather, 'its "thinking" is the "Thinking of thinking"' (νοήσεως νόησις), i.e. the principle and *sine qua non*, but not the activity of thinking. In other words, 'it thinks only itself' (αὐτὸν ἄρα νοεῖ) 'throughout eternity' (τὸν ἅπαντα αἰῶνα), without distinction of subject from object, for where both are immaterial 'the thesis is both the operation and the thought' (ὁ λόγος τὸ πρᾶγμα κὶ ἡ νόησις), 'thought and what is thought of are one and the same' (ἡ νόησις τῷ νοουμένῳ μία[5]); Mind, 'becoming everything' (πάντα γίνεσθαι), is what it knows. Furthermore, it is eternal and beautific (ἥδιστος) Life, the Life (ζωή) of God himself. The second mind is creative (ποιητικός), and an 'efficient cause (τὸ αἴτιον καὶ ποιητικόν) in that it makes everything'[6] (τῷ πάντα ποεῖν); it is passible (παθητικός) and mortal, and thinks of contingent things, not always of itself. It is on a plane still lower than that of its creative activity that the mind is 'sensitive' (αἰσθητικός = παθητικός).[7]

These two (or three) minds are the same as Plato's two (or three) parts of the soul, one immortal, and the other mortal, the latter in its best part active and courageous, and in its worst part passively affected by and subject to emotions and reactions provoked by sensation (αἰσθήσις). The two minds are the 'natures' in the universal doctrine of 'one essence and two natures'.[8] As three, they correspond to the contemplative and active lives and the life of pleasure.

In these distinctions of the theoretical from the practical mind, and in the identification of the former (Mind) with the Life (ζωή) of God and of its Thinking with its Thesis, or why not say 'Word' (Λόγος)? there is a veritable prediction or fore-telling of St John's 'In the First Principle (as the Scholastics so often interpret *in principio* = Skr. *agre*, not so much 'in the beginning' as 'at the top') was the Word, and the Word was with God, and the Word was God'. The 'Word' that, as Aristotle says, the First Mind thinks, when in its act of being it thinks itself, is for St John the Christ, the Son of God, 'through whom all things were made' and whom St Augustine therefore calls 'as it were, God's art' (*De Trin.* VI.10)[9]—the art *by* which all things were made. 'Word' and 'Mind' (λόγος, νοῦς) are for Plato often interchangeable, while if for Aristotle the Word is what the First Mind thinks, and the Thinker and the thought are one, it is clear that one might safely paraphrase St John by 'In the First Principle was the Mind, and the Mind was with God, and the Mind was God.[10]

Having so far outlined the immediate background and implications of our text, it may be shown that these are also universal, and in particular, Indian conceptions; in saying which we are very far from suggesting or implying that in their Hellenistic context they are of Indian origin. As before, and to simplify the presentation, we shall combine the evidence of several texts, notably *Bṛhadāraṇyaka Upaniṣad*, I.a 4.10, IV. 1.6, IV. 3.28, 30, 32, *Kena Upaniṣad*, I. 2 and 5 and *Maitri Upaniṣad*, VI. 34.6, with *Śatapatha Brāhmaṇa*, X. 5.3.1 'In the beginning (or rather, 'at the top')[11] there was just That Mind' (*agre . . . tan-mana evāsa*); a paraphrase of *Ṛg Veda*, X. 129, 1 'There was That One (*tad ekam . . .āsa*), naught else whatever'.

To the question, 'what was it that Brahma knew, whereby he became the All?' it is replied, 'In the beginning, verily, this (Self)[12] was Brahma. It knew just Itself (*ātmānam-evāvet*), thereby It became the All' (*sarvam abhavat*). And as to this Gnosis, 'Verily, though he (who can say, 'I am Brahma') does not think (*na manute*) or know (*na vijānati*), yet is he one who thinks and knows, albeit he does not think or know (contingently). Forsooth, there cannot be a dissipation of the Knower's knowing, because of his imperishability. It is not, however, any second thing, divided from Himself, that he should know . . . That is his highest station, that is his Beatitude' (*ānanda*).

And 'What is that Beatitude? Nothing but Mind (*mana eva*). Verily, my King, it is by his Mind that He possesses himself of the Woman (i.e. *vāc*, the Voice, Theotokos),[13] a Son is born of Her, in his image (*pratirūpaḥ*); that is his Beatitude. Verily, my King, the Imperial, Supreme Brahma is just Mind.' As expressed in Thomist phraseology, the generation of the Son is a vital operation, *a principio conjunctivo*.

Aristotle's 'Thinking of thinking', i.e. non-discursive principle of discursive thought, is the 'Mind of the mind' (*manaso manas*) of the *Kena Upaniṣad* where, to the question 'By whom (*kena*) impelled and sent forth does the mind fly?'[14] it is answered that is by 'the Mind of the mind', and that 'the Contemplatives, wholly relinquishing (*atimucya*, sc, their own mind), when they depart from this world, become immortal'. A subsequent verse says that 'He has It in mind, who does not think It; he who thinks It, does not know It; It is unknown to those who "know It", but known to those who "know it not" '; and that is precisely the thesis of Nicolas of Cusa's *Docta Ignorantia*, while 'wholly relinquishing their own mind' corresponds to Philo's 'He that flees for refuge from his own mind, flees for refuge to the Mind of all things' (I. 93).[15]

And so, as the *Maitri Upaniṣad* says, 'The mind is said to be twofold,[16] clean and unclean: unclean, by admixture with desire, clean when separated from desire[17] . . . The means of bondage and release;[18] of bondage, when it clings to the objective, of liberation, when disconnected from the objective'.

Is it not then true, as Jeremias said, that *'in den verschiedenen Kulturen findet man die Dialekte der einen Geistessprache?'*

NOTES

1. In which the distinction is implied of *esse* from *essentia*, existence from being, γένεσις from τὸ ὄντως ὄν.

2. Meister Eckhart quotes the gloss, *Quod in mente est, vivit cum artifice; quod fit, mutatur cum tempore.*

3. Henceforth I use the capital when the First Mind is referred to.

4. Just as for Plotinus, *Enneads*, IV. 4.6, the Gods 'never learn' and 'do not remember': and for the same reason, viz. that where there is no forgetting, there is no occasion for learning or remembrance. It is only for the second and variable mind, our mind that has forgotten so many things, that to be taught and so reminded is desirable. What it can be taught is what it has forgotten (*Meno*, 80, etc., and also Indian doctrine), and so, as Meister Eckhart says, 'Not till the soul knows all that there is to be known can she pass over to the Unknown Good'.

5. To restore 'that original nature in which the knower and the known are alike' is for Plato life's highest purpose (*Timaeus*, 90D); it is the beautific 'synthesis' (*samādhi*) for which the discipline of Yoga is undertaken, and in which it culminates.

6. Cf. Maheśvarānanda, *Maharthamañjarī*, p. 44, where 'The suchness called Sadāśiva (*sadā*, 'eternal') is prior with respect to the principle called Īśvara (Lord, κύριος), which latter, by the splendour of its practical power becomes the demiurge of all things in their manifested likeness'. Cf. John, 'through whom all things were made', and Skr. Viśvakarma, 'All-maker'.

Aristotle's Τὸ αἴτυον καὶ ποιητικόν (*De anima* III.5, 430 12) reflects *Phaedrus*, 97C νοῦς . . . πάντων αἴτιος. Cf. Hermes Trismegistus *Lib* I. 9 'And the First Mind, which is Life and Light, gave birth to another mind, the maker of things' (δημιουργός).

7. 'Aesthetic' (or 'pathetic') is, properly speaking, the science of the feelings, whether of plants, animals or men. Art has to do with the making of things for good use, physical and mental.

8. As in *Bṛhadāraṇyaka Upaniṣad*, II.3.1 (*dve rūpe*); *Maitri Upaniṣad*, VII.11.2. (*dvaitībhāva*) etc.

9. Meister Eckhart's *'bildner aller dingen in sīnem vater'* (Pfeiffer, p. 391). In the same way the human artist works *per verbum in intellectu conceptum* (St Thomas, *Sum. Theol.*, IA. 45.6)

10. 'The Mind was God': cf. *Śatapatha Brāhmaṇa*, X. 5.3.1 'Mind' (*manas*) = *Ṛg Veda* X. 129.1 'That One' (*tad ekam*).

'Mind is the male, Voice the female . . . He, by Mind had intercourse with the Voice' (*Śatapatha Brāhmaṇa*, I.4.4.3, 4, VI. 1.2.8); so we call a thought a concept, implying that it is the produce of a vital operation.

11. Rather than 'in the beginning', since it is to a before the beginning (*ante principium*) that the text refers.

12. Not, as rendered by Hume, 'this world'; for we are told that He *became*, not that He *was*, the All. 'This' contrasted with 'All' can be only 'One'.

13. Separated from Himself (Prajāpati, the Father) as a mother of whom to be born, *Pañcaviṃśa Brāhmaṇa*, VII. 6; as *Agni*, *Jaiminīya Upaniṣad Brāhmaṇa*, I, 51.5.

14. 'Mind is the swiftest of birds' (*Ṛg Veda*, VI. 9.5).

15. 'The Lord of Mind, the Lord of all minds' (Śaṅkarācārya on *Vedānta Sūtra*, IV. 4.8).

16. 'There are two minds, that of all, which is God, and that of the individual' (Philo, I. 93). Hence the possibility of a 'repentance', or rather, 'change of mind' (μετάνοια). Cf. my 'On Being in One's Right Mind', [see chapter 3 of present volume].

17. 'Desire, first seed and child of Mind' (*Ṛg Veda*, X. 129.4). To be 'minded to' is to desire, and when we 'mind' *things*, then there is 'wishful thinking'.

18. 'By what (*kena*) ladder does the sacrificer ascend to heaven? . . . by the Mind' (*Bṛhadāraṇyaka Upaniṣad*, III. 1.6). 'I am born a new being of God, and I see now not with the eye but by the Mind's act' (Hermes Trismegistus, *Lib*. XIII. 11a).

It will be understood that the First Mind, throughout, is *intellectus vel spiritus*, and the other a purposeful and constructive mentality; the First, or theoretical (speculative) Mind 'cares for nothing but the Truth', the other is pragmatic, and contented with fact.

TWENTY

Athena and Hephaistos

IN the production of anything made by art, or the exercise of any art, two faculties, respectively imaginative and operative, free and servile, are simultaneously involved; the former consisting in the conception of some idea in an imitable form, the latter in the imitation (*mimesis*) of this invisible model (*paradeigma*)[1] in some material, which is thus in-formed. Imitation, the distinctive character of all the arts, is accordingly two-fold, on the one hand the work of intellect (*nous*) and on the other of the hands (*cheir*).[2] These two aspects of the creative activity correspond to the 'two in us', viz. our spiritual or intellectual Self and sensitive psycho-physical Ego, working together (*synergoi*). The integration of the work of art will depend upon the extent to which the Ego is able and willing to serve the Self, or if the patron and the workman are two different persons, upon the measure of their mutual understanding.

The nature of the two faculties, which are respectively the formal and efficient causes in the production of works of art, is clearly stated in Philo's account of the building of the Tabernacle, 'the construction of which was clearly set forth to Moses on the Mount by divine pronouncements. He saw with the soul's eye the immaterial forms (*ideai*) of the material things that were to be made, and these forms were to be reproduced as sensible imitations, as it were, of the archetypal graph and intelligible patterns . . . So the type of the pattern was secretly impressed upon the mind of the Prophet as a thing secretly painted and moulded in invisible forms without material; and then the finished work was wrought after that type by the artist's imposition of those impressions on the severally appropriate material substances,[3] and in more general terms by St Bonaventura, who points out that 'the work of art proceeds from the artist according to a model existing in the mind; which model the artist discovers (*excogitat* = *cintayati*) before he produces, and then he produces as he has predetermined. Moreover, the artist produces the external work in the closest possible likeness of the interior model'.[4]

The work of art is, then, a product at once of wisdom and method, or reason and art (*sophia* or *logos*, and *techne*).[5] It may be noted here that the primary references of the words *sophia* and *episteme*, cf. Hebrew *hochmā* and Sanskrit *māyā*,[6] are to the artist's 'cunning' or 'science', from which the sense of 'wisdom' develops; and that while '*techne*' can often be rendered by 'art' as opposed to 'artless labour' (*atechnos tribe*)[7] this distinction is the same as that of mere 'industry' (*tribe*) from 'method' (*methodos*).[8] It amounts to the same thing to say that in matters of handicraft or manufacture (*cheirotechnike*) there is one part more allied to science (*episteme*), and another less, and that 'without enumeration, measurement and weighing, the arts (*technai*) would be relatively worthless . . . and a matter of mere practice and toil',[9] or to distingish art (*techne*) and mere experience (*emperia*) from science (*episteme*), though the artist needs both.[10] All these dicta provide a background for the medieval: *Ars sine scientia nihil* and *Scientia reddit opus pulchrum*.

We recognise that for anything to be 'well and truly made' the cooperation of the hands as efficient cause and intellect as formal cause is indispensible. The purpose of the present article is to call the attention to the expression of this mythologically in terms of the relation of Athena to Hephaistos, the former being the Goddess of Wisdom who sprang from the head of her father Zeus, and the latter the Titan smith whose wonderful works are produced with the help of Athena as co-worker (*syntechnos*).[11] Athena and Hephaistos 'Share a common nature, being born of the same father' and live together in a common shrine (*hireon*) or as it were in one and the same house[12]: she is 'the mind of God' (*he theou noesis,* or *nous*), and called also Theonoe, and he 'the noble scion of light'.[13] From them all men derive their knowledge of the arts, either directly or indirectly; 'Hephaistos, famous for his art (*klytometis*),[14] aided by Athena of the gleaming eyes, taught glorious works to men on earth';[15] or it was Prometheus who stole from them 'immanent artistic wisdom (*entechnon sophian*) and fire', and gave them to men 'as a divine portion (*moira*)'.[16]

Here the words *entechnos* and *moira* imply that the human 'artist in possession of his art' (*entechnos demiourgos*)[17] is such by participation (*methexis, metalepsis*) in the Master Architect's creative power. Athena and Hephaistos, in fact, 'agreeing in their love of wisdom and of craftsmanship (*philosophia* and *philotechnia*), both together chose this land of ours as being naturally fitted to be the home of virtue and wisdom, and therein they planted as native to the soil good men, and set in their minds the structure of the art of government'.[18] All this means that the human artist—say, the blacksmith at his forge—in possession of his art has within him both a wisdom and a method, a science and a skill; and that as a whole man, responsible for both operations, free and servile, and capable alike of imagination and of execution, is of the nature of Athena and Hephaistos both: it is Athena who inspires what Hephaistos effects. So we have Phereclus 'whose hands were knowing (*epistato*) to fashion all manner of wondrous works (*daidala*), because Athena loved him',[19] and the carpenter who is called 'a master of wisdom as to form, by the promptings of Athena.[20] In this relationship Athena's function, in that she is the source of the formal cause or pattern of the work to be done, is essentially authoritative and paternal rather than receptive or feminine, we need not be surprised to find that the artist's 'inspiration' (*empnoia, empneusis*), or 'the divine power (*dynamis* = *śakti*) that moves him', is referred to often as 'the God', the immanent 'Daimon', or Eros, that is to say the Spirit to whom the very word 'inspiration' points.[21]

On the other hand when the servile operation alone is performed by the merely 'productive mechanic' (*banausikos*) who does not understand what he is doing, however industrious he may be, then his service becomes a matter of only 'unskilled labour' (*atechnos tribe*)[22] and he is reduced to the condition of the mere slave who earns money for a master,[23] or mere 'hand' (*cheirotechnes*) rather than an architect or lover of wisdom.[24] This is precisely the position of the modern chain-belt worker, in whom the industrial system whether capitalistic or totalitarian, has divided Athena from Hephaistos.[25]

NOTES

1. An imitation—'for if it did not effect that, it [painting] would be held to be an idle playing with colours' (Philostratus, *Vit. Ap.* II. 22.). Of an invisible model—cf. Plato, *Timaeus*, 51E, 92, *Republic*, 484C, 510D, E, 596B, *Laws*, 931A; Plotinus, *Enneads*, V. 9.11. 'It is in imitation (*anukṛti*) of divine forms that any human form is invented here . . . [for instance] this divine harp, of which the human harp is an imitation' (*Aitareya Brāhmana*, VI, 27, *Śānkhāyana Āraṇyaka*, III, 9). The painter is to 'put down on the wall what has been seen in contemplation' ('*tad dhyātam*', Someśvara, *Abhilāṣitārthacintāmaṇi*, I, 3. 158).

Plato of course, by 'imitation' means an iconography of things unseen, and deprecates the making of 'copies of copies', or realism in the modern sense of the word. It is in the same way only that Apollonius, in Philostratus, *Vit. Ap.* VI. 19, calls 'imagination (*phantasia*) a wiser artist (*demiourgos*) than imitation', because the work of the creative artist depends upon 'the imagination even of what has not been seen',—if, indeed, it is not better to make 'no images of Gods at all . . . inasmuch as the intuitive mind (*gnome*) can draft and represent (*anagraphei . . . kai anatypoutai*) better than any artist'. This last is what would be called in India a purely 'mental' (*manasū*) or 'subtle' (*sūkṣma*) worship.

2. Philostratus, *Vit. Ap.* II. 22. cf. *Śatapatha Br.* III, 2. 4. 11: 'Were it not for intellect, the word would babble incoherently', and *Kauṣītaki Up.* III, 6, 7: 'When intellect is their rider then all things are effected by the two hands . . . for indeed, without the cooperation of intellect the two hands would make nothing intelligible', i.e. would not know what they were doing.

3. Philo, *Moses*, II, 74–76.

4. St Bonaventura, *De red, artium ad theologiam*, 12.

5. *Homeric Hymns*, IV, 483, in connection with music. Otherwise expressed, in the case of metalwork, it is by art and reason (*he techne kai ho logos*) that the material causes, fire and steel, etc. are dominated (Plutarch, *Mor.* 436 A. B). Cf. references in notes 2, and 1.

6. *Māyā*, '*von mā* = "man", vgl. "*metis*" . . . *goettliche Kunst*' (Grassmann, *Woererbuch zum Rigveda*); cf. Liddell and Scott, s. vv. *mao* and *metis*.

7. Plato *Phaedrus* 260E, cf. 270B.

8. Aristotle, *Soph. Elench.* III, 18.

9. Plato, *Philebus*, 55D—56A.

10. Plato, *Republic*, 422C, *Ion*, 532C. 536C.

11. Plato, *Statesman*, 274C. for an example of their cooperation cf. Homer, *Cypria* 5.

12. Plato, *Critias*, 109C, 112B.

13. Plato, *Cratylus*, 407B. For Theonoe as a type cf. Euripides, *Helen*, passim, e.g. 530, where she 'knows all things truly', Hephaistos is more properly to be connected with *Aph* to kindle; fire being *phlox Hephaistoio*, *Iliad*, XVII, 88. Characteristic epithets of Hephaistos are *klytometis*, 'famed for his art', *klytotechnes* 'famed for his craft', and *klyto-ergos*, 'famed for his work'. Athena is *Chariergos*, 'she who—by her wisdom, or science—gives the work its grace or beauty' (*Anth. Pal.* VI, 205)—hers is the 'formal cause', or 'exemplary cause', or 'art in the artist' by which he works. 'Noble' (*gennaios*), characterising Hephaistos may refer to the common paternity of Hephaistos and Athena (*Critias*, 109C), but may rather mean 'faithful', by no means implying that his function is not servile, cf. Euripides, *Helen*, 729, 1641, where *gennaios* goes with *doulos*, and implies a freedom only of the mind (*nous*), in the sense of Philo's *Quod omnis probus liber sit*; cf. Aeschylus, *Prometheus*, 45, where Hephaistos works for Zeus at a task that he 'hates'.

14. For *metis* = *māyā* see note 4. Cf. *Iliad*, x. 19 *syn metin . . . tektagaito* and Pindar, *Olympian Odes*, IX, 78 where *technais* = *māyābhiḥ*. Metis as a person is the first wife of Zeus, reborn from his head as Athena (Hesiod *Theogony*, 886); the story implying that 'the chief god has Wisdom always within him' (H. J. Rose, *Greek Mythology*, p. 50) *Metieta* (for *metietes*) as an epic epithet of Zeus corresponding to Sanskrit *māyin*; so that 'if you would create an image of Zeus you must intuit, or conceive (*ennoein* = *excogitare*, Skr. *dhyai*) encampments, art (*metin*), and the artistic skills (*technas*), and how she flowered forth from Zeus himself' (Philostratus, *Vit. Ap.* VI. 19). Athena is a 'worker' (*ergane*, Sophocles, fr. 724), as in Latin *operosa Minerva* with Vulcan; and it may be observed that *energeia* = *ousia* and is contrasted with *hyle* (Aristotle, *Metaphysics*, VII, 2. 1, and 6), as *logos* and *techne* are contrasted with the material they control (Plutarch, *Mor.* 436A, B). Just as, also, for St Thomas, the artist works *per verbum in intellectu conceptum, Sum. Theol.* I, 45.6.

15. *Homeric Hymns*, XX; Plato, *Critias*, 109 C. D.

16. Plato, *Protagoras*, 321D—322A.

17. Plato, *Laws*, 903C; cf. *Phaedrus*, 277B, where *to entechnon kai me* are distinguished according to an author's knowledge or ignorance of that of which he treats, and *Symposium*, 209A, distinguishing 'inventive' (*heuristikoi*) from other artists. For Aristotle, *Rhetoric*, I. 1. 11. and I. 2.2, the distinction is that of one whose work is done according to 'the laws of art' (*entechnos methodos*) from one who is not such an expert (*atechnos*). With *entechnos* cf. *entheos*, *energeia*, *ennoia*, 'inwit', etc.

18. *Critias*, 109C, D. For the art of government (*politeia*) as tantamount to the arts in general see *Republic*, 342—every art (*techne*) being a ruler of and stronger than that of which it is an art and for the sake of which it operates.

19. *Iliad*, V, 61. Hardly to be distinguished from the Sophia to Hephaistos is 'the Sophia of Daidalus' (Plato, *Euthyphro*, 11E); and the like must hold good for Regin, Wayland and the other great mythical smiths.

20. *Iliad*, XV. 410–411.

21. On inspiration see my *Figures of Thought or Figures of Speech*, 1946, pp.25–28, and s. v. in *The Dictionary of the Arts*.

22. Plato, Phaedrus, 260E, cf. 270B.

23. Xenophon, *Mem.* III. 11.4.

24. Aristotle, *Metaphysics*, I.1. 17; Xenophon, *Vect.* V. 4.

25. All this is, of course, perfectly well known. 'Validation of success in terms of externals has become the mark of our civilisation. In such a value-system human relations take on the values of the salesmen . . . Under such conditions men everywhere become nasty, brutish, and cruel . . . Unless Western man is able to release himself from the degrading tyranny of his enslavement to the religion of economics he is as certainly doomed to self destruction as all the portents indicate that he is' (M. E. Ashley Montagu in *School and Society*, vol. 65, no. 1696, 1947). 'Today, under the centralised economic order, we appear to be descending below the level of the beast, hating, exploiting and destroying each other on a world scale, and reducing the average man to a standardised automaton incapable of thinking and acting for himself' (Bharatan Kumarappa, *Capitalism, Socialism, or Villagism?* 1946, p. 194). There are two positions: that of the tradesman, that 'however much . . . individuals suffer, progression in line with the manufacturing enterprise of civilisation must be allowed free course' (Sir George Watt, in *Indian Art at Delhi*, 1912), and that of the humanist, that 'however much an economic system may succeed in bringing riches it will be unstable and prove a failure if in the process it causes human suffering, or in any way hinders people from a full life' (Bharatan Kumarappa, *ibid.* p. 112). Let us choose between them.

Index